DEMOCRACY IN IRAQ

For Lyndal

University of Plymouth
Charles Seale Hayne Library
Subject to status this item may be renewed
via your Primo account

http://primo.plymouth.ac.uk
Tel: (01752) 588588

Democracy in Iraq

History, Politics, Discourse

BENJAMIN ISAKHAN
Australian Research Council Discovery (DECRA) Research Fellow,
Centre for Citizenship and Globalization, Deakin University, Australia.

ASHGATE

Published by
Ashgate Publishing Limited
Wey Court East
Union Road
Farnham
Surrey, GU9 7PT
England

Ashgate Publishing Company
Suite 420
101 Cherry Street
Burlington
VT 05401-4405
USA

www.ashgate.com

British Library Cataloguing in Publication Data
Isakhan, Benjamin, 1977-
Democracy in Iraq : history, politics, discourse. -- (Law, ethics and governance)
   1. Democracy--Iraq. 2. Democracy--Iraq--History.
   3. Democracy--Religious aspects--Islam. 4. Iraq--
   Politics and government.
   I. Title II. Series
   321.8'09567-dc23

Library of Congress Cataloging-in-Publication Data
Isakhan, Benjamin, 1977-
Democracy in Iraq : history, politics, discourse / by Benjamin Isakhan.
    p. cm.
   Includes bibliographical references and index.
   ISBN 978-1-4094-0175-9 (hardback) -- ISBN 978-1-4094-0176-6 (ebook)
   1. Democracy--Iraq--History. 2. Iraq--Politics and government. 3.
   Islam and state--Iraq. I. Title.
   JQ1849.A91I73 2012
   320.9567--dc23

ISBN 9781409401759 (hbk)
ISBN 9781409401766 (ebk)

2012007263

MIX
Paper from
responsible sources
FSC FSC® C018575
www.fsc.org

Printed and bound in Great Britain by the
MPG Books Group, UK.

Contents

A Note on Translation and Transliteration

Transliterating Arabic and Kurdish words into English is no easy thing, especially for someone who does not speak either language. I have tried to be as simplistic as possible; I have avoided the use of diacritical marks in an effort to keep the book palatable to the unaccustomed reader and in the hope that linguists and native speakers will recognize the simplified English. The translations that appear herein are therefore the work, in most cases, of the original cited authors. Where such translations were not available, I have consulted various Arabic–English and Kurdish–English dictionaries, bi- and multi-lingual colleagues and friends, and a number of reputable websites. I have made every effort to ensure that both the translations and transliterations are correct and consistently applied throughout the book.

Prelude: In the Beginning

This project begins before the age of humankind. It begins before the heavens had been named and before the earth had taken form. It begins with the steady rise and fall of the tides controlled by the primal mother, Tiamet, the goddess of the salty waters.[1] For eons her waters ebbed and flowed according to her whim. Over time, she surged up onto the land and stretched herself northwards, reaching into the plains of lower Mesopotamia and forming those two mighty rivers, the Tigris and Euphrates. It was here that she met the god of the sweet pure waters, Apsu, the great begetter of life. As the saline and the fresh waters blended and bubbled, Tiamet and Apsu came together as one. And from this mighty union came forth the mud beings Lahmu and Lahamu.

In time, Lahmu and Lahamu gave birth to the upper firmament, which they named Anshar and the lower firmament, which they named Kishar. Together Anshar and Kishar produced a wonderful son, the god of the sky, Anu. It was Anu, the mightiest and most sovereign of gods, who was to be the leader of the great council. He was to rule over the universe and his word became the divine law that bound all things. Beside him stood his son, the most ferocious of gods, Enlil, the Lord of the Storm. Before them sat the other five senior gods and goddesses who held particular weight among the divine assembly. The council was made up 50 gods and goddesses in total and together they constituted the Ordained Assembly of the Great Gods.[2] This assembly was called together when the gods needed to make decisions regarding any number of issues and constituted the highest authority in the universe.

Before engaging in their binding political rhetoric, the gods ate the finest of foods and drank their fill of strong wines. Following this, they each took an oath to abide by the decisions of the council and then either Anu or Enlil would usually broach a topic and the discussions would begin. At times, the gods argued heatedly but they would always listen until the pros and cons of each issue were clarified and a virtual consensus emerged. When the council reached full agreement, the seven senior or 'law-making' gods would announce the final verdict and each of the members would voice their approval with a stern 'Let it be'. This unified

---

1   Much of this section is a re-telling of the Ancient Mesopotamian myth of Enuma Elish. For a version of the myth in full, see *Myths and Legends of the Ancient Near East* (Storm, 2003: 39–50).

2   For an erudite discussion of the democratic practices of the Ordained Assembly of the Great Gods that the myth of Enuma Elish reveals, see Thorkild Jacobsen's essay 'The Cosmos as a State' (Jacobsen, 1977 [1951]).

command meant that the will of the assembly had become divine law; it was the decree of Anu and the duty of Enlil.

Eventually, however, the deliberations of the gods disrupted the slumber of their own mother, the great sea goddess, Tiamet. She was angered by their insolence and sought the counsel of her fellow sleepless gods. Together, they decided to wage war against the elite members of the Ordained Assembly. After many of the gods had visited Tiamet in an attempt to placate her, dissuade her from the attack or defeat her, Lord Marduk, son of Ea came forward and volunteered his services. In return, he demanded of Anshar, the father of Anu, 'If I am to be your champion, if I am to defeat Tiamet and save your lives, call an assembly, name a special fate for me and make it known that henceforth I, not you, shall have control over what comes to pass. My word shall be the law!' (Storm 2003: 43).

After much impassioned debate, the Ordained Assembly of the Great Gods eventually elected Lord Marduk as the new king of the gods. Like Anu before him, his word became the divine law of the universe, he was bestowed with the insignia of royalty – a sceptre, a throne, and a staff, and he was given an invincible weapon with which to smite his enemies.

Bravely, Marduk then set off to engage Tiamet in battle. The fight was long and arduous, but Marduk finally beat Tiamet. The primal mother, the great goddess of the salty waters, lay dead.

After returning to a reception worthy of such a victory, Marduk's position as king and master of all the gods of heaven and earth was confirmed. He assembled the Ordained Assembly of the Great Gods, and he listened to their concerns and heeded their advice. When it came time to reach a final decision, Marduk stood and told them, 'You elected me, and that election must stand firm and supreme ... It is I who make the laws' (Storm 2003: 49). Together, the great gods then set about creating much of the known universe, including their new home which they called Babylon. To look after their city, the gods created the first slaves, human beings, who were put on earth to do their bidding.

Thus began the age of humankind.

Acknowledgements

All scholarly pursuits result from a mixture of solitude and collegiality. There are long periods in which the researcher is completely cut off from the world – perusing the literature, making notes, carefully studying various materials, writing and then editing each chapter. However, a scholar who works alone is never challenged or criticized, is never encouraged to prod in new directions or re-frame ideas in light of contrary information or difficult questions. This vital interaction with others not only improves the quality of academic work, but it makes the hours spent alone seem so worthwhile. Throughout the duration of this project there have been innumerable friends, colleagues and students who have helped tease-out, clarify and solidify a number of the initial ideas and intellectual curiosities I had about democracy in Iraq. I am grateful to all of them.

Throughout the development and completion of this manuscript, I have been fortunate enough to hold four prestigious research fellowships at three exceptional Australian universities. At Griffith University I must thank the staff of the Griffith Islamic Research Unit, Mohamad Abdalla, Halim Rane and Mahmood Nathie, who took a very keen interest in my work on Iraq. I am even more indebted to other Griffith University staff such as Stephen Stockwell and Nigel Krauth who read early versions of the manuscript and their helpful editing enabled a more coherent narrative and cogent argument. At La Trobe University, I would like to thank the staff of the Centre for Dialogue, especially Joseph Camilleri, Michalis Michael, Luca Anceschi and Larry Marshall for their in-depth knowledge of world affairs and dedication to scholarship of the highest order. Finally, at Deakin University, I must thank the staff of the Centre for Citizenship and Globalization, especially Fethi Mansouri, who is first among others who have taken an interest in my work and have challenged many of my ideas about history, politics and discourse. Most recently, I have been fortunate enough to receive an Australian Research Council Discovery Early Career Researcher Award (DE120100315), a fellowship which has allowed me to complete this volume.

More broadly, I would also like to pay tribute to Muhsin Al-Musawi, Alan Knight and Jennifer Kloester who read a version of the manuscript in its entirety and provided invaluable criticisms and comments. Beyond them is a network of people across the world that have read sections of the book, taken an interest in my work and encouraged me to continue. I must also thank the staff of Ashgate, especially Alison Kirk, for her initial support and editorial and administrative assistance. While I rest none of the blame for any remaining problems, oversights or errors made throughout the pages that follow on any of the abovementioned shoulders, any credit received must be tempered by an acknowledgement of their contribution and dedication.

On a more personal note, I would like to thank my family. In many ways my own genealogy – half Western (Australian), half Middle Eastern (Assyrian) – has been central to my own need to scrutinize and question the received wisdoms that many hold in the Western world regarding the political nature of the Orient. In addition to the gift of mixed ancestry, my family has provided the kind of support that has been critical to the project's completion. There are also various other relatives and friends that have helped me in their own way throughout the years and although I cannot list all of them here, my heartfelt thanks go out to them all. However, I must make special mention of my wife, Lyndal, whose patience and understanding are the real reason this book exists at all.

Finally, I must pay tribute to the many Iraqi friends and colleagues who have been very happy to quench my thirst for knowledge about their country and its rich and complex history. I can only hope that, in some small way, this project contributes to a better understanding of this past and enables a more peaceful and democratic future.

Introduction

The events in Iraq do create opportunities to examine democracy, power, tyranny, military force, cultural differences, law, civil liberties, Islam, Christianity, economic development, and even human nature. We ought to understand these issues, because they arise in our own lives and communities; because they are intrinsically interesting and morally serious.

Levine 2004: 22

Democracy in Iraq

On 7 March 2010, the sun rose over the city of Baghdad much as it had since the dawn of human civilization. As the call to prayer rang out across the city, the seven humble families of one particular apartment block in Karkh[1] (Western Baghdad) went about their usual morning rituals: the devout among them prayed, the children stirred and played games, the women prepared breakfast for their families, and the men completed the first of their morning chores. However, today was no ordinary day. Today was the day of Iraq's latest round of national elections. Today held the promise of moving Iraq beyond the violence and trauma of the US-led occupation, beyond the 35 years of Baathist oppression, and beyond the succession of largely ineffective governments that had ruled over Iraq since its creation by the British in the 1920s. For these seven families – and indeed for all Iraqis – today represented an opportunity to ponder these hardships and to elect a government that might represent the needs and interests of the heterogeneous Iraqi population and deliver them a more stable, secure and democratic future. The residents of the small apartment block in Karkh were thus more reflective than usual.

Sadly, this mood of quiet contemplation was soon shattered. At around 7am a deadly explosion tore through the building. In an instant the place these families called home had transformed into a pile of rubble, pinning them under the weight of the twisted debris. Neighbours and friends rushed to the scene and were soon joined by rescue teams and ambulances, all searching for survivors. Tragically, four innocent Iraqi civilians were killed in the explosion and seven others were badly wounded. Seeing the bodies of their friends and family lying prostrate and bleeding on the street, the women embraced the limp and lifeless bodies, tears streaming down their faces as they wailed with grief. The men, overwhelmed with sorrow, beat their heads with their hands and fell to the ground. The people in the

---

1 The story of this household in Western Baghdad is taken from an article written by Qassim Al-Hilfi and published in the Iraqi newspaper *Al-Sabah* (The Morning) (Al-Hilfi, 2010).

crowd shifted awkwardly on their feet, unsure of where to look or how to help as another tragedy unfolded in Iraq. Gradually, the survivors pulled themselves together and said their goodbyes to the dead, making the appropriate arrangements for the bodies to be sent to the local mortuary.

Remarkably, these seven grief stricken families were still determined to vote. They began searching through the rubble in the hope of finding their official documents so that they could proceed as planned to the nearest polling station. Once they had the documents, they set out together on foot, walking for miles before lining up and then placing their ballot paper in the plastic tubs provided. Among them were Abu Nour and his wife Um Nour who had lost two of their children in the blast. Reflecting the bravery of the Iraqi people, as well as their determination to create a more democratic future, through her tears Um told reporters that she knew there were 'still terrorists supplied by actors who are against the success of democracy in Iraq. We pay with our blood and our children to sacrifice for our nation which is our salvation and our home' (Um Nour cited in Al-Hilfi 2010). Despite his pain, her husband agreed:

> This process must have sacrifices ... I was chosen by God to be one of those who sacrifice pure blood to enable the right way and state-building which are sought by all good people in this country and the sacrifices are required ... But our response [to the terrorists] was greater because we bid farewell to our martyrs and then we went to the polls to say 'yes to Iraq and no to all its enemies' (Abu Nour cited in Al-Hilfi 2010).

In total, around 11.5 million Iraqis joined with Abu and Um in saying 'yes to Iraq and no to all its enemies' by taking part in the 2010 elections. Although the security clamp-down had left the streets of the nation eerily quiet in the lead up to the vote, this soon changed as scores of Iraqi citizens – men and women, young and old, Sunni and Shia, Kurd and Arab, Christian and Muslim – filled the streets with their chatter and excitement. Some had arrived early and now paraded their purple ink-stained index fingers to the growing crowds; others arrived later, preferring to wait in the long queues as a sign of their solidarity and to discuss politics, religion and football with their friends and fellow citizens. Like Abu and Um Nour, each had their own tragic story to tell of war, loss and oppression, and each was acting in defiance of the violence and chaos of post-Saddam Iraq, ignoring the blood-curdling threats issued by various insurgents and terrorist networks.

However, these were not the first successful elections to have been held in Iraq since the US-led invasion and occupation began in 2003. Just over 12 months earlier in January 2009, Iraq witnessed relatively free and fair elections for 14 of Iraq's 18 provincial councils.[2] These elections were preceded by a series of democratic elections and a referendum that were held throughout the nation in 2005. These included the January elections which saw some 8.5 million Iraqis vote

---

2   The remaining four Kurdish provinces held separate local elections in July of 2009.

to nominate a national assembly which went on to draw up the Iraqi constitution. A draft of the constitution was then circulated to the citizens of Iraq via the nation's diverse media sector before they gave their verdict in a nationwide referendum in October. This time their ballot paper posed a simple question printed in both Arabic and Kurdish: 'Do you support the draft constitution?'. Approximately ten million Iraqis answered this question and, despite some opposition, the overwhelming majority replied in the affirmative. With the constitution officially accepted, the Iraqi people went to the polls for the third time in December 2005 when 11 million Iraqis elected their own government.

The series of democratic elections that have occurred throughout Iraq since 2005 have attracted the attention of scholars, foreign policy pundits and journalists from across the political and ideological spectrum. While such coverage is critiqued and problematized throughout this book, it is worth noting here that, for the most part, coverage of Iraq since 2003 has emphasized horrific violence through depictions of suicide bombings, kidnappings, mortar attacks, improvised explosive devices, sectarian hostility and the threat of all-out civil war. One might argue that the tendency of the 'Western'[3] media, academics and other commentators to focus on the daily atrocities of post-Saddam Iraq has largely obfuscated the positive political developments and seen successful stories of Iraq's fledgling democracy buried beneath a seemingly endless reel of bloodshed and chaos. Where attention has been paid to the political landscape in Iraq it has tended to privilege disagreements and disunities among Iraq's myriad ethno-religious factions over the complexity of Iraqi politics and the highly inclusive and progressive nature of the democratic deliberations being conducted.

Much of the coverage has also argued that Iraq simply lacks the social and political prerequisites necessary to build towards democratic forms of governance. For example, only months after the relatively free and fair elections of 2005, *USA Today* published an editorial by former US army officer, Ralph Peters, in which he discussed his concerns about Iraq and expressed his opinion as to why democracy would not take root there. It is worth citing at length:

> Iraq is failing. No honest observer can conclude otherwise. Even six months ago, there was hope. Now the chances for a democratic, unified Iraq are dwindling fast ... Iraq still exists on the maps, but in reality it's gone. Only a military coup – which might come in the next few years – could hold the artificial country together ... Yet, for all our errors, we did give the Iraqis a

---

3   The use of the terms 'West' and 'East' throughout this project is in itself problematic given that it relies on a Eurocentric vision of the world. Unlike the terms 'North' and 'South' which have a clearly defined geographical boundary in the equator, the terms 'East' and 'West' are ideological, originating in Europe to divide the Eurasian landmass between the European or 'Western' world and the Asiatic or 'Eastern' world. Despite their Eurocentric origin and their geographical inaccuracy, these terms remain in common parlance and will be used throughout this book.

unique chance to build a rule-of-law democracy. They preferred to indulge in old hatreds, confessional violence, ethnic bigotry and a culture of corruption. It appears that the cynics were right: Arab societies can't support democracy as we know it. And people get the government they deserve. For us, Iraq's impending failure is an embarrassment. For the Iraqis – and other Arabs – it's a disaster the dimensions of which they do not yet comprehend. Iraq was the Arab world's last chance to board the train to modernity, to give the region a future, not just a bitter past. The violence staining Baghdad's streets with gore isn't only a symptom of the Iraqi government's incompetence, but of the comprehensive inability of the Arab world to progress in any sphere of organized human endeavour. We are witnessing the collapse of a civilization (Peters 2006).

On the one hand, balanced assessments of the deep-seated and intractable problems that Iraqi democracy faces along with an open acknowledgement of the failures of the US occupation and the Iraqi government are welcome. On the other, it is instructive to note how often assessments like Peters's seek to connect such concerns to a series of widely held assumptions about Iraq's political history (or, more broadly, that of Arabs or Muslims). For Peters and those of his ilk, whatever problems Iraqi democracy faces, they are not the fault of the invading and occupying forces of the West, nor of the political system they tried to install, but indicative of the backward and barbaric nature of the Iraqi people. Not only is Iraq 'failing' but, even when offered a way out in the form of democracy and freedom, Iraqis prefer 'to indulge in old hatreds, confessional violence, ethnic bigotry and a culture of corruption'. Arab society as a whole has not only missed the 'train to modernity' and failed to 'progress in any sphere of organized human endeavour', it is also incapable of supporting 'democracy as we know it'. Arabs are locked inside an anti-democratic cage built by their own 'culture', their 'bitter past', and their 'civilization'.

The central argument of this book is that not only are such notions remarkably common in discussions of the entire effort to bring democracy to Iraq, but also that they are – sometimes unwittingly, sometimes deliberately – couched in a series of very old ideas about the supposed political divide between East and West. This divide relies on a distinct dualism: the West is seen as having a unique inclination towards democracy, it tolerates diversity and opposing points of view, it encourages innovation and excellence, and it supports freedom, equality and the rule of law. Paradoxically, the East purportedly is driven by impulses that give way to vice and violence, that rely on stagnant traditions and out-dated modes of culture, that limit freedom and expression, and that give rise to unimaginably cruel tyrants who rule by fear, oppression and bloodshed. These are, of course, overly simplistic ways of looking at both the political history of the Occident and the Orient. Not only do they reduce rich and complex histories to a storybook narrative, but they routinely ignore the myriad places and times in which the West itself has acted oppressively and tyrannically, while the East has practised tolerance, cooperation and the rule of law. Repeated and recycled with little critique, this simple dualism has amounted to an intellectual orthodoxy that helps explain away complex realities: the West has a duty to spread democracy among the uncivilized 'lesser breeds' but the project is futile because the East is trapped in an unescapable web of barbarism and bellicosity.

The aim of this book is to demonstrate the myriad ways in which – despite all its obvious flaws and inherent racisms – this dichotomy has been brought to bear on discussions of the complex political history of Iraq. It then seeks to expose the manufactured and arbitrary nature of this false dichotomy by examining Iraq's long and complex history of struggling towards egalitarianism, collective governance and democratic reform. From ancient Mesopotamian assemblies, through Islamic philosophy and doctrine and, despite foreign interference and autocratic tyrants, Iraq has a democratic history of its own. This alternative history of Iraq forces us to acknowledge that democracy is not 'ours' to give to the Iraqis; it is a dynamic system of governance underpinned by virtues of justice, equality and liberty. Virtues that the people of Iraq (or Arabs or Muslims) have at least as much historical claim to as anyone in the West.

Critical Theory, Orientalism and the Democratic History of Iraq

In order to challenge this intellectual orthodoxy and to unearth the democratic history of Iraq, however, this study must first come to terms with a body of scholarship referred to here as critical theory. For Max Horkheimer, such critical theories set out to challenge 'The world that is given to the individual and which he must accept and take into account' and is therefore 'wholly distrustful of the rules of conduct with which society as presently constituted provides each of its members' (Horkheimer 2007 [1937]: 350, 352). In other words, critical theory can be seen to involve the questioning of ideologies – that nexus of received wisdoms, beliefs, values and attitudes inherited from the world around us. In critical theory, these ideologies are scrutinized in order to highlight the assumptions that underpin their claims to truth, their processes of inclusion and exclusion, their relation to other ideological positions and assumptions, and the problematic nature of their universal application.

Arguably, the most influential example of this kind of ideological critique is Karl Marx's[4] body of work relating to the rise of capitalism. Here, Marx proposed a radical new approach to history, focusing on the ways in which the ruling elite sought to justify and maintain the imbalances that came with capitalism by making capitalism itself appear as a legitimate mode of production (Marx 1977 [1887]-a, 1977 [1887]-b). As Marx and his long-time collaborator, Freidrich Engels, articulated elsewhere, the ruling elite were successful in doing this because,

---

4 It is worth noting here many of the scholars discussed here like Marx, Gramsci and Foucault also relied heavily on Orientalist stereotypes throughout their work. This problematic legacy in the Western humanities and social sciences – and especially its consequences for thinking about the history of democracy – is examined in detail in Chapter 1.

> The ideas of the ruling class are in every epoch the ruling ideas: that is, the
> class which is the ruling material force in society is at the same time its ruling
> intellectual force ... In so far, therefore, as they rule as a class and determine the
> whole extent of an epoch, it is self-evident that they do this in their whole range
> and thus, among other things, rule also as thinkers, as producers of ideas, and
> regulate the production and distribution of the ideas of their age: thus their ideas
> are the ruling ideas of the epoch (Marx and Engels 1974 [1846]: 64).

By propagating these 'ruling ideas' the elite are also able to establish a certain
degree of consent from the masses. In other words, as Antonio Gramsci put it,
cultural hegemony is achieved when otherwise ordinary ideas are repeated and
recycled to such an extent that they become what everybody knows, but few dare
to question (Gramsci 1971 [1929–1935], 1978 [1921–1926]).

Perhaps the best application of this critical-theoretical approach to political
history and political discourse is found in the work of Michel Foucault. Throughout
his work, Foucault developed a model of history which 'breaks off the past from
the present and, by demonstrating the foreignness of the past, relativizes and
undercuts the legitimacy of the present' (Poster 1984: 74). To do this, Foucault
attempted to move the debate over issues of power away from the hegemonic
proliferation of dominant ideologies (or 'ruling ideas'), towards a more complex
understanding of the constituent layers of power (or 'discourses') which criss-
crossed the social world. Foucault was able to demonstrate that these various
discourses converge to provide a given society a particular view of the world
(or 'episteme') which can unwittingly be underpinned by discontinuities and
distortions that are embedded within the discourses themselves (Foucault 1970).
Despite its potential to be grievously flawed, each successive episteme both drives
and unifies intellectual production and thereby constitutes itself as the legitimate
and righteous view of the world (Foucault 1981, 1991 [1979], 2005 [1969]). In
this way, overly simplistic and often erroneous ideas – such as the suggested
incompatibility of democracy with Iraqi / Arab culture or the Islamic religion –
are fed into the complex matrix of political, social and cultural discourses that
surround us. They are taught in the classroom, they form the plotlines of comic
books, novels and cinema blockbusters, they are repeated by journalists in the
nightly news, and are used by politicians and pundits to justify imperial expansion
and epic wars.

Another seminal theorist, Jacques Derrida urged us to 'deconstruct' such
discourses by paying close attention to the binary oppositions that underpin ideology
(Derrida 1973 [1967], 1976 [1967], 2003 [1967]). For Derrida, these binary
oppositions help to make sense of the world by reducing complex phenomenon to
an austere and overly simplistic set of polar opposites that are generally thought
to be at odds with each other such as 'good v. evil' or 'Occident and Orient'. The
process of deconstruction is first to expose these binary oppositions, to establish
their inherent contradictions, marginalities and structured silences and then to
challenge the lineage of discourses on which they are premised. This project

seeks to expose the assumptions that underpin the binary opposition between the West's alleged tendency to democracy and the East's proclivity for violence. By deconstructing the binary oppositions inherent in such assumptions it becomes possible to demonstrate that, not only do they privilege generalizations over nuance and depth, but also that they are based on suppositions and false dualisms about the politics of both the East and the West.

Arguably the most erudite example of this critical–theoretical approach to the binary between East and West is the work of Edward W. Said (Said 1979, 1981, 1994 [1993]). In his seminal *Orientalism*,[5] Said deconstructed an astounding number of academic, bureaucratic and literary texts from the Colonial period. What he found was that the Colonial period had seen the West (or more specifically the European Colonial powers) approach the East (and here Said focuses on the Arab world) with a sense of superiority – intellectually, politically, culturally and militarily. This sense of superiority not only permeated an entire episteme of interdependent discourses, institutions and practices in Europe, but also served to create an ideological fantasy that bore no relation to the reality and complexity of Middle Eastern society – its myriad of cultures, religions, peoples, customs, and histories.

This Orientalist fantasy served to homogenize, demonize and stereotype the Middle East according to fairly reductive and negative terms, such that the Oriental was viewed as the 'other'. During the nineteenth century this creation of the 'other' transformed from loose assumptions and general 'ideas about the Orient – its sensuality, its tendency to despotism, its aberrant mentality, its habits of inaccuracy, its backwardness – into a separate and unchallenged coherence' (Said 2003 [1978]: 205). Clearly the unquestioned tendency to view the people of the Orient as deficient and inferior 'others' served the Colonial agenda and its practice of continuing to dominate and control sections of the East. The ideological fantasy of Orientalism had the effect of marginalizing or, more accurately, silencing, the histories and cultures of these 'others'. Said concluded that the people of the Orient have been 'rarely seen or looked at; they were seen through, analyzed not as citizens, or even people, but as problems to be solved or confined or – as the Colonial powers openly coveted their territory – taken over' (Said 2003 [1978]: 207).

Central to Orientalism was therefore a binary opposition between an assumed Western superiority and Eastern backwardness. As is argued in Chapter 1, this dualism is indicative of a particular sub-set of the Orientalist fantasy on which studies of the political history of both the Orient and Occident have so often relied; that of Western democracy and Oriental despotism. These discourses of democracy have a parallel history that can be traced back through the Western scholarly canon. From the time of the ancient Greeks, through the Crusades, the

---

5   It should be noted here that while Said's *Orientalism* is widely recognized as an unprecedented breakthrough in understanding and critiquing Western conceptions of the non-European world, it was somewhat pre-empted (and paralleled) by the work of several scholars (Abdel-Malek 1963, Alatas 1977, T. Asad 1973a, 1973b, Grossrichard 1998 [1979], Jameelah 1971, Tibawi 1964, Turner, 1978).

Reformation and the founding of modern representative democracy, most scholars have contributed to our belief of the West as unique in its propensity for democratic governance and the East as simply incapable of such an advanced political system. Continuing through the eighteenth, nineteenth and twentieth centuries such discourses achieved the status of a received wisdom, they proliferated an ideological uniformity that was rarely critiqued or negated, and they helped bolster the more ambitious claims of so-called experts on the Orient. However, to argue that this dialectic belongs to the annals of history severely underestimates the impact that this discursive lineage continues to have on scholarship, foreign policy and journalism that concerns itself with the Middle East. As Peters' opinion editorial demonstrates, the notion that the Middle East and its 'culture', 'bitter past', and 'civilization' is somehow antithetical to democracy remains a central tenet of discussions of the region today.

Said's work not only encourages us to deconstruct the binaries that exist between 'Western democrats' and 'Oriental despots', however, but to move beyond these by asserting counter-histories free from prejudices and simplistic dualisms. As Franz Fanon reminds us, 'Colonialism is not satisfied with merely holding a people in its grip and emptying the native's brain of all form and content. By a kind of perverted logic, it turns to the past of the oppressed people, and distorts, disfigures, and destroys it' (Fanon 2005 [1963]: 210). The task therefore of many Post-Colonial scholars has been to retrieve the silenced histories that lay behind the roar of Western power, 'both in terms of the objective history of subaltern or dominated, marginalized groups, "counter-histories", and in terms of the subjective experience of the effects of Colonialism and domination' (Young 1995: 58).

In this vein, the study being conducted here also holds up to scrutiny the notion that the West has a particular penchant for democracy and is therefore more civilized than the non-European world. This is a central premise of the work of Post-Colonial scholar Homi K. Bhabha who noted that the guiding discourses of the modern Western world – justice, democracy, liberty – were created at exactly the same moment that the West was involved in the tyranny of the Colonial project (Bhabha 1994, 1995 [1990]). Bhabha elaborates on this point in an interview with Jonathan Rutherford, where he states that:

> I think we need to draw attention to the fact that the advent of Western modernity, located as it generally is in the eighteenth and nineteenth centuries, was the moment when certain master narratives of the state, the citizen, cultural value, art, science, the novel, when these major cultural discourses and identities came to define the 'Enlightenment' of Western society and the critical rationality of Western personhood. The time at which these things were happening was the same time at which the West was producing another history of itself through its Colonial possessions and relations. That ideological tension, visible in the history of the West as a despotic power, at the very moment of the birth of democracy and modernity, has not been adequately written in a contradictory and contrapuntal discourse of tradition. Unable to resolve the contradictions

perhaps, the history of the West as a despotic power, a Colonial power, has not been adequately written side by side with its claims to democracy and solidarity (Bhabha 1990: 218).

Bhabha's assertion is of particular importance in the context of this work because he exposes a more sophisticated history of the modern Western world from the eighteenth and nineteenth centuries onwards. On the one hand, this era of Western history witnessed a series of social upheavals and political struggles in Britain, Western Europe and in North America which paved the way for modern, representative forms of democracy. On the other hand, as Bhabha observes above, at precisely the same time that the West was confronting its own political instability and forging states based on egalitarian models of social justice and representative democracy, it was spreading out across much of the globe in the quest for resources and power. In other words, while the Western world fought for a government that acknowledged and responded to the needs of the citizen at home, it was simultaneously involved in subjugating, capturing, enslaving and, in many cases, exterminating, the people of the non-Western world.

This points to the need for a more complex view of the political history of the West, and the arguably more urgent need for a sophisticated understanding of the political history of the Orient. Behind the constituent layers of Orientalism as conceived by Said and the fantasies it propagated and projected onto the region is a complicated heritage. As in the West, there are long periods in which violence and despotism triumphed and, in other times and places, epochs in which ordinary people came together to practise forms of government akin to what is today called democracy. Unfortunately, the notion that democracy could have been practised in non-Western contexts has been overwhelmingly ignored in traditional accounts of the history of democracy. Instead 'the standard history of democracy' privileges the keystone moments of Western civilization: the achievements of the ancient Greeks and Romans, the later development of the British parliament, the American Declaration of Independence and the French Revolution, and the gradual global spread of democracy since the end of the Cold War. However, as recent research has begun to demonstrate 'there is much more to the history of democracy than this foreshortened genealogy admits. There is a whole "secret" history, too big, complex and insufficiently Western in character to be included in the standard narrative' (Isakhan and Stockwell 2011: 1).

Drawing on this research and employing a critical-theoretical approach, this book focuses specifically on the political history of Iraq in order to demonstrate the nation's rich democratic heritage. To do so, it is necessary to briefly outline what is meant by the term 'democracy' in this context. While there is not space enough here to document the varied debates and definitions of democracy that have been asserted over time, suffice it to say that democracy itself is a complex and contested concept with little consensus on its precise character or on an exact definition (Isakhan 2012b). There are ancient Grecian attempts to understand democracy, mostly by those who were not in favour of it (Aristotle 1943 [350 BCE],

Plato 1975 [380 BCE]) and there are accounts by those who witnessed the dramatic sequence of events that led to the emergence of modern representative democracy in Europe and America (de Tocqueville 1864 [1835], Paine 1856 [1791]). More recent times have brought us minimalist empirical definitions (Schumpeter 2011 [1947]) and an emphasis on certain preconditions, such as economic prosperity (Downs 1957, Lipset 1971 [1959]), autonomous social classes (Dahl 1971, Lijphart 1977), a certain civic culture (Almond and Verba 1989 [1963]), strong political institutions (Dahl 1971, Huntington 1968) and the presence of a political elite who must be determined to see democracy grow and spread (Dahl 2005 [1961]). Paralleling this literature are various philosophical models detailing what a more democratic world might look like, including calls for wider participation (Pateman 1999 [1970]), a radical strategy to undermine the hegemony of the Western liberal model (Laclau and Mouffe 1985) and the need for greater degrees of rational-critical debate (Habermas 1996 [1992]) and deliberation (Dryzek 2000).

From this corpus it is possible to offer a definition of democracy that is both succinct enough to eschew the myriad differences between the empirical and normative peculiarities of the literature, and at the same time practicable enough to be applied to the political past. Such a definition of democracy would necessarily consist of three fundamental parts. First, any claim to democracy must be constituted by a group of more or less equal individuals (the citizen body) who have similar access to certain rights (such as freedom of speech) that come with parallel responsibilities (such as respect for other opinions). This citizen body should also be vested with some power to determine key decisions facing their community (such as how and by whom they are governed). Second, this citizen body should be governed by a set of laws or norms that serve to both protect their rights and responsibilities and to hold those in power to account. Finally, for democracy to work the citizen body must be prepared to do three things equally: they must contest (offer contrary points of view, join an opposition party); they must co-operate (accept the result of an election, form a civil society organization); and they must participate (attend assemblies, vote and get involved in politics).

This study will therefore assess the successes and failures in Iraq's own history of democracy by applying the above criteria across five key epochs in Iraqi history. In Chapter 2, these criteria are applied to the pre-Athenian democratic developments that occurred throughout the ancient Middle East from approximately 3000 BCE to the modern age. Despite the common misconception that the ancient Middle East was home to a lineage of megalomaniacal kings and their savage empires, there is evidence that the practices of democracy were found throughout the region from the smallest city-states to the largest kingdoms. Chapter 3 analyzes the participatory forms of government and egalitarian social movements found throughout both the history and doctrine of Islam. From the life of the Prophet through to the Ottoman era, the history of various Islamic empires and the teachings of a range of clerics and philosophers reveal a picture very much at odds with the overwhelming consensus in the West that the religion of Islam is antithetical to democracy and works against inclusion, diversity and debate.

Together, these two chapters raise important questions about the discourses of democracy: they not only illustrate that democracy was at work in the Orient long before the rise of Athens and the birth of Western civilization, but also that it was kept alive by the Islamic world as much of Europe declined into the inequity of much of the medieval period.

In Chapters 4–6, the focus shifts slightly. It builds atop the above analysis to also examine the extent to which Iraq developed a 'public sphere'. For Jurgen Habermas the public sphere is defined as 'that [which] connects society with the state and thus has a function in the political realm' (Habermas 1996 [1989]: 28). In other words, the public sphere is constituted by those institutions and practices that engender a culture of open and 'rational-critical' debate towards 'democratic deliberation' (Habermas 1987 [1981], 1996 [1992]). These are added here because the public sphere is usually associated with institutions and practices that were not known in ancient Mesopotamia or the classical Islamic world. These include the extent to which rational-critical debate is supported by a robust media sector, the political landscape is constituted by oppositional parties, and an engaged civil society is made up of various actors who co-ordinate activities such as mass protests which agitate for civil rights, air grievances or work towards a more inclusive political order.

In Chapter 4 these criteria are discussed in relation to Colonial Iraq (1921–58) and the role that Iraq's complex media and political landscape played in fostering an engaged public sphere as the country navigated the thorny issues of nationhood and occupation under the auspices of British Colonialism and the installed Hashemite monarchy. Chapter 5 follows with a re-examination of Post-Colonial Iraq (1958–2003), an era which not only witnessed the ascension of a number of repressive regimes but also a number of clandestine Iraqi opposition groups from across various ethno-religious and political divides who began producing their own media outlets and calling for democratic change. Finally, Chapter 6 focuses on Re-Colonial Iraq (2003–11) following the invasion and occupation of Iraq by the 'Coalition of the Willing'. This era has seen an unprecedented upsurge in oppositional political parties, critical media outlets and virulent protest movements – from religious clergymen to secular civil society actors – who have worked together to call for an end to foreign occupation, to rally against corruption and to demand more democracy. Far from a benighted Iraq prone to Oriental despotism these three chapters reveal an alternative vision of modern Iraqi history in which one finds a sophisticated political culture, deeply concerned with the issue of democratic governance.

Taken together these chapters demonstrate that Iraq has a very different history to the one with which it is usually associated. Care must be taken not to over-emphasize the depth and breadth of these democratic moments in Iraq; participatory assemblies, egalitarian beliefs and a lively public sphere cannot be taken in lieu of a robust democracy. As with all Western democracies, which have had their own problems and inconsistencies – from ancient Greek slavery to modern US apathy – Iraqi democracy often falls short of the democratic ideal. Nonetheless, this alternative account of Iraq's political history does provide a more complex lens through which to view Iraq's past and present. It illuminates a democratic potential greatly at odds with the lineage of Orientalist tropes and motifs that have been used to categorize and understand Iraq in the West.

However, this is not the first attempt to unearth a more nuanced and detailed assessment of Iraq's political history. Several studies have revealed that Colonial Iraq was home to a varied media landscape, a thriving religious and secular intellectual scene, myriad political parties and movements, and prolific literary and artistic discourses (Bashkin 2009, 2010, Dawisha 2005a, Wien 2006). Others have provided unique insights into Post-Colonial Iraq and noted that while a succession of autocratic leaders sought to control and manipulate the political discourse of Iraq in order to situate the Iraqi people into a position of forced acquiescence, they simultaneously gave rise to a virulent culture of resistance and opposition (Baram 1991, Batatu 1982 [1978], Bengio 1998). Taking more of a longitudinal approach, there are several excellent studies of Iraq's political history from the British Mandate through to the fall of Saddam (Marr 2004 [1985], Stansfield 2007, Tripp 2007 [2000]). These include those which have offered a more detailed examination of the cultural formations and intellectual life of Iraq with particular emphasis on the literary, intellectual and political cultures which have openly called for Iraq's liberation and discussed the possibilities for a cohesive and democratic future (Al-Musawi 2006, Davis 2005b, Dawisha 2009).

Despite the strength and importance of this body of work and its assertion of a more complex assessment of Iraq's political culture and history, none of these studies provide a sustained critical analysis of the discourses which have been brought to bear on Iraq's recent democratization. In addition, none of these works have attempted to problematize and unhinge these discourses by juxtaposing them against a thorough analysis of the indigenous roots of democracy in Iraq. Another problem with the aforementioned studies is their narrow historical focus and the virtual absence of important epochs such as ancient Mesopotamia and the Islamic period, not to mention the successes and failures of democracy in Iraq since 2003. Finally, none of these studies provide a discussion of the ways in which Iraq's democratic legacy might be used as a tool in re-thinking the history of democracy and in building, stabilizing and legitimizing democracy across Iraq today. This project therefore attempts to fill this lacuna by couching modern Iraqi experiences with democracy in a broader discussion of its rich political history.

In conducting a project such as this there are several key problems and limitations. First among these is the fact that it is difficult to analyze and discuss with any sense of finality Iraq's democracy. At the time of writing, daily reports from across Iraq continue to document the chaos and turmoil of the nation, including the grim and complex battles fought between the occupying forces, the Iraqi security services, various insurgent groups and terrorist organizations, as well as those between competing ethno-sectarian factions. This is not to mention the plights of so many ordinary Iraqis (such as the seven families sharing the apartment block in Karkh) who continue to endure the countless struggles and hardships of the post-Saddam era. Furthermore, such violence continues to take its toll on the democratic process in Iraq which itself is ongoing. Despite the fact that Iraqis have participated in a series of relatively free and fair elections, seen parties and governments form and citizens elected to the ranks of Prime Minister and President, the nation is by no means a stable and robust democracy. The government, its ministries and institutions are still relatively weak and the basic infrastructure of Iraq remains well below minimum acceptable standards in much of the country. Compounding all of this is the fact that the US withdrew all of its forces at the end of 2011, leaving an uncertain future beyond occupation.

This also raises another limitation of this research project, namely that studying Iraq – its history, its political culture and especially its current situation – is decidedly difficult to do from the other side of the world. The various issues, risks and costs associated with researching Iraq have meant that while this study includes many primary sources and up-to-date information based on contacts within Iraq, it also relies on existing secondary information. While it is important to acknowledge here that such a methodology brings with it certain limitations to the scope of the study and the inferences it can make, the author has made every attempt to cite reputable and established works and to cross-reference these against other materials where available. It is also important to note that this book does not represent a comprehensive political history of Iraq, if indeed such a thing is possible. This book is a deliberately potted history, emphasizing those moments in Iraqi history when people engaged with democratic principles, ideas and practices.

Finally, determining whether or not Iraq will become a robust and stable democracy is beyond the scope of this study. This book is about the ways in which Iraq and its democratization have been constructed according to certain discourses which have for so long underpinned Western understandings of the Middle East. In addition, this project is also about scrutinizing these discourses and closely examining the assumptions on which they are based by re-examining the long and rich political history of Iraq. In the interest of establishing a stable and democratic Iraq, this book concludes that the democratic history of Iraq might be used as a powerful political and discursive tool where the Iraqi people may come to feel a sense of ownership over democracy and take pride in endorsing it. This could go a long way towards mitigating the conflicts across the nation and in stabilizing and legitimating its democratic order. This book therefore argues that there is much scholarly work left to be done in order to broaden the narrative of democracy and move beyond the overly simplistic framework provided for us by the discourses of Western democracy and Oriental despotism. By asserting alternative histories and emphasizing their democratic potentials, a step is taken not only towards a more nuanced picture of Iraqi politics *per se*, but also towards salvaging the utopian promise of democracy from the intersecting discourses which have constructed it for us.

Chapter 1
Discourses of Democracy

In sum, the theory of oriental despotism was crucial not just to 'explain' Asian backwardness but, no less importantly, to cement the identity of Europe – both past and present – as the birthplace of advanced, democratic civilization.

Hobson 2004: 228

The Discourse of Western Democracy

The etymology of the English word 'democracy' can be traced back to the sixteenth century when it was adapted from the French word *democratie*. Further back, the Late Latin term *demokratia* had its origins in a Greek word that is itself a composite of two other words, *demos* and *kratos*. The latter translates to mean 'power' or 'rule' and appears today in English words such as aristocracy (rule by the *aristoi*, the best or elite), autocracy (rule by the *autos*, the self), monarchy (rule by the *monos*, alone or one), and oligarchy (rule by the *oligoi*, the few or little) to name only some. The word *demos*, on the other hand, was a protean word that had several different, but related, meanings such as 'citizen body', or 'lower classes' that can be generally translated to mean 'the people'. Together, then, *demokratia* literally means 'people power / rule', or perhaps more eloquently, 'rule by the people'.

The word *demokratia* is believed to have first appeared in the writing of the 'Father of History', Herodotus, around 460 BCE. In his seminal text, *The Histories*, Herodotus presents the origins, context and events of the Greco-Persian Wars of 490 BCE and 480–479 BCE with a remarkable penchant for detail and a vast knowledge of cultures and lands beyond those of his native Greece. Throughout his work, Herodotus repeatedly praises the freedom and democracy of Greece. For example, when Athens is liberated from the despotic rule of Pisistratidae (who owed his allegiance to Persia instead of Greece), Herodotus seizes the opportunity to praise the strength of Athenian democracy. Having thrown off the shackles of despotism,

Thus did the Athenians increase in strength. And it is plain enough, not from this instance only, but from many everywhere, that freedom [elsewhere translated as democracy (see: Forsdyke, 2001: 333)] is an excellent thing; since even the Athenians who, while they continued under the rule of tyrants, were not a whit more valiant than any of their neighbours, no sooner shook off the yoke than they became decidedly the first of all. These things show that while undergoing oppression, they let themselves be beaten, since then they worked for a master; but so soon as they got their freedom, each man was eager to do the best he could for himself. So fared it now with the Athenians (Herodotus 1996 [460 BCE]: V.78).

Athenian democracy emerged when the aristocracy issued Kleisthenes a mandate in 508/7 BCE to formulate a political system that would eschew the centralization of power. Kleisthenes, an adept and popular politician who had long advocated a system of 'rule by the people', devized a sophisticated method of participatory democracy centred on the notion of the *polis*, meaning the 'city and its citizens' (Aristotle 1984 [332 BCE]: 20–2). To govern the *polis*, the Athenians convened in an assembly, an outdoor meeting which presided over issues as vast as 'war and peace, treaties, finance, legislation, public works, in short, on the whole gamut of governmental activity' (Finley 1973: 18–9). All adult male citizens were encouraged to attend these assemblies, which convened about 40 times a year, and were permitted to *isegoria* – the freedom to voice their concerns in front of their fellow citizens. Furthermore, the assembly elected a few key officials and experts to positions of authority, while every citizen had more than a good chance of being chosen by lot for a short-term position in public office. While the developments in Athens remain among the most significant democratic moments of the ancient world, it must be remembered that the sheer size of the Grecian assembly would have prevented a robust exchange of views and that many citizens (women, foreigners, slaves etc.) were excluded from the proceedings. It should also be remembered that *demokratia* was very unpopular among many prominent Greeks. Plato believed that democracy was very far from an ideal form of government as it privileged the will of the uneducated lower classes; instead, he argued in favour of a republic presided over by a wise philosopher-king (Plato 1975 [380 BCE]). Despite such criticism, the Athenian experiment lasted around two centuries before it was overthrown by the superior military might of the Macedonians, who replaced it with their own oligarchic system in 322 BCE.

Concurrent to the rise and fall of *demokratia* in Athens, was the development of the Roman Republic. Interestingly, the etymology of republic comes from the Latin words *res* (meaning 'thing' or 'affair') and *publicus* (or 'people') which together make 'the affairs of the people', not altogether dissimilar to the Greek notion of 'rule by the people'. While in the earliest years of the Republic, the workings of the Senate (originally composed of the heads of clans) and the *Comitia Curiata* (the general assembly of all arms-bearing men) were complex and relatively egalitarian, the Republic quickly descended into the kind of oligarchic power structures that the Athenians had been so determined to avoid. Nonetheless, scholars such as Polybius and Cicero went to great lengths to defend the Republic, arguing that it came closer to the ideal vision espoused by many earlier Greek philosophers because it combined elements of democracy with a virtuous ruling elite (Cicero 1998 [54 BCE], Polybius 1889 [150 BCE]). Despite such optimism, there can be no denying that Rome was at best a robust oligarchy in which the interests of a small number of wealthy, land-owning nobles almost always trumped the will of the plebs (or 'common people'). Although the *plebs* did eventually gain access to the inner workings of the Republic after having fought vehemently for the privilege, the Republic remained the domain of the elite and, as the empire spread out across the known world, an increasing number of citizens were disenfranchised. Eventually, the authority of Rome was undermined by a series of wars, corruption scandals, and a decline in the civic spirit that had underpinned the birth of the Republic.

Thus, the concept of 'the affairs of the people' administered by popular governance is commonly understood to have vanished from Europe for around a thousand years (Bryce 1921, Dahl 1998, Dunn 1992). Although the Vikings and the Venetians held assemblies as far back as the fifth century, it is generally thought that it wasn't until the northern city-states of Italy began to develop systems of popular rule around 1100 that democracy began to re-emerge on the continent. This period saw a thriving socio-economic and cultural atmosphere that paralleled that of ancient Greece and is now acknowledged as having given rise to the Renaissance. Although the authority over the early political machinations of these city-states was restricted to the aristocracy, who were granted supreme judicial authority, the system eventually evolved to include the *popolo* (the people of the middle classes). By the middle of the thirteenth century there were written constitutions which guaranteed each individual state their own 'elective and self-governing arrangements' (Skinner 1992: 57). Shortly after this however, these city-states descended into economic hardship and forms of oligarchy and autocracy replaced these increasingly unstable and short-lived democracies.

Meanwhile, in Medieval England, King John was forced to raise taxes due to an escalating number of military defeats. This greatly enraged the powerful English barons and Catholic bishops who drew up a list of restrictions they wanted to enforce on the actions of the king and rights they wanted to secure. By 1215 the king was forced to sign the *Magna Carta* (Latin for 'Great Paper') which prescribed that the authority of the king was to be shared with a Great Council constituted mostly by noblemen and ecclesiastics. Eventually, this Great Council evolved into the more familiar Parliament (from the French *parler*, 'to speak') during the reign of Edward I. Under the leadership of his grandson, Edward III, the parliament was split into two chambers in the middle of the fourteenth century: the Upper Chamber, which went on to become the House of Lords and represent the interests of the elite, and the Lower Chamber which became the House of Commons and was constituted by representatives of the nation's counties and boroughs. Although the introduction of the House of Commons has clearly influenced the development of representative democracy, it must be remembered that it consisted of borough representatives who had been elected by the mere 10 per cent of the adult male population who were eligible to vote. Nonetheless, the rising power of the two chambers came to the fore during the seventeenth century when the Parliament became increasingly critical of the monarchy. This paved the way for the English Civil War (1642–51) which, in turn, brought about the passing of the Bill of Rights in 1689 and the Act of Settlement in 1701, both of which upheld the powers of the Parliament and serve as seminal moments in the story of British democracy.

Paralleling these developments, the middle of the fourteenth century had seen German national Johannes Gutenberg convert a winepress into the world's first movable-type printing press thus giving birth to the modern mass media. Following the onset of the Thirty Years War in 1618, Europe was inundated with fledgling newspapers and, by the middle of the seventeenth century, 'political newspapers had the largest circulation of all contemporary forms of printed material, or were at any rate the most widely distributed form of secular reading matter' and these papers 'exemplified a norm of neutrality that has remained unequalled ever since' (J. Weber 2006: 399, 402). The common newspaper also played a critical role in transforming the once esoteric world of kings, courtiers, politicians and ecclesiastics into legible fodder for the common person; they fed into the emerging bourgeois civil society that was to prove so influential in the series of political events and revolutions that paved the way for the materialization of modern democracy. At the time of the French Revolution many previously clandestine newspapers, journals and pamphlets flooded the streets of the nation, garnering the force of public opinion and 'undermining the credibility of established authority and spreading new ideas of religious scepticism, social criticism and reform' (Fontana 1992: 111). This led the rebellious few who constituted the representatives of France's Third Estate (the middle classes and peasants) to found the National Assembly and vow to revolt against the existing monarchy, advocating a system of 'popular sovereignty vested in the whole of the French nation' (Fontana 1992: 114). This call was heeded by the citizenry and a bloody rebellion swept across much of France. Chanting *Liberté, Egalité, Fraternité, ou la Mort!* ['Liberty, Equality, Fraternity, or Death!'] the insurgents went on to storm the Bastille prison in Paris on 14 July 1789, effectively setting in motion a series of events that ended with the usurpation of the French monarchy. Later the same year, the French Constituent Assembly adopted 'The Declaration of the Rights of Man and of the Citizen', which, in 1791, formed the preamble for the constitution and set in place a representative democracy with near universal male suffrage.

The next chapter in the unfolding story of democracy occurred not in Europe, but in the newfound colony of America. Here, according to Alexis De Tocqueville's seminal study *Democracy in America*, the emigrants who arrived on the shores of New England from the beginning of the seventeenth century created a situation in which 'A democracy more perfect than antiquity had dared to dream of started in full size and panoply from the midst of an ancient feudal society' (de Tocqueville 1864 [1835]: 35). The Americans were able to overthrow their foreign monarch in the American Revolution, prompting their 1776 Declaration of Independence. The Framers of the United States Constitution then went on to deliberate over and re-draft their document until it was completed in Philadelphia in 1787. Although, the constitution had its imperfections, it was cleverly crafted to eschew the authority of a monarch while retaining what Americans saw as the merits of the English system. Finally, in 1789 the new republic began operating under the authority of the document following its ratification. As part of their effort to protect civil liberties, the United States also then issued the Bill of Rights in 1791 which included a series of amendments to the Constitution.

Just over a decade later in England, journalists were granted access to the House of Commons in 1803, allowing the birth of a more critical British journalism. The space where these media professionals sat came to be known as the 'Fourth Estate', a term which came to symbolize the media's responsibility in not just reporting the news but in serving as the people's 'watchdog' over the elite. In other words, the journalist's democratic responsibility was to 'highlight problems and weaknesses in government policies and performance, in order that corrective action might be taken' (Romano 2005: 8). In this watchdog role, the media helped to hold governments accountable to their constituents, highlighting abuses of power such as corruption, detailing incompetence and scrutinizing government policy and administration. Beyond this, the media played a central role in the emergence of modern democracy by creating an informed citizenry with a propensity for varied debate and discourse, which, as has been discussed, Habermas referred to as the 'public sphere' (Habermas 1989 [1962], 1996 [1989]).

To state that the developments in England, France and America were heralded as a triumph is something of an understatement. Having witnessed European events first-hand, French philosopher Destutt de Tracy stated that 'Representation, or representative government, may be considered as a new invention ... [it] is democracy rendered practicable for a long time and over a great extent of territory' (de Tracy 1811: 19). Later, the oft cited British political scientist, John Stuart Mill claimed that

> There is no difficulty in showing that the ideally best form of government is that in which the sovereignty ... is vested in the entire aggregate of the community; every citizen not only having a voice in the exercise of that ultimate sovereignty, but being ... called on to take an actual part in the government, by the personal discharge of some public function (J. S. Mill 1962 [1861]: 57).

Throughout much of the nineteenth century, Europe also witnessed the rise of the Industrial Revolution. This engendered a system of capital whereby the wealthy continued to cultivate their riches and the masses were increasingly forced to work in abhorrent conditions for less and less recompense. These harsh conditions led to a series of further democratic revolutions across Britain and Europe through the mid-nineteenth century. In France, bloody protests led to the formation of the Second Republic with an emphasis on universal suffrage and unemployment relief. News spread quickly of the events in Paris and it was not long before a series of violent protests and subsequent democratic reforms occurred across the Habsburg's Austrian Empire, Germany, Italy and Poland.

Following the end of the First World War and the dissolution of the great Prussian, Ottoman and Austro-Hungarian empires, several nominally democratic states emerged across Europe. However, such developments were countered by the effects of the Great Depression which brought with it significant economic hardships and a widespread dissatisfaction with the existing political order. Under these conditions the 1920s and 1930s witnessed 'the establishment of varied forms of dictatorship and totalitarianism of the left and the right in Russia, Germany, Italy, Japan and other countries' (Saward 2003: 37) as well as the emergence of non-democratic regimes in parts of Eastern Europe, Latin America and Asia. As David

Held has pointed out, these events suggest that democracy is a 'remarkably difficult form of government to create and sustain' and that the forces of 'fascism, Nazism and Stalinism came very close to eradicating it altogether' (Held 2006 [1987]: 1).

However, with the success of the Allied powers at the conclusion of the Second World War, 'all of the main alternatives to democracy either disappeared, turned into eccentric survivals, or retreated from the field to hunker down in their last strongholds' (Dahl 1998: 1). This, coupled with the successful democratization of the occupied nations of Germany and Japan as well as the growing economic strength of the West during the 1950s and 1960s, meant that democracy was once again flourishing across much of Europe and the Western world, even spreading to parts of South America and Asia during the 1970s and 1980s. However, the end of the Second World War also saw the USSR emerge as one the world's two leading superpowers and the power vacuum created by the defeat of Nazism led to the 'mutual suspicion and vilification, arms building, proxy confrontation and ideological posturing of the Cold War' (Saward 2003: 43). But the economic pressures of the 1980s, as well as internal resentment of communist oppression and external demands for democratization, caused the socialist republics of the Eastern Bloc gradually to give way to form more liberal, democratic governments. Then, in 1991, under the weight of these same pressures, the USSR disbanded and the long Cold War was over.

The end of the Cold War prompted many libertarian Western intellectuals to herald the triumph of the Western world and its ideology of free market-based liberal democracy. Foremost amongst this body of work was Francis Fukuyama's controversial thesis that the world was witnessing 'not just the end of the Cold War, or the passing of a particular period of post-war history, but the end of history as such: that is, the end point of mankind's ideological evolution and the universalization of Western liberal democracy as the final form of human government' (Fukuyama 1989: 1). Whether or not Fukuyama's central thesis is correct, democracy certainly continued to spread across much of the globe throughout the 1990s and into the 2000s. Much has been made of this *Third Wave* (Huntington 1991) or *Global Resurgence* (Diamond and Plattner 1996 [1990–1995]) of democracy. Along these lines, one influential Freedom House Report claimed that the twentieth century had been 'Democracy's Century', an era which witnessed the transformation of democracy from a handful of 'restricted democracies' in 1900 to a situation where more than half of the world's population lived and thrived in 'electoral democracies' by the end of the century (*Democracy's Century* 1999). Since the coming of the new millennia, democracy has continued to flourish with developments across much of the globe. Perhaps most telling has been the modest successes of a series of people's movements in the former states of the USSR, including the 'Rose Revolution' (Georgia, 2003), the 'Orange Revolution' (Ukraine, 2004) and the 'Tulip Revolution' (Kyrgyzstan, 2005). Similarly, recent developments in countries such as Thailand, Iran, Burma, Pakistan and Nepal indicate, at the very least, the popularity of democracy and its continuing support amongst various people's movements opposed to oligarchic or autocratic forms of power. Even the tiny Himalayan nation of Bhutan recently held its first general election (March 2008), ironically enough under the orders of the king himself. Most recently, the 'Arab Spring' of 2010 and 2011 has not only toppled long-standing regimes in Tunisia, Egypt and Libya, but also served as a mechanism for people across the region to express their disdain for authoritarian and oppressive forms of government (Isakhan, Mansouri, and Akbarzadeh 2012). It is fair to say that recent history has witnessed democracy spread across much of the globe to stand today as the preferred method of human governance.

As democracy spreads, it is interesting to note the degree to which it is understood according to the lineage of events, practices and movements outlined above. Clearly, these developments – from as far back as the Greek concept of *demokratia* and the Roman Republic, but more directly since the establishment of the British Parliament, through the American Declaration of Independence, the French storming of the Bastille and the apparent global spread of democracy since the fall of Communism – have had a profound impact on our understanding of the Western world today. This extraordinary sequence of events has frequently been invoked throughout the various political and social movements that litter Western history. For example in Walter Benjamin's essay 'On the Concept of History', he discusses briefly this connection between Europe's political past and more contemporary events. He states that 'The French Revolution viewed itself as Rome incarnate. It cited ancient Rome exactly the way fashion cites a bygone mode of dress' (Benjamin 2003 [1940]: 395). More broadly, the Western story of democracy has been invoked among people's movements across the globe. Consider the intriguing paradox recounted by Jack Goody in which citizens of Burkina Faso (then known as the Upper Volta) protested against French occupation in the 1950s under banners reading *Liberté, Egalité, Fraternité* (Goody 2006: 246).

Today, concepts such as human rights, justice, liberty, personal freedoms and minority representation are said to have a long and rich narrative that can be traced backwards through the great moments of Western civilization. Underpinning this understanding of the origins and development of modern Western society is a particular discourse of democracy. Here, the body of knowledge and lineage of events outlined above have come to generate a very specific understanding of the nature of democracy itself where 'rule by the people' has come to signify those political moments and traditions of Western Europe and the United States. It has also engendered an understanding of Western civilization as underpinned by an inherent tendency towards egalitarianism and methods of collective governance. In this way, the Western world has asserted itself as the rightful legatee of legitimate forms of democracy and therefore believes in its dissemination and emulation across the globe. It is this combination, the understanding of Western civilization as the product of this genealogy and, at the same time, the notion of this civilization's unique propensity for and propagation of democracy which converge to form what is termed here the discourse of Western democracy.

This discourse of Western democracy – like the discourses uncovered by Foucault that had constituted the clinic, the asylum and the prison for example

(Foucault 1961, 1990 [1976], 1991 [1979]) – has been established within the parameters of the West's own episteme. It is inherently Eurocentric in nature, reflecting events, institutions, practices, social movements, revolutions and participations from within a relatively narrow historical narrative. The link formed between the history of Western politics and the discourse of democracy is made explicit by John Hobson when he argues that

> Eurocentrism typically extrapolates backwards the modern conception of political democracy all the way to Ancient Greece. It then fabricates a permanent picture of Western democracy by tracing this conception forwards to Magna Carta in England (1215), then to England's Glorious Revolution (1688/9), and then on to the American Constitution (1787/9) and the French Revolution (1789). In this way, Europe and the West is (re)presented as democratic throughout its long rise to power (Hobson 2004: 290).

In a sense, this means that discussion of democracy is not only describing something often seen as exclusive to the West, but is also actively defining it against those 'others' who have not formed part of this larger narrative. Along similar lines Larbi Sadiki argues that 'From Hellenic times down to the present, it seems that democracy has mostly been a narrow conception at least in two ways: the philosophers and seminal thinkers who constructed it; and the "publics" they constructed democracy for' (Sadiki 2004: 6). In terms of the first point, Sadiki goes on to demonstrate that the individuals who have debated and defined democracy over the years have (until very recently) belonged to a very exclusive group, that of Western males, mostly from the elite class in their respective societies. Perhaps because of this elite patriarchal lineage, democracy has also almost always been about inclusion and exclusion. Clearly this might firstly involve women, minorities, slaves, and the working poor who for so much of democracy's history have been excluded from its practices and narratives from within the very Western culture which is so often assumed to have a history of egalitarianism and human rights. More to the point, the discourse of Western democracy is therefore also defined as not non-Western. As Sadiki notes,

> The story of democratic achievement in the modernist metanarrative is exclusively equated with its inception in parts of the Western world, especially England, France and the United States. If those societies which are exemplars of democracy are, for instance, distinguished by rationalism, secularism, urbanism and individualism, then those societies which are characterized by the absence of these 'universal laws' are condemned to continuous democratic impasse (Sadiki 2004: 149).

In this way, the discourse of Western democracy has largely ignored the Middle East and the broader non-Western world and tended to disregard its systems of governance, its revolutions and civil movements and, more specifically, its methods and models of 'rule by the people'. As Said has pointed out, where any attention has been paid to the complexity of Middle Eastern politics it has tended to rely on Orientalist assumptions regarding their tendency to authoritarian or despotic rule, their abhorrence of collective governance and their general inability to democratize (Said 2003 [1978]). This has led to the assumption that Middle Easterners – even when offered democracy and freedom – either cannot rise above their cruel, brutal nature or are simply unable to grasp the complexities of this Western concept. Essentially, this reflects the Colonialist adage that lies at the heart of Orientalism, that it may well be impossible to reform the savage. This notion depends on a binary opposition between the two historical discourses outlined in this chapter, the discourse of Western democracy which marks the West as the hallmark of the modern, civilized and democratic world and that which constructs the East as its antithesis, the backward, barbaric and despotic nether region, as characterized by the discourse of Oriental despotism.

The Discourse of Oriental Despotism

The antecedents of the discourse of Oriental despotism can be traced back as far as that of its binary opposite, Western democracy. In some of the earliest examples of classical Greek literature, including Homer's *Iliad*, Aeschylus's *The Persians*, and Euripedes' *The Bacchae*, the Orient was associated with a kind of mystical backwardness and a tendency towards irrational violence and immoral depravity (Aeschylus 1961 [472 BCE], Euripedes 1973 [400 BCE], Homer 1950 [700 BCE]). Patricia Springborg argues that entrenched in the 'seemingly innocent, archaically quaint or apparently arbitrary elements' of the writings of individuals such as Polybius, Plato, Hesiod, Diodorus, Isocrates and others, there are tropes and motifs which can be seen 'to shore up racial and elite hegemony quite deliberately' (Springborg 1992: 1–2).

More specifically, while key Greek thinkers such as Herodotus and Aristotle are widely recognized for their contribution to the understanding and formulation of *demokratia*, they were simultaneously amongst the first to discuss the concept of despotism, which they often attributed to the Orient. Herodotus' re-telling of the events of the Greco-Persian Wars not only represents the first serious scholarly attempt at writing history, but also, the first comprehensive attempt 'to translate "others" into the terms of the knowledge shared by all Greeks, and which, in order to make credible these "others" whom it is constructing, elaborates a whole rhetoric of "otherness"' (Hartog 1988 [1980]: xxiv). This is evident in the contrast drawn between the tyranny, oppression and civic weakness of the despotic Persian empire and the liberty, egalitarianism and civic strength of the Greek model of *demokratia* (Herodotus 1996 [460 BCE]: V.78; VII.102–4, 139). Another method employed by Herodotus to construct the Persian other was to both over-estimate the size of the Persian empire and also point out the inferiority of their weapons and military skills (Herodotus 1996 [460 BCE]: VII.209–13). This is perhaps best illustrated in

Herodotus' re-telling of the battle at Thermopylae, where the brave 300 Spartans and a loose collection of other Greek soldiers are reported to have made a stand against the encroachment of a total of five million Persians (Herodotus 1996 [460 BCE]: VII.183–6). The cumulative effect of this construction of the Persian 'other' not only underlined Greek superiority and bravery, but also stipulated the need for Greek unity against the fundamental threat posed to the freedom and liberty of Greece by the dark, despotic peoples to the East.

The assumptions that Herodotus made about the inferiority of Oriental politics are well illustrated by his passage covering a debate among seven noble Persians over which governmental system is most suitable for the Persian empire (Herodotus 1996 [460 BCE]: III.80–7). Of the seven nobles, Otanes is said to have argued in favour of democracy, Megabyzus in favour of oligarchy, while Darius, eyeing the throne of the world's foremost superpower, argues in favour of monarchy. In his powerful address, Darius claims that both democracy and oligarchy lead to violent disputes until a single individual 'stands forth as champion of the commonalty, and puts down the evil-doers. Straightway the author of so great a service is admired by all, and … appointed king; so that here too it is plain that monarchy is the best government' (Herodotus 1996 [460 BCE]: III.82). The remaining four Persian nobles then vote in favour of installing a monarch and, through a clever ruse, Darius himself is able to ascend the throne. Through this story, Herodotus cleverly demonstrates to his audience the backwardness of the Persians via their failure to recognize the superiority of democratic governance and the fact that they were tricked into succumbing to a monarchy, a situation which would presumably never occur in democratic Greece.[1]

These themes are reiterated in Xenophon's *The Persian Expedition*, in which he recounts the story of 10,000 Greek mercenaries who had been hired in 401 BCE by Cyrus the Younger of Persia in a plot to usurp the throne of his brother, Attaxerxes II (Xenophon 1986 [360 BCE]). The 10,000 travelled all the way from Greece to central Mesopotamia, making it as far as Cunaxa, just north of ancient

---

1   On the one hand, it is little wonder that figures such as Herodotus – or the many listed below like Pope Urban II or Martin Luther – portrayed the Middle Eastern other as brutish, backward and inferior. These people lived through times of great conflict and rivalry between East and West and it is an unfortunate reality that during such periods even the most intelligent commentator is often prone to reductionist stereotypes. This is not just an Occidental phenomenon and the same can certainly be said of Persian portrayals of the Greeks or Arab portrayals of the Christian Crusaders for example. On the other hand, as Patrick Porter points out in his *Military Orientalism*, ever since the ancient Greeks obsessed over the threat posed by the expansive army of Xerxes, the West has been drawn to the exotic nature of Oriental warfare. Feared, revered or commandeered, eastern warriors have played a central role in western imaginings of the dark and brutal territories that lie beyond the Occidental–Oriental line. These imaginings have contributed much to the development of Orientalist sentiments in the West. Such deep-seated notions remain embedded in the western consciousness and resurface in new guises and with renewed impetus each time Western civilization is seen to be under threat from the Eastern barbarian (Porter 2009).

Babylon and in the middle of modern day Iraq. The circumstances that unfolded left the 10,000 Greeks stranded deep in enemy territory and they had to fight their way northward, enduring countless battles and betrayals by the Persians, Kurds, Chaldeans, Armenians and various other so-called 'barbarians'. Throughout his tale, Xenophon frequently contrasts the tendency towards despotism amongst these 'barbarians' against the civility and democratic nature of the Greeks. This clear divide in Xenophon's work is uncritically acknowledged in George Cawkwell's 'Introduction' to a recent edition of the text:

> On every page of the *Anabasis* the contrast between Greek and barbarian is sharply drawn – the barbarian world vast and diverse, feudal and ancient or tribal and savage, the Greek world compact and united by the sea, and, despite variety, essentially one in its approach to life. The Greek was pre-eminently a 'political animal,' and the Ten Thousand are all the Greeks in miniature. When they are left leaderless, the crisis is not resolved by authority or seniority. They assemble and debate. Arguments and the art of words prevail. The army is really a polity on the move. Let barbarians fall to the ground in submission to whoever wins the contest for the crown. The Greeks will give their allegiance to the man whose reason, not his blood, proves his fitness to lead (Cawkwell 1986 [1972]: 9–10).

At around the same time that Xenophon was transcribing the struggle of the 10,000 through the hostile Orient, Aristotle was compiling some of the earliest known writings on topics as diverse as philosophy, physics, poetry, logic, biology and ethics. Amongst his writing, Aristotle took particular interest in politics, outlining the key parameters of the various political systems of his time. As with Herodotus and Xenophon, Aristotle tended to equate the Occident with democracy and the Orient with despotism, arguing that the hotter climates of the East had created peoples who were susceptible to oppression by forms of total power. Along these lines, *Aristotle* claims in Politics that,

> There is another sort of monarchy not uncommon among the barbarians, which nearly resembles tyranny. But this is both legal and hereditary. For barbarians, being more servile than Hellenes, and Asiatics than Europeans, do not rebel against a despotic government. Such royalties have the nature of tyrannies because the people are by nature slaves; but there is no danger of their being overthrown, for they are hereditary and legal (Aristotle 1943 [350 BCE]: III.14).

In the years that followed, the works of these early Greek writers were reiterated and confirmed across Europe as empires such as that of Alexander the Great (who was a student of Aristotle) and later the Romans expanded. Later, the teachings of Christianity eventually spread out from the Levant and up into Europe. While this brought with it something of a renewed interest in the Orient across the West, ironically it also enabled a new way for marking many of the people of the region as the 'other': they were the descendants of Abraham's eldest son, Ishmael, who had been cast out by Abraham into the desert, condemned to a life of tribalism and barbarity. In this way, well before the rise and spread of Islam in the middle of the seventh century, terms such as Ishmaelite or Saracen were used pejoratively across Europe. These terms signified the inferiority of the people of the Middle East, rather than indicating an enemy posing a credible threat (Rodinson 2002 [1980]: 3–5).

This discourse was to evolve somewhat as the religion of Islam expanded and the armies of Arabia were able to launch successful attacks on Christian territories. Having little if any information about the actual tenets of the Islamic faith it was not the religion that concerned Europe so much as the threat of military invasion. Europe was, at first, unable to fully grasp how the Ishmaelites had been able to wage such sophisticated attacks on the might and virtue of Christendom (Beckett 2003: 1–13, Daniel 1979: 107–8). Both the confusion and burgeoning sense of threat experienced in Europe are perhaps most evident in the literature of the Anglo-Saxon period in England where renowned biblical scholars such as the Venerable Bede (673–735) merged both contemporary politics and theology in his interpretation of the story of Abraham's son Ishmael (Genesis 16:12) to claim

> This means that Ishmael's seed was to dwell in the desert, and without fixed habitations. These are the nomadic Saracens who raid all the peoples on the edge of the desert, and who are attacked by all. But this was long ago. Now, however, his hand is against all men, and all men's hands are against him, to such an extent that the Saracens hold the whole breadth of Africa in their sway, and they also hold the greatest part of Asia and some part of Europe, hateful and hostile to all (Bede 2008 [700]: IV.16:12).

A pivotal historical era in the continuation of the binary opposition between Occident and Orient were the Crusades of the late eleventh century through to the thirteenth century. Throughout this epoch, Christian Europeans captured important cities across Anatolia and the Levant including the Holy City of Jerusalem which had been conquered by the Muslims in 638. This era was also witness to the first Latin translation of the *Quran* and a more developed understanding of the religion and practices of Islam. Perhaps because this growing body of knowledge was largely sponsored by the Church, it served to focus European energy against the Muslim threat, rather than to foster any sense of tolerance or genuine scholarship.

In the lead up to the Crusades, Pope Urban II gave a public address at Clermont in south-east France in 1095. In it, the pontiff attempted to invoke the wrath of European Christians over the capture of Jerusalem as well as Islam's expansion across Asia, North Africa and even into Spain (some 300 hundred years earlier). In a series of powerful rhetorical turns, the Pope relied on a number of Orientalist clichés to build his case for war, arguing that the Turks and Saracens are 'miscreants' and 'the enemies of God' who 'eagerly anticipated' their conquest of Europe and that they were cowardly and underhanded in battle (Pope Urban II cited in Malmesbury 1895 [1120]: 359–61). Interestingly, and in ways not at all dissimilar to Aristotle some 1500 years before him, Pope Urban II asserts that environmental factors are to blame for Asiatic backwardness, where 'every race, born on that region, being scorched with the intense heat of the sun, abounds more in reflexion, than in blood' (Pope Urban II cited in Malmesbury 1895 [1120]: 361). This speech is widely recognized for having set in motion roughly two centuries of conflict between the worlds of Christendom and Islam, with one renowned Middle East historian, Philip K. Hitti having referred to it as 'probably the most effective speech in all history' (Hitti 1968: 168).

It is at this point – at the height of the Crusades – that the Occidental/Oriental relationship took on a new dimension. Until the Crusades any tension between the two regions had been largely framed in terms of territories, ethnicities and cultures, rather than between religions. While these earlier differences remain embedded within the broader discourse, the Crusades saw many adherents of both Islam and Christianity become increasingly antagonistic towards each other. Instead of viewing the other religion as a compatible alternate theology, some began to view the other as apostates and blasphemers, a distinction which remains prominent in many quarters today.

This cultural legacy regarding Western perceptions of the Orient was passed down from the Greco-Persian Wars, through the Crusades and into modern Europe. Here, new technologies such as the printing press not only enabled the dissemination of political and religious materials, but *Volkskalender*'s, early lunar calendars that also contained lengthy poems of a political nature (Brévart 1988). The first example extant is the *Turkenkalender: An Urgent Appeal to Christendom Against the Turks* (printed in late 1454) which, as its name suggests, urges the leaders of Christian Europe to take up arms against the Turks after their capture of Constantinople in 1453. The pamphlet begins by asking God to help 'us Christians against our enemy, the Turks and pagans … and to avenge the atrocities committed against the Christians of Constantinople' (Simon 1988: 7). From here, the pamphleteer moves on to incite each of the heads of Europe 'to take up arms against the Turkish infidel' and to leave 'no Turk alive in Turkey, Greece, Asia and Europe' (Simon 1988: 7, 10). In this way, the text sharply contrasts the Turks as 'enemies', 'pagans' and 'infidels' who deserve no less than complete extermination, against Europeans who are portrayed as 'noble', 'privileged' in possession of 'superior and spirited strength' and are therefore required to 'support the battle for our faith and eternal salvation' (Simon 1988: 11–12).

Later, as the Ottoman Empire expanded through Belgrade and Hungary, the printing press continued in its role as the disseminator of early Orientalist propaganda. Across Germany pamphleteers ran-off scores of polemical texts against the Turks and Islam, creating a whole new genre known as *Turkenbuchlein* (Bohnstedt 1968). Even the highly esteemed monk and theologian, Martin Luther, whose challenges to the papacy gave birth to modern Protestantism, wrote several treatizes against the Turks (Edwards 2003, R. O. Smith 2007). At the time there was much debate in Europe about the correct response of Christianity to the Muslim encroachment and, in 1529 as the Turks reached Vienna, Luther's tract *On War Against the Turk* sought to make clear his own personal opinion that the Turks were the 'servants of the Devil', 'wild and barbarous people' who lead 'an abandoned and carnal life' full of 'wickedness and vice' (Luther 1974 [1529]: 126–30). Here, invoking the kind of rhetoric that is indicative of Orientalism, Luther states:

> In the first place, the Turk certainly has no right or command to begin war and to attack lands that are not his. Therefore his war is nothing but an outrage and robbery with which God is punishing the world, as he often does through wicked scoundrels, and sometimes through godly people. The Turk does not fight from necessity or to protect his land in peace, as the right kind of ruler does; but, like a pirate or highwayman, he seeks to rob and ravage other lands which do and have done nothing to him. He is God's rod and the devil's servant; there is no doubt about that (Luther 1974 [1529]: 125).

Throughout the seventeenth, eighteenth and nineteenth centuries, the technology of the printing press improved and literacy rates climbed across Europe, bringing with them a burgeoning market for printed books, journals, pamphlets and newspapers. While these early media formats are so often lauded for their role in fostering the bourgeois civil society that was to provide the impetus for the emergence of modern representative democracy, they have rarely been critiqued for their contemporaneous use of Orientalist discourses. One particularly popular example is the early travelogue in which wealthy aristocratic British and French explorers recorded their adventures. In *Sir Jean Chardin's Travels in Persia* for example, the narrative exposes the drunken, brutal and arbitrary despotism of the Persian king through the eyes of a rational French merchant and diplomat. The king is seen to command absolute obedience to his every whim, no matter how heinous his request or how inebriated he is at the time of his demands. This is perhaps best illustrated in the relationship between the king and his Prime Minister who admits to the king 'I am your Slave, I will ever do what your Majesty shall command me' (Chardin 1720 [1686]: 16). Despite such submission, the king repeatedly humiliates the Prime Minister in front of the court by using ill language, by striking him, by throwing wine in his face and 'a thousand indignities of this nature' (Chardin 1720 [1686]: 17). Such despotism was reported back to Europe as indicative of the Persian – and by implication, Eastern – model of governance, a model of drunken cruelty that would have contrasted sharply with the apparent civility of Europe at the time (Grossrichard 1998 [1979]).

Drawing heavily on Chardin's accounts of Oriental despotism, French philosopher Charles Louis Montesquieu attempted to illustrate that despotic power benefited no one by using Persia as the model despotic empire which he viewed as representative of a broader Oriental despotism that pervaded all aspects of Asiatic life[2] (Montesquieu 1923 [1721]). In *The Spirit of the Laws* Montesquieu

---

2   It should be noted here that while Montesquieu's work relied heavily on the notion of Oriental despotism, this aspect of his work received criticism from scholars such as Francois-Marie Voltaire and Francois Quesnay who held very positive views on India, China

went on to claim – in a similar vein to both Aristotle and Pope Urban II before him – that climate and geography predisposed certain regions to particular political systems. In vast, hot lands Montesquieu argued, the 'effeminacy of the people ... has almost always rendered them slaves' (Montesquieu 1949 [1748]: 264). 'This', Montesquieu continues, 'is the grand reason of the weakness of Asia, and of the strength of Europe; of the liberty of Europe, and of the slavery of Asia ... Hence it proceeds that liberty in Asia never increases; whilst in Europe it is enlarged or diminished, according to particular circumstances' (Montesquieu 1949 [1748]: 266). This line of reasoning leads Montesquieu to the conclusion that 'Power in Asia ought, then, to be always despotic', because, 'it is impossible to find in all the histories of that country [Asia] a single passage which discovers a freedom of the spirit' (Montesquieu 1949 [1748]: 269).

The eighteenth and nineteenth centuries witnessed not only the series of events and upheavals across Europe and the United States that were to pave the way for modern representative democracy, but also saw the Colonial project extend its reach to subjugate much of the world under Occidental control (Bhabha 1990, Said 2003 [1978]). This period also brought with it the cementation of familiar stereotypes regarding the Oriental 'other' into a series of received wisdoms that were frequently drawn upon without scrutiny or independent research. This is evident in the works of influential scholars such as the German philosopher Georg Hegel who developed a Eurocentric approach to world history in which the Asiatic civilizations that had once contributed to the narrative of human history, now lay at its periphery (Bernal 1991 [1987]: 294–6, Gran 1996: 2–3). While Hegel is considerably more generous to the kingdoms of the Near East than he is to those of the Far East, this is only because 'They are related to the West, while the Far Eastern peoples are perfectly isolated' (Hegel 1952 [1837]: 235). In discussing the Persian Empire he argues that its success was enabled by its ability to quell the natural barbarousness of the people. He argues that

> It was not given to the Asiatics to unite self-dependence, freedom, and substantial vigour of mind, with culture, *i.e.*, an interest for diverse pursuits and an acquaintance with the conveniences of life. Military valour among them is consistent only with barbarity of manners. It is not the calm courage of order; and when their mind opens to a sympathy with various interests, it immediately passes into effeminacy; allows its energies to sink, and makes men slaves of an enervated sensuality (Hegel 1952 [1837]: 242).

This picture of the Orient as naturally despotic, barbarous, enslaved, disorderly, degenerate, culture-less and effeminate was particularly useful to the imperial forces of Europe in justifying their control over, and abuses of, the increasing number of territories and peoples who came under their control.

---

and Persia, arguing that they had made some of the greatest contributions to humankind (Quesnay 1946 [1767], Voltaire 1963 [1756], 1994 [1779]).

Similar sentiments are also evident in James Mill's six volume *The History of British India*. Mill reiterates the notion of Oriental despotism as he imagined it to be in India throughout his work, claiming that 'Among the Hindus, according to the Asiatic model, the government was monarchical, and, with the usual exception of religion and its ministers, absolute. No idea of any system of rule, different from the will of a single person, appears to have entered the minds of them, or their legislators' (J. Mill 1972 [1817]: 212–213).

These ideas are also present in Alexis de Tocqueville's writings on the French occupation of Algeria. While Tocqueville was so generous in his appraisal of *Democracy in America* (de Tocqueville 1864 [1835]: 35) and so certain that it would continue to flourish there, he was equally as certain that, despite the best efforts of the French to civilize the Arabs, the Arabs would never overcome their penchant for violence and tyranny. This theme is reiterated throughout his many letters and essays that deal with Algeria – known collectively as *Writings on Empire and Slavery* (de Tocqueville 2001 [1833–47]). In one particularly revealing passage, De Tocqueville writes

> that for quite a long time – we cannot know how long – domination of the Arabs will be onerous. This is because of the social organization of this people, their tribal organization and nomadic life, something we can do nothing about for a very long time, perhaps ever. Very small, nomadic societies require great effort and expense to be held in an order that will always be imperfect. And this great governmental effort produces very little, because the same causes that make them so difficult to govern also make them poor, needing little and producing little (de Tocqueville 2001 [1841]: 62).

Similarly, Karl Marx[3] also inherited notions of Oriental despotism and the Asian propensity for stationariness. Overall, Marx tended to view the Orient through a series of stagnations or absences – those of civil society, bourgeoisie culture, private property, propensity for social change and modernization. He further believed that the only route for Asian salvation was for the Orient to undergo 'Europeanization' (Avineri 1968, Turner 1978). In this sense, Marx provided

---

3   While this book is guided by the work of Karl Marx in the sense that he provided a revolutionary approach to the ways in which bourgeoisie culture is able to legitimate and propagate its elite position via the assertion of certain ideologies, this work is also conscious of his position as both an inheritor and producer of Orientalist stereotypes. It was Said who not only recognized and critiqued the presuppositions that Marx relied on in formulating his understanding of the Orient, but who also understood that, while Marx's work was clearly problematic along these lines, it was also ironically valuable as a tool for comprehending the same lineage of Orientalism of which Marx was himself a part. In this way, this project parallels Said's work if only because it can be seen as both a utilization of key aspects of critical theory (such as Foucault's work on discourse and the power/knowledge nexus) which developed out of the work of Marx and, at the same time, a substantial critique of the ways in which these methods have served to construct the Middle Eastern / Islamic / Arab 'other'.

some justification for European colonization, particularly in the contemporaneous instance of British India, about which he stated,

> England, it is true, in causing a social revolution in Hindostan, was actuated only by the vilest interests, and was stupid in her manner of enforcing them. But that is not the question. The question is, can mankind fulfil its destiny without a fundamental revolution in the social state of Asia? If not, whatever may have been the crimes of England she was the unconscious tool of history in bringing about that revolution (Marx 1973 [1853]: 493).

Central to Marx's understanding of the Orient was his formulation of what came to be termed the 'Asiatic Mode of Production'. Asia was thus stifled by the constant dynastic change and the centralized ownership of property and production. The people were reduced to being the slaves of their despotic ruler, forced into menial labour and thereby unable to form civil movements or become upwardly mobile (Krader 1975, Sawer 1977, and Turner 1994).

Together, scholars such as Hegel, Mill (and his son John Stuart Mill), De Tocqueville and Marx contributed much to the modern world's understanding of the benefits and pitfalls of representative democracy. They were also certain that, while Europe had a unique proclivity for democracy, the non-European world was destined to stagnate under oppressive forms of governance. To argue, however, that such notions are isolated to the works of nineteenth century European scholars is to profoundly underestimate the pervasiveness of this discourse (Isakhan 2010b). This rubric continued to develop in the works of several notable early twentieth century scholars, such as Maximilian Weber who began his work on the sociology of religion by writing *The Protestant Ethic and the Spirit of Capitalism*. Following Hegel and relying mostly on secondary Orientalist sources, Weber developed a profoundly Eurocentric view of world history. Weber believed that the religious dichotomy between East and West had a profound effect on the realms of politics and law, arguing that

> all Indian political thought was lacking in a systematic method comparable to that of Aristotle, and, indeed, in the possession of rational concepts. Not all the anticipations in India (School of Mimamsa), nor the extensive codification especially in the Near East, nor all the Indian and other books of law, had the strictly systematic forms of thought, so essential to a rational jurisprudence, of the Roman law and of the Western law under its influence. A structure like the canon law is known only to the West (M. Weber 1992 [1904–5]: 14).

Furthermore, Weber viewed Islam as a religion guided by instability which thereby prevented Muslims from successfully challenging the political order and instigating social change (Salvatore 1996, Turner 1974, 1996 [1981]). Despite the fact that Weber spent much of his life writing about Oriental cultures and religions, he rarely bothered to challenge his erroneous assumptions regarding the superiority of the West over the East. Perhaps even more problematical is the fact that his work went on to have a profound impact on European scholarship of Islam where, at least until very recently, 'the great majority of studies of social movements in Islamic societies tended (either implicitly or explicitly) to be situated within the Weberian tradition' (Burke 1988: 20).

Building on the work of Weber and Marx, Karl Wittfogel argued that Oriental societies demanded the centralization of authority and the subjugation of the peasantry under the auspices of an agro-bureaucratic state. Wittfogel went on to claim that such a 'hydraulic state is not checked by a Beggars' Democracy. Nor is it checked by any other effective constitutional, societal, or cultural counterweights. Clearly it is despotic' (Wittfogel 1957: 126). In addition, such hydraulic states were also required to maintain their hegemony over the people via the obliteration of any civil movements that may challenge the existing political order. In this way, according to Wittfogel, the Oriental understood total submission to authoritarian rule.

By the middle of the twentieth century, Orientalism had developed into an academic discipline in and of itself. Here, scholars such as Gustave von Grunebaum and, more recently, Bernard Lewis focused their analysis of Middle Eastern socio-political history less on agricultural factors and more on the practices and rituals of Islam. Although it has to be stated that such scholars contributed enormously to the body of work on Islam and the Middle East, they have nonetheless been heavily criticized for their propagation of Orientalist ideologies including their understanding that 'Despotism was implicit in the very core of Islam' (Sadowski 1993: 16). For example, Grunebaum argues that the potential for egalitarian and collective models of governance in Islam had been steadily decaying since as far back as the ninth century. Accordingly, he asserted that it was doubtful the political model of 'the caliphate as designed by the legists ever had any real existence' and that Islamic law thereby descended to a point where the 'believer was thought under obligation to obey whosoever held sway' (Grunebaum 1946: 168). By the eleventh century, as Grunebaum goes on to claim, 'the tendency natural to despotism and orthodoxy' were responsible for Islamic civilization having become 'Arrested in its growth' where it 'remained an unfulfilled promise' and 'stagnated in self-inflicted sterility' (Grunebaum 1946: 322). As Mohamad Abdalla points out, Grunebaum ignored the 'rise, rather than the decline of science in the Muslim world after the eleventh century' (Abdalla 2007: 67).

Similarly, Bernard Lewis has made a number of sweeping statements about the nature of Middle Eastern politics under the authority of the caliphs, which he saw as an era of 'almost unrelieved autocracy, in which obedience to the sovereign was a religious as well as a political obligation' (Lewis 1964: 48). According to Lewis, this is a rather predictable consequence of the fact that Islamic law itself

> knows no corporate legal persons; Islamic history shows no councils or communes, no synods or parliaments, nor any other kind of elective or representative assembly. It is interesting that the jurists never accepted the

principle of majority decision – there was no point, since the need for a procedure of corporate collective decision never arose (Lewis 1964: 48).

Perhaps more controversially, Lewis argued that because Christendom was able to eventually overcome the historic threat of Islam, a vacuum had been created in which 'Muslim Rage' emerged and it was only 'natural that this rage should be directed primarily against the millennial enemy' of Christian Europe and its colonies (such as the United States) (Lewis 1990: 49). According to Lewis this, along with the Islamic world's alleged failure to separate church and state and the advancement of the West since the Crusades brought about 'a feeling of humiliation – a growing awareness, among the heirs of an old, proud, and long dominant civilization, of having been overtaken, overborne, and overwhelmed by those whom they regarded as their inferiors' (Lewis 1990: 55). The convergence of this sense of rage and humiliation is supposed to have led to the rise of Islamic fundamentalism, which will bring about a 'Clash of Civilisations' between Islam and the West in which these Islamic fundamentalists will react against 'our Judeo-Christian heritage, our secular present, and the worldwide expansion of both' (Lewis 1990: 56).

It was this final section of Lewis' article which was to provide the impetus for Samuel P. Huntington's essay and later book in which he expanded the notion of a 'Clash of Civilisations'. As early as 1984 Huntington was arguing that 'among Islamic countries, particularly those in the Middle East, the prospects for democratic development seem low' (Huntington 1984: 216). In his later work, Huntington argued that, each region of the globe had its own individual religio-cultural essence that plays a large part in determining receptivity to democratic systems (Huntington 1987: 24). He isolated Islam and Confucianism as 'profoundly anti-democratic' and claimed that they would 'impede the spread of democratic norms in society, deny legitimacy to democratic institutions, and thus greatly complicate if not prevent the emergence and effectiveness of those institutions' (Huntington 1991: 298–300). The 'Clash of Civilizations' was therefore based on the fundamental differences between these anti-democratic civilizations and the West (Huntington 1998 [1996]). Here, Huntington reserves particular vitriol for the world of Islam which he accuses of never having successfully grasped the concept of the nation state, preferring the macro-level politics of a succession of pan-Islamic empires such as the Caliphates and the Ottomans. Later in the book, Huntington draws out his notion of a looming threat between Islam and the West via a historical account that relies heavily on the work of Bernard Lewis and other Orientalists. He concludes by arguing that 'The underlying problem for the West is not Islamic fundamentalism. It is Islam, a different civilization whose people are convinced of the superiority of their culture and are obsessed with the inferiority of their power' (Huntington 1998 [1996]: 217).

More recent scholars of the Middle East have continued the long Orientalist tradition of defining the Middle East and Islam according to its absences. Patricia Crone has argued that when the *Shariah* (Islamic law) was first codified around the middle of the eighth century, it was embedded with the nuances of the existing tribal laws. This meant that Islamic politics was predisposed towards encouraging the long-held divisions between the various sects and peoples (Crone 1980). Similarly, Daniel Pipes and John Hall claim that these medieval events have left Islamic society with only a very tenuous understanding of politics and precluded it from developing an active civil society or model of democracy (Hall 1985, Pipes 1983). Taking this a step further, Mehran Kamrava states that 'it is the forces of primordialism, informality and autocracy that have shaped and continue to shape the parameters of life in Middle Eastern societies' (Kamrava 1998: 32). It is this fundamental lack of a democratic history, Kamrava goes on to argue, that has left the Middle East without the prerequisite social and cultural dynamics to foster various democratic movements, institutions and classes that make up a thriving civil society and give rise to democratic governance (Kamrava 1998: 31–2). This assertion is made even more explicit when Anthony Black concludes that

> the very idea of a constitution, the rule of law, procedures which precisely define legitimate tenure of power, presupposes a separation of authority from the individual. In the Islamic world, authority remained tied to the outstanding individual and dynasty … This affects political culture and practise today, making a peaceful transfer of power and the introduction of new blood through elections very difficult (Black 2001: 351).

Returning briefly to the work of Bernard Lewis it is worth noting that, since the events of September 11 2001 and the subsequent 'War on Terror', Lewis has published several works that have continued to foreground the perceived dialectic between the Orient and Occident. In one article, which appeared only a few months after 9/11, Lewis opened with the following paragraph:

> In the course of the twentieth century it became abundantly clear that things had gone badly wrong in the Middle East – and, indeed, in all the lands of Islam. Compared with Christendom, its rival for more than a millennium, the world of Islam had become poor, weak, and ignorant. The primacy and therefore the dominance of the West was clear for all to see, invading every aspect of the Muslim's public and even – more painfully – his [her] private life (Lewis 2002: 43).

This tendency to reduce 'all the lands of Islam' down to a homogenous entity and to describe them as 'badly wrong' and 'poor, weak, and ignorant' against the 'primacy and therefore the dominance of the West' is, as has been demonstrated above, a tendency that harks back through the canon of Western scholarship to its earliest formal roots in classical Greece. From Herodotus to Huntington, a whole list of reasons have been cited by Western scholars who wish to explain away Middle East politics and justify its exclusion from what Derrida would call the 'emancipatory promise' of democracy (Derrida 2006 [1993]: 74).

Conclusion

The discourses of Western democracy and Oriental despotism create a political distinction between East and West. While the Occident is constructed as forthright, righteous and democratic, the Orient becomes the 'other', known only for its backwardness, its moral deficiencies and its tendency towards violence, barbarity and despotism. Paralleling one another, these twin discourses of democracy have an ancestry that dates at least as far back as classical Greece, where several scholars not only sketched out the Western propensity for *demokratia*, but clearly delineated it from the Eastern world which was condemned to the rule of tyrants and autocrats. The lineage of these competing discourses continued through many key moments in Western civilization, from the Anglo-Saxon era, the Crusades, the Reformation and through the Colonial period right up until today. To say that this Eurocentric lineage has had a profound effect on Western understandings of the Middle East throughout the twentieth and early twenty-first century is an understatement. Here, a collection of Orientalists have claimed that the Middle East has little tradition of power sharing, tolerance or egalitarian government and that certain cultural and religious factors continue to thwart any attempts to democratize the region.

The problems relating to this lineage of Orientalist discourse are manifold. One such problem is the fact that these discourses are so firmly embedded in the canon of Western scholarship. For example, the modern Social Sciences and Humanities is constituted by those authors who repeatedly make a distinction between the democratic nature of the West and the despotic tendencies of the East: History students are taught the works of Herodotus, Xenophon and William of Malmsbury; Political Scientists read Aristotle, John Stuart Mill and Huntington; Sociology and Philosophy majors sit through long lectures on Hegel, Marx and Weber; Theologians scour the works of Bede, Pope Urban II and Luther; and students of the Middle East frequently cite the works of Grunebaum and Lewis. What is rarely stated explicitly throughout these lectures, courses and readers is the Orientalist nature of these texts, their reliance on presuppositions about the Orient that are long-standing, ubiquitous and provide for us a certain picture of the region's inability to democratize. It is little wonder then that these assumptions penetrate into wider society and are drawn upon by policy-makers, politicians, journalists, film-makers and artists who so often resort to a kind of Orientalist short-hand in order to explain away events involving the Middle East or Islam. It is also little wonder that, as we shall see, this rich discursive heritage has so often been brought to bear on Iraq's political history.

However, uncovering the lineage of these discourses of democracy is one thing, but asserting the genealogy of an alternative set of discourses and uncovering their genealogy is quite another. To do so, it is essential to expose and critique the assumptions which envelop our understanding of democracy and its history and investigate marginalized narratives and histories. As Said argued shortly before his passing in 2004, 'There was never a misinterpretation that could not be revised, improved, or overturned. There was never a history that could not to some degree be recovered and compassionately understood in all its suffering and accomplishment' (Said 2004: 22). It is the central premise of this project that Iraq's history has been profoundly misinterpreted and that it must be 'revised, improved, or overturned'. The ensuing chapters are an attempt at 'recovering and compassionately understanding' the democratic history of Iraq 'in all its suffering and accomplishment'.

Chapter 2
Democracy in Ancient Iraq

> In comparison with Greek and Hellenistic cultures, Mesopotamian culture at first
> sight, undeniably, seems alien and strange. The better one has learned to understand
> it, however, the more it has come to resemble our own culture. Its strange and
> exotic features conceal within themselves an invisible world of ideas more familiar
> to us, which resurfaces in new garments but largely identical in content in classical
> antiquity.

> Parpola 2000: 30

The Political Significance of Ancient Iraq

In asserting an alternative history of Iraq – one that emphasizes rather than ignores
its democratic potential – the analysis must begin well before the time of the
ancient Greeks; a time which preceded the false binaries between Greece and
Persia, between the Occident and Orient, between Christianity and Islam, between
Europe and her colonies and between Western democrats and Oriental despots.
Reaching back into the annals of the ancient past, a number of early city-states
began to appear across Mesopotamia[1] around 3200 BCE. As is now commonly
understood, this era witnessed the development of some of humankind's earliest
agricultural and architectural feats, including early farming practices and animal
domestication, complex irrigation networks, sophisticated artistic and structural
wonders as well as a relatively complex, urbane and cosmopolitan society.
Very early on, these complex societies – with their large hydraulic projects and
complicated temple and city economies – prompted the development of the world's
first written language. This involved using a split reed to create the distinctive
wedge-shaped marks now known as cuneiform on clay tablets which evolved
from early markings concerning systems of weight and measurement through to
a rich body of literary texts (Oppenheim 1967, Silvestro, 1965). As time passed,
a plethora of overlapping and successive empires spread out across and beyond
Mesopotamia, each bringing their own complex histories and cultures.

This rich history of the ancient Middle East became politically significant long
before the birth of the modern nation-state of Iraq in 1921, as various early Pan-Arab
and Iraqi nationalist groups utilized its symbology in their rhetoric to encourage
unity amongst the ethnically diverse population (Davis 2005b: 13). This was to

---

1   The term 'Mesopotamia', as with the term 'demokratia', is a composite word that
is thought to have first appeared in the work of Herodotus. The word 'Meso' translates to
mean 'middle' while 'Potamia' means 'river', thus making 'the middle of the rivers' (more
commonly translated as 'between the two rivers') in reference to the Tigris and Euphrates.

continue throughout the British occupation and the rule of the Hashemite monarchy from 1921–58, an era which also saw the creation of the Iraqi Museum and a vibrant archaeological scene. Throughout this period, as Magnus Bernhardsson has cogently articulated, the ruling elite utilized the country's ancient Mesopotamian past in order to build a sense of nationhood amongst Iraqis of differing religious persuasions and ethnicities (Bernhardsson 2005). Similarly, the Arab Baath Socialist Party underwent an extensive and sustained cultural campaign in which the successes of the nations past became a symbol of Iraq's potential as a united and prosperous state. One epoch on which the Baath focused much of their attention was that of ancient Mesopotamia. They attempted to 'Arabize' Iraq's ancient past by radically transforming it in the minds of the Iraqi people from *Al-Jahiliya*, the pre-Islamic period of 'ignorance', to that of the 'Arabs before Islam' (Davis and Gavrielides 1991: 134–5). To do this, the Baath ordered the annual re-enactment of ancient Mesopotamian spring festivals across the nation which included traditional music, folktales, poetry, dances and arts, all linked to the early Near East. The regime also funded extensive archaeological excavations, re-built the ancient city of Babylon in the late 1980s, decorated various buildings and monuments with Mesopotamian symbols, and constructed museums dedicated to great leaders of the ancient past, such as Nebuchadnezzar and Hammurabi.

In Amatzia Baram's studies of Baathist manipulation of Mesopotamian symbology and folklore he demonstrates the ways in which the Baath were able to re-appropriate and manipulate Iraq's ancient history in order to both encourage national unity and patriotism as well as to garner submission to the central ruling elite (Baram 1983, 1991, 1994). Baram's examination not only emphasizes the political significance of the ancient Middle East to contemporary Iraqis, but also demonstrates the degree to which the Baath understood the maintenance and legitimation of hegemony via the manipulation of cultural and social artefacts to gain the consent of the people and maintain power. Here, Saddam and the Baath understood that by emphasizing Iraq's Mesopotamian heritage they could eschew many of the more contemporary schisms which divide Iraqi society such as those between the Kurds, Shia Arabs and Sunni Arabs (Isakhan 2011b).

What is particularly problematic about these contemporary invocations of Mesopotamian history as a political tool is that, aside from its role in fostering some degree of national unity, it has also been used to justify the ruling elite of the time via a vague connection to a long line of 'Oriental despots'. Take for example the grandiose murals and portraits that scattered Iraq in the time of Saddam Hussein in which he was frequently cast alongside infamous Mesopotamian kings such as Nebuchadnezzar in scenes riddled with ancient symbology and motifs (Al-Khalil 1991, Reid 1993). Up until recently, the political history of the ancient Middle East had long been assumed to reveal a lineage of autocratic tyrants and the grand, menacing armies they gathered together in order to conquer and rule the region by fear, bloodshed and domination. 'In the traditional view of Historians,' as Daniel Bonneterre points out, 'Mesopotamia has stood out among the lost civilizations as a pessimistic world under the dark shadow of violence … [which]

emphasized terror and ferocious actions' (Bonneterre 1995: 11). The result of this misunderstanding, which arguably dates back to ancient Greece, 'is a simplistic book image of the ancient Near East civilizations as naturally despotic and most savagely cruel' (Bonneterre 1995: 11).

So pervasive is this perception of the ancient Middle East and its tendency to despotism that commentators such as Sandra Mackey invoked several of the key assumptions about Oriental despotism and its ancient origins by claiming, in the lead up to the invasion of Iraq in 2003, that

> the kings of Assyria never accepted the reality that empires, like modern states, survive only through a measure of consent by the governed. Like a series of ancient Saddam Husseins, each failed to lay the basis of a durable state (Mackey 2002: 37).

Another example of this can be found in Mark Etherington's *Revolt on the Tigris*. Etherington was the British governor of the Wasit province under the authority of the Coalition Provisional Authority (CPA) during 2003–04. Etherington's legitimate concerns about the prospects of democracy in Iraq are connected to its ancient society – or lack thereof:

> Iraq's 'otherness' had been accentuated by its political isolation ... There was no all-embracing society in Wasit to speak of, but rather a series of camps and cliques – miniature societies – each with its own place. Most were quick to denounce the others, and compromise was rare. Each clique was self-sufficient because it was built around a source or sources of power. Like ancient city-states they traded with one another, made alliances and broke them, declared wars and negotiated peace; and occasionally one vanished because the strength sustaining it had waned. When power was fed into Wasit's ancient system this great flotilla would tremble as it absorbed new realities – and then steadily re-align itself as it had done for centuries ... To speak of 'democracy' as a theme, or of 'Iraq' as a rallying point or social adhesive, was thus less than effective because few Iraqis saw the advantage of thinking in that way ... If the prospect of a democratic state is among the world's most potent political rallying cries, it meant little to most Iraqis who simply sought to transmute it into the old currency (Etherington 2005: 84–5).

Here, Mackey and Etherington suggest that the key challenge facing Iraq's democracy is its ancient culture of stagnant tradition. In ways that ironically mimic the Baath, they use broad brush strokes to connect the 'kings of Assyria' or Iraq's 'ancient city-states' to more contemporary political problems such as the rule of Saddam or the political wrangling and violence of the post-Saddam era. This understanding of the ancient Middle East as the precursor to more contemporary instances of Oriental despotism is clearly problematic in that it serves to further entrench the view of a backward East.

However, the archaeological excavations and anthropological work that were carried out across the region throughout the nineteenth and twentieth centuries have begun to uncover a very different image of the processes of power and authority in the ancient Middle East. This has provided an understanding that the history of modern democracy, which is usually understood to have begun around 500 BCE in Greece, can be traced further back to early Mesopotamia. As is illustrated in some detail below, this work therefore provides evidence that

> When the Mesopotamian state first emerged in the early periods, royal power did not play an important role and only many centuries later did it become despotic. Originally kings were merely the first among equals and were obliged by laws or by long social traditions to respect the rights of the various groups of the population. In addition, royal power was restricted by popular assemblies which sometimes had a real and even decisive influence and which made citizens proud of their civil rights (Dandamayev 1995: 23).

Ancient Mesopotamian and Middle Eastern Democracies

The crystallization of Mesopotamian civilization from around the middle of the fourth millennium BCE, saw the development of the framework that these civilizations would use to formulate their deepest questions, evaluate the world around them and develop their cultural legacy and societal institutions. Evidence for such advanced thought is found in the early myths and legends of ancient Mesopotamia, such as the inner functioning of the Ordained Assembly of the Great Gods. This assembly was made up of 50 gods and goddesses in total, with both genders playing an active role in the deliberations, and was the highest authority in the universe. As Min Suc Kee notes, this body served as 'a vital decision-making agency responsible for juridical judgements', where the gods would listen and debate until the pros and cons of each issue were clarified and a virtual consensus emerged (Kee 2007: 259, n1). When the council reached a full agreement, the seven senior gods would announce the final verdict and each of the members would voice their approval with a 'Let it be'. This unified command meant that the will of the assembly had become divine law. While this body largely served as the judicial court of the universe, passing judgement on the wrongdoings of gods and humans alike, the assembly was also vested with the authority to elect and depose the kings of both the divine and earthly realms.

A specific example which demonstrates such advanced forms of governance is the ancient Mesopotamian myth of creation, *Enuma Elish*. As recounted in the Prelude to this book, in this particular myth the gods form an assembly in order to elect a leader or 'champion of the gods' who will defeat their powerful enemy, the primal mother, Tiamet. After much debate and deliberation, the Ordained Assembly of the Great Gods elect Lord Marduk as the new king of the gods. Armed with an invincible weapon, Marduk is able to smite Tiamet and, after returning home to a reception worthy of such a powerful and victorious god, Marduk sets about creating the known universe including the first slaves: human beings, who are put on earth to do the bidding of the gods.

Such myths can be understood as a form of allegory, whereby ancient humankind projected the world around them onto the realm of the gods. This notion of myth is reinforced when Henri Frankfort and H. A. Frankfort argue that myth 'is nothing less than a carefully chosen cloak for abstract thought. The imagery is inseparable from the thought. It represents the form in which the experience has become conscious' (Frankfort and Frankfort 1977: 7). In this way, the myths come to reveal more than the political machinations of the council of the great gods; at the very least they indicate just how long the will to democracy has been alive in human society. Beyond this, many have speculated that these myths also reveal the actual systems whereby ancient humankind governed itself. The general consensus is that, in order for the people of ancient Mesopotamia to have attributed such complex democratic systems to their gods, they must have experienced analogous assemblies themselves (Easton 1970: 82–3).

Following on from the myths and their likely connection to earthly assemblies, is the significance of the ancient Mesopotamian epics which reflect an epoch some one to two centuries later than the myths, around 2800–2700 BCE. These epics differ substantially from the earlier myths in that they centre 'around a human or semi-human hero, [such as] Enmerkar, Lugalbanda, Gilgamesh, etc. rather than around a god' (Jacobsen 1970 [1957]: 143). The most famous of these ancient Mesopotamian epics is the *Epic of Gilgamesh* which dates from around 2800 BCE (Storm 2003: 62–99). Uruk, the city of which Gilgamesh is ruler, is under threat from the armies of Kish. Instead of commanding the armies according to his will, Gilgamesh consults the bicameral congress of the city, which are striking in their similarity to those already discussed. First, he consults with the conservative council of the elders who appear to have been made up of the heads of the powerful families within the state, who advise Gilgamesh against fighting the armies of Kish. However, Gilgamesh has the authority to veto their decision and appeal to a second assembly of all arms-bearing men. This assembly decides to fight and Gilgamesh – despite the advice of the elders – goes into battle for the freedom and liberty of Uruk. In the epic of Gilgamesh, there is, as Jacobsen concludes, 'a state in which the ruler must lay his proposals before the people, first the elders, then the assembly of the townsmen, and obtain their consent, before he can act. In other words, the assembly appears to be the ultimate political authority' (Jacobsen 1970 [1943]: 163).

Although there can be no doubt that the assemblies held at Uruk during the time of Gilgamesh were less advanced than those held in later Greece or Rome, the situation that brought about the convening of Uruk's bicameral assemblies is not dissimilar to the one that ancient Greece faced some 2400 years later. Sumer, like Greece, was made up of a number of independent city-states, each of them vying for power and supremacy over the region and its people. In a reversal of the veto power that the assembly of the arms-bearing men had over the elders in Uruk, the Spartan elders (a council of twenty-eight men, all over sixty years of age) had the power to overrule any 'crooked decree' that was passed by the popular assembly. Further parallels can be drawn between the *Epic of Gilgamesh* and the deliberative practices of the Roman Republic in the prelude to their war against Carthage (around 265 BCE). In Rome, the senate refused to authorize the war and therefore the consuls summoned the *Comitia Centuriata*, or military assembly, which gave the final approval for war (Easton 1970: 83 n1).

To describe the democratic practices found in myths such as *Enuma Elish* and epics like *Gilgamesh*, the renowned Danish Assyriologist Thorkild Jacobsen coined the term 'Primitive Democracy' (Jacobsen 1970 [1943]). This political mechanism functioned more like a classical (participatory) than a modern (representative) form of democracy in the sense that it was

> a form of government in which internal sovereignty resides in a large proportion of the governed, namely in all free adult male citizens without distinction of fortune or class. That sovereignty resides in these citizens implies that major decisions – such as the decision to undertake a war – are made with their consent, that these citizens constitute the supreme judicial authority in the state, and also that rulers and magistrates obtain their positions with, and ultimately derive their power from, that same consent (Jacobsen 1970 [1943]: 157).

Jacobsen also goes on to justify his use of the word 'Primitive' to describe this early form of democracy, by stating that 'the various functions of government are as yet little specialized, the power structure is loose, and the machinery for social coordination by means of power is as yet imperfectly developed' (Jacobsen 1970 [1943]: 157).

These democracies seem to have functioned much like the aforementioned divine assembly. Although they were called together to make decisions regarding matters as diverse as irrigation projects, trade missions, land surveying, administrative issues and to judge the serious offences of citizens, it was primarily assembled when the security of the city-state was under threat. This formed the nucleus of the city-state's municipal administration and allowed the collective resources of the community to be pooled in order to reach consensus for concerted action. These councils further mirrored that of the gods by functioning as a bicameral assembly in that it was divided between 'an upper house of "elders" and a lower house of "men"' (Kramer 1963: 74). Although the elder men or 'fathers' seem to have held most of the power, some research suggests that these assemblies also resembled those of the gods in the fact that, 'women as well as men took part in decision-making – sometimes with a dominating role' (Saggs 2004: 30). During an assembly each of the citizens had the right to express their opinion and discussion would continue until a virtual unanimity was reached and the final decisions were then announced by the elders. Just as the gods elected Marduk their king when under threat from Tiamet, so too did the early city-states of Mesopotamia convene for the specific purpose of electing a king when the security of the city-state was under jeopardy, usually from threat of attack by a neighbour. Although this meant that the new king became the supreme leader of the people and was able to implement new law, the appointment was to be held for a limited term by each incumbent and expired when the pending emergency had been resolved.

However, what makes Jacobsen's use of the term 'primitive' here particularly problematic is that considerable evidence has emerged which suggests that over time these relatively simplistic models of direct and participatory democracy became increasingly sophisticated. More recent work has questioned the notion that the region's experiments with democratic governance were in any way more 'primitive' or inferior to later examples like Athens. They must instead be acknowledged as an important chapter in the complex and multifaceted story of democracy and its history, one that began across the Mediterranean and Eurasian landmass of the ancient world, rather than in specific and isolated corners (Isakhan 2007a, 2011c, 2012a).

One such example is the extended kingdom of Ebla, which ruled a modest empire that dominated parts of modern day Syria, Lebanon and Iraq. Excavations at the capital (modern Tell Mardikh in north-western Syria) in 1976 revealed astonishing details about this kingdom of some 250,000 people, which had been at the height of its power from around 2600–2240 BCE (Bermant and Weitzman 1979, Matthiae 1980). The 15,000 cuneiform tablets that were unearthed by archaeologists, exposed a sophisticated political culture involving some 11,000 public servants, providing arguably the 'best evidence we have for a government by an impersonal bureaucracy' in the ancient world (Springborg 1992: 8). The bureaucrats developed a system of governance whereby the king of Ebla was elected for a seven-year term and shared power with a council of elders. After serving his first term, the incumbent was entitled to run for a second and, in the event that he was not re-elected to office, the former king was able to retire on a state pension.

Geographically closer to the early developments of Mesopotamia already discussed the city-state of Shuruppak (modern Fara, Iraq) had its political and economic zenith from 2600–2350 BCE. Political power was firmly rooted in an oligarchy led by the temple priests, but serving underneath this powerful elite was a second chamber of magistrates or governors who formed a plural executive, had limited powers and a revolving tenure (Bailkey 1967: 1218). Perhaps more democratic, the people of Kish (modern Tell Al-Uhaymir, Iraq) held a general election to nominate their king around 2300 BCE. This particular king even took the 'throne-name *Iphur-kish* (Kish assembled) to emphasize the popular basis of his rule' (Saggs 2004: 132).

At around the same time, the people of Lagash (modern Tell Al-Hiba, Iraq) were embroiled in an early struggle against the upsurge of despotic regimes. It seems as if the power of the throne had seduced the authorities of Lagash to the point of bloodthirsty megalomania and that they were prepared to deny their citizens the basic political, social and economic freedoms that they had come to expect from a free state. Here, corrupt judges had sided with the rulings of the elite and turned much private and temple land into state property. This created a 'bitter struggle for power between the temple and the palace – the "church" and the "state" – with the citizens of Lagash taking the side of the temple' (Kramer 1963: 79). In states such as Lagash, the temple community wielded enormous political power and 'showed a strongly democratic character' (Frankfort 1978 [1948]: 221). Not only were all citizens of the state – irrespective of their status or wealth – expected to contribute some labour to the maintenance and harvest of temple land, but the authorities of the temple also fulfilled a vital watchdog function over the government, monitoring instances of corruption and other abuses of power. The extent of the temples' role in balancing the authority of the state is evident by the fact that it both generated and advocated resistance amongst the people of Lagash towards state-imposed terror and despotism. This constituted some of the earliest evidence of collective political action against oppressive systems of power and the first recorded use of the word 'freedom' (Kramer 1963: 79). In the wake of such a struggle, Urukagina (king of Lagash around 2300 BCE) established liberty as one of the main tenets of the society, 'meaning the removal of abuses of the oppressed and the restoration and safeguarding of their rights' (Bailkey 1967: 1231). He sought to establish the basic equality of all citizens by freeing the poor of their debts, re-installing the collective and egalitarian policies of the temple, renegotiating the rights of the citizen, working to eradicate hunger and oppression, and by returning the commandeered land to the people, making him 'the first known social reformer in history' (Bailkey 1967: 1221).

In the central Babylonian plain, approximately half-way between Lagash in the south and Kish in the north, the people of Nippur (modern Nuffar in Afak, Iraq) had long been familiar with democratic forms of governance. From as far back as the Early Dynastic Period (3000–2750 BCE) the elected elite of the various city-states of Mesopotamia had met in assemblies at Nippur for the purpose of debating and resolving broader regional issues and conflicts as well as the election of a temporary king to rule over the collective states under the confederacy known as the 'Kengir League'[2] (Jacobsen 1970 [1957]: 139–40). Similar in practise to the archaic Greek amphictyony, such as the Delphic League, or to the modern day United Nations, the 'Kengir League' demonstrates an extraordinarily advanced political culture where the differences and disputes between the various city-states were addressed and hopefully resolved via the extensive debate and deliberation of the kings, emissaries and league officials. While it would seem that the political climate of Nippur might tempt the more ambitious members of the society to overthrow such isonomous models of governance, the city managed to preserve its democratic tendencies well into the Ur III period (2150–2000 BCE). While many of Nippur's neighbours had since witnessed the rise of a centralized authority under the blood-line of a particular king, Nippur remained 'governed by a heterogenous collective, the assembly of Nippur citizens, the governor (*Ensi*) of the city, and the highest priests of the Enlil and Ninurta temples' (Leick 2001: 159).

Underpinning the democratic practices found across ancient Mesopotamia was an extensive set of legal codes developed across the region to ensure that justice was served in cases as diverse as crime, slavery, agriculture, debts and loans, marriage, property rights, sexual offences and theft. As one example, the city-state

---

2   'Kengir' is the Sumerian word for the Mesopotamian region.

of Isin (modern Ishan Al-Bahriyat, Iraq), which flourished from 1953–1730 BCE, was governed by the Law Code developed by Lipit-Ishtar (1934–1924 BCE).[3] Through the 50 laws, the king demonstrated his concern for the democratic virtues of social justice, equality and peace. In the Epilogue to the Law Code, he claims that the code was developed 'in order to establish justice in the land, to eliminate cries for justice, to eradicate enmity and armed violence, to bring well-being to the lands of Sumer and Akkad' (Roth 1997 [1995]: Epilogue I). Although concerns about justice are not inherently democratic, they do reflect, at the very least, the presence of an elite concerned with the wellbeing of the citizen.

Similar concerns about justice existed in the northern Mesopotamian city-state of Sippar (modern Tell Abu Habbah, Iraq) which managed to retain models of collective governance until surprisingly late. From approximately 1890–1590 BCE, the city appears to have been governed by a bicameral assembly comprising an upper house made up of nobility and a lower house made up of free adult males. Here, the upper house consisted of the more senior, qualified and wealthy members of the society who rotated leadership of the various magisterial and administrative positions on an annual basis. Unfortunately, as the city of Sippar gradually came under the jurisdiction of the central Babylonian government, the elite citizens who made up the upper house were infiltrated by royally appointed officials. Thus the emphasis shifted away from the original impetus of serving the citizens towards the role of a mediating body between the authority of the king and the subjugation of Sippar. Even in this situation, however, the upper house retained its judicial role and presided over particular cases that required a higher body to exact justice. These judges were always local citizens and, if dissatisfied with their verdict, a citizen could appeal for a royal verdict (Leick 2001: 176, Oppenheim 1969: 9–10).

More generally, the grand empires of the time – namely, the Babylonian, the Assyrian and the Egyptian – also appear to have had democratic tendencies despite the common misconception that they were the very epitome of Oriental despotism. During the early Old Babylonian period (2006–1595 BCE), the Mesopotamian region fell into an epoch not at all dissimilar to that faced by Greece after the fall of Attica: a period of political instability and factionalism, extreme divergences in wealth and poverty, and incessant bellicosity. To counteract the chaos of such a dangerous political landscape, Hammurabi the 'King of Justice' (1792–1750 BCE) who ruled Babylon (modern Al-Hillah, Iraq), devised a set of legal prescriptions commonly referred to as the Code of Hammurabi. These laws are the best organized, longest and most detailed of ancient Mesopotamia and consist of a lengthy prologue, 275–300 laws and an epilogue. What is particularly interesting about these laws is that they frequently make reference to an assembly of judges who preside over complicated legal issues, interpreting the law and applying them to difficult real-world situations. Indicating the importance of the judges and the judicial assembly, the first four laws concern the penalties for giving false

---

3   In all instances throughout this book, the dates that follow the name of a ruler indicate the years of rule, not life.

testimony before the assembly, which in many cases was death.[4] The fifth law
states that:

> If a judge renders a judgement, gives a verdict, or deposits a sealed opinion,
> after which he reverses his judgement, they shall charge and convict the judge of
> having reversed the judgement which he rendered and he shall give twelve-fold
> the claim of that judgement; moreover, they shall unseat him from his judgeship
> in the assembly, and he shall never again sit in judgement with the judges (cited
> in Roth 1997 [1995]: Law 5.6–30).

Beyond this, the Code of Hammurabi also asserts several prescriptions concerning
the rights and limitations of citizenship. For example, it distinguishes between
people, not on the basis of age, gender, ancestry or military service, as was the
case in ancient Athens, but on the basis of class. This ancient Babylonian concern
for the rule of law and the rights of the citizen was extended into the reign of later
Babylonian kings. The people of Babylon also highly valued personal liberty and
the kings frequently prescribed freedom for various groups, by securing the rights
of citizens, cancelling obligations to the state and granting freedom to slaves who
had fulfilled their duty or had been held as guarantors for loans (Martin and Snell
2005: 404, Snell 2001: 64). In addition, later Babylonian rulers also advocated
a judicial system in which the more important and complex cases were brought
before the whole town in the form of an assembly. This assembly tried both civil
and criminal cases and had the power to issue the death sentence, with their final
decision being ceremonially confirmed by the king. As Jacobsen points out, this
judicial system was democratic in nature, with the major decisions over right
and wrong or life and death vested in the assembly, a forum open to the entire
community of citizens (Jacobsen 1970 [1943]: 159–63). Overall, the kings of
ancient Babylon did not rule despite public endorsement; they operated according
to it, always remembering that their incumbency depended upon the consent of
their constituents.

The population of the Assyrian capital, Ashur (modern Qalat Sherqat, Iraq),
were able to congregate in an assembly which reached agreement under the
guidance of the more senior, wealthy and influential members of the community.
Knowing all too well the popularity and power of the elders to influence the wider
community of citizens, the kings of Assyria were 'always careful not to offend
their high administrative officials, whose loyalty to the dynasty they at times had
to secure by oaths and agreements' (Oppenheim 1964: 103). When differences of
opinion between the king and the elders did occur, the elders 'were quite ready
to revolt against the king if they did not approve of his policies' (Oppenheim
1964: 103). In particularly serious matters, the elders would convene an assembly
of the free citizens and work with them in writing a letter addressed to the king.

---

4   There are many laws within the Code of Hammurabi that concern the role of the
judges in trying cases of civil law (cited in Roth 1997 [1995]: Law 9, 13, 168, 172, 177).

In this way, the citizens of Ashur were able to fight for exemptions and privileges, 'make legal decisions, sell real estate within the city that had no private owner, and assume corporate responsibility in cases of murder or robbery committed even outside the city, within a specified distance' (Oppenheim 1964: 12).

In addition, the power of the Assyrian elders can be seen in the fact that the king was not able to directly appoint his own successor, but instead nominated a potential heir who was then subject to the consent of the council. More broadly, the power of the state was also mitigated by a thriving private sector as the merchants of the Assyrian empire grew in wealth and, subsequently, in influence. The great merchant families appear to have convened in a building commonly known as the 'city house' where they 'made decisions on commercial policy, fixed the rates of export tax ... acted as a diplomatic body ... and controlled relations with Anatolian rulers on whose cooperation and protection the caravans and resident merchants relied' (Leick 2001: 203). From among this body of wealthy merchants, one member was chosen annually by lot to serve as the chairman of the board. This individual was conferred with the highest honours underneath the authority of the king and 'was responsible for public works, for overseeing the judiciary, and took a leading part in the city's religious and ceremonial rites' (Leick 2001: 203).

Speaking generally about the democratic developments across Mesopotamia during the time of the Babylonian and Assyrian empires, Yves Schemeil notes that 'historical documents describe assemblies of citizens deliberating for days, each session including new members' (Schemeil 2000: 104). It appears that due to the size of the community it was often hard to garner consensus and therefore the circle of delegates became wider as deliberations continued, often involving commoners, teenagers and women. At every stage, the assemblies appear to have been lively places, with participants openly pointing out the contradictions and inconsistencies in their opponents' arguments. Freedom of speech was paramount and, when each of the participants had been given a chance to state their case at least once, the proceedings ended before debate became cyclical, emotional or counter-productive. When the time came for the citizens to vote, they did so by either kneeling or walking to the speaker to approve or by sitting to disapprove (Moran 1992: 401–2, n24). Although 'majority votes were often sought and reached ... it was always possible that minority views would raise the problem again if its legal solution was a failure' (Schemeil 2000: 104). Similar to the Ordained Assembly of the Great Gods, the proceedings of these later assemblies were concluded by the chair sternly pronouncing, 'Let it be'.

As with Babylon and Assyria, the ancient Egyptian Empire[5] is often assumed to have been governed by Oriental despotism. However, ancient Egypt practised

---

5 The Egyptian Empire, as with other examples discussed below including the Hittites, the Israelites and the Phoenicians, never directly ruled over the region now called Iraq. However, each of these empires did rule significant parts of the Middle East, North Africa and/or the Levant and shared borders with Mesopotamian empires, states and kingdoms. Egyptian, Hittite, Israelite and Phoenician histories are deeply enmeshed in the neighbouring

forms of democratic governance including an array of councils who 'convened on the palace stairs, a place where all opinions expressed by courtiers, civil servants, and members of the king's inner circle, all of whom met separately at the building's four corners, could be easily conveyed and explained to the Pharaoh' (Schemeil 2000: 104). The individual charged with the prestigious but onerous task of liaising between the various councils and the Pharaoh was known as the 'Vizier'. Originally, this position was occupied by a prince of royal blood, but was later bestowed upon a nobleman of considerable ability who became the head of every governmental department and therefore the most powerful officer of the state. Essentially the role of the Vizier included 'not only a daily report to his sovereign on the state of the nation but also the delivering of judgements in his audience hall, [and] the receiving and issuing of instructions to the various branches of central government' (Aldred 1998: 196). The central government included several different departments, such as the Treasury and the Ministry for Agriculture, while the Vizier himself was supported by 'a legion of scribes, stewards, runners and guards' (Aldred 1998: 196). Having strict guidelines to follow, a Vizier would call into session a 'hearing' or 'council of the mat' made up of the leaders of these various departments from across the empire. During this council of the elite, the Vizier would sit with his numerous advisors, curators and scribes by his side. In front of him were scrolls filled with the laws of Egypt and beyond them were the forty senior officials, each of whom was to be heard in due course (the higher ranking officials spoke first, followed by those of lesser importance). Although usually occupied by well educated men, government positions were not limited to those of a particular bloodline, class or colour but were filled by promising young men who had been specifically groomed for the role (Frankfort 1968: 85, 90, Gardiner, 2004: 101). The expectations on these men were enormous, with sentences of capital punishment dealt out to any member of the district council found to be practising injustices.

In such assemblies, the Vizier 'presided over important civil cases referred to him from lower courts; he dealt with questions of land tenure and the witnessing of wills; and he considered criminal cases requiring heavy sentences' (Aldred 1998: 196). However, even this council of the elite could not bring new laws into effect without them being duly debated and deliberated across a variety of separate councils and assemblies before garnering either the approval or denial of the Vizier. Such systems were moreover employed for the discussion of military campaigns where lengthy debates on strategy sometimes led to the amendment of royal policy, as in Tuthmosis III's and Ramses II's expedition to Syria (Schemeil

---

Babylonian and Assyrian empires as well as the other kingdoms and city-states of the region. These empires are considered here, not because they are 'Iraqi' in any respect, but for their democratic practices and for their certain cultural influence and diplomatic relations with their Mesopotamian neighbours. It is more than conceivable that the methods and models of participatory governance that were practised in Memphis, Hattusas, Jerusalem and Tyre were well known and even imitated in Babylon, and vice versa.

2000: 104). Beyond this, the various separate councils appear to have wielded considerable power over the day-to-day agricultural affairs of their individual regions. Interestingly, an individual citizen could appeal directly to the Vizier regarding decisions made by a council on rural affairs. The Vizier would then consult with the relevant officials and usually suspend the verdict so that it could be reconsidered for a designated period of time before the final decision was put into action. Although this was not democracy in the pure sense of direct participation in decision making, it certainly provided avenues through which the common Egyptian could 'participate' in regional politics (Van den Boorn 1988: 13, 47, 168–71). In addition, this kind of sophisticated appeal process undermines notions of Oriental despotism to reveal instead an egalitarian bureaucracy concerned with the individual rights of citizens and an aversion to corruption.

Apart from these examples where democratic practices formed part of the governing structures of the major empires of the ancient Near East, one also finds examples from across their colonies. Kanesh, one of the outlying merchant colonies of the Assyrian empire, serves as a case study. With archaeologists uncovering some 16,000 cuneiform tablets, a picture of Kanesh's thriving economic and trade systems emerged. Located in Turkey's Cappadocia region, Kanesh flourished from 2000–1800 BCE with evidence suggesting that a number of Assyrians moved there, purchased land and settled for long periods. Here, Geoffrey Evans finds parallels between the governmental machinations employed in Kanesh, and those used by the people of Uruk during the time of Gilgamesh – some 800–1000 years earlier. Although he rightly points out that there were a number of significant changes, he goes on to state that 'the assemblies of Kanesh remain of the first importance historically. They possess features similar to the earlier ones, and we possess a little more information about the manner in which they operated' (Evans 1958a: 4).

It appears that because these remote and generally wealthy citizens of the Assyrian empire preferred their governance to be closer to home, they were able to retain significant autonomy until surprisingly late periods. The more successful and influential among them formed the council of the elders and there can be no doubt that oligarchic tendencies and nepotism emerged within the group. Although they remained the subjects of the king and therefore subscribed to his law, the elders presided over many domestic issues, including both political and judicial decision making. In these assemblies, there appear to have been rather advanced forms of voting whereby the congregation would divide into three groups and each group would deliberate and vote independently before reconvening in a plenary where the final votes were counted (Larsen 1976: 319–23). However, when the elders failed to agree, matters were brought before the full assembly of all adult males, which was 'called into session by a clerk at the bidding of a majority of [the elders]' (Jacobsen 1970 [1943]: 159). There is also evidence to suggest that once this assembly had convened, the citizenry of Kanesh also voted, although perhaps in a far less sophisticated manner. What is certain is that beyond the deliberations of the assembly was a civic culture and a complex bureaucracy that extended out into the social world of the ancient Middle East where citizens were accorded freedom of speech, where they discussed and debated social issues, and where they often formed loose political alliances (Gibson and Biggs 1987, Larsen 1976: 161–70). Although Evans is initially reluctant to cite these practices as democratic he later concedes that the various political procedures practised in Kanesh 'strongly suggest a liberal and democratic spirit among this small group of local dignitaries. In such an atmosphere, democratic procedures within the group might easily arise' (Evans 1958b: 114–5).

En route between Ashur and Kanesh, caravans of traders, individual travellers and the messengers of the Assyrian empire passed through Mari. A much smaller empire that came to prosperity after the turn of the second millennium BCE, Mari dominated that part of the north-western Euphrates that now falls across the borders of Syria and Iraq. The ancient city of Mari (modern Tell Hariri, Syria) was excavated by French archaeologists from 1933 onwards uncovering, amongst other things, 'an archive of over twenty thousand cuneiform tablets, mainly administrative and economic documents and letters' (Saggs 2004: 64). It is these clay tablets that Daniel Fleming has claimed provide the 'ideal resource for the study of many aspects of ancient political life' (Fleming 2004: 19). In Mari, as in Kanesh, there seem to have been few who would openly and directly challenge the authority of the king. However, Mari kingship was not despotic, but instead 'actual power seems to be a matter of constant negotiation, as he [the king] engages a panoply of traditional leaderships, each with its own constituencies and assumed prerogatives' (Fleming 2004: xv). Through the immense resource uncovered at Mari, it is possible to trace the communicative patterns between and across a broad spectrum of sites of power. Collective forms of governance appear to have held some influence over the state and, reminiscent of earlier examples, 'they appear most prominently in decisions of war and peace' (Fleming 2004: 223).

The reason for Mari's dispersed power structure was due to the fact that it was a loose collective of various nomadic, tribal and village peoples. This resulted in a number of chiefs, officials, elders, assemblies and governors who vied for power and influence under the authority of the king. Fleming studied in detail the small Mari towns of Tuttal, Imar and Urgish, concluding that collective forms of governance were most prominent in such small communities and that it is likely to have been this way since the third millennium BCE. Although collective decision making appears to have occurred mostly in smaller groups of the elite, there were occasions where 'both the pastoralists of the steppe and the residents of towns … gather[ed], not only to receive word from an outside king but even to speak for the group' (Fleming 2004: 234). Ultimately, these antediluvian governmental systems evolved from simple tribal gatherings to incorporate decision-making aspects and wield influence over the higher authority of the king. It is therefore conceivable that a king genuinely wanting to unite this heterogeneous region would encourage such collective decision making and accept the inherent challenges of a kingdom consisting of various systems and sites of power.

However, Fleming is reluctant to use the nomenclature of democracy to describe the political machinations of the Mari, preferring the anthropological terminology of 'corporate polity' (Fleming 2004: 174–80, 222–8). Essentially, Fleming's reluctance stems from his concern that the term 'democracy' may serve as a 'barrier to understanding the diverse Near Eastern tradition of group-oriented decision making that may somehow stand behind the remarkable development of Athens' (Fleming 2004: 16). Beyond his concern over the loose application of the term 'democracy', Fleming also reveals that the Athenian *polis* is not without precedent. While it is commonly assumed that Western democracy arose triumphantly out of a dark history of despotic rule, cases such as the Mari and other Mesopotamian examples suggest a cross-section of egalitarian and collective traditions spread over the wider region that rival, pre-date and probably influenced the much later developments of ancient Greece.

Another example of early Middle Eastern democracy can be found among the Hittites. These Anatolian peoples formed their state and later their empire out of Hattusas (modern Bogazkale, Turkey) and ruled from approximately 1600–1200 BCE. This burgeoning city was just north of the former merchant colony of the Assyrian empire, Kanesh. The Hittite empire, much like the examples discussed above, developed a number of sophisticated diplomatic and bureaucratic bodies as is evidenced by the uncovering of an abundance of treaties, diplomatic texts, indictments, edicts and letters. Here, power rested across a complex web of parochial townships and villages, each with their own loose systems of collective governance, usually under the guidance of a council of elders who would 'normally deal with local administration and in particular with the settlement of disputes' (Gurney 2004 [1952]: 70).

As the Hittites gradually moved from these loose satellites of governance towards a central authority under the king, the earlier systems of power would have had little choice but to streamline and offer their submission to the new ruler. This does not mean that the elders forfeited their power in any way, but rather that the position of king did not equate to absolute control. O. R. Gurney proposes that the Hittite monarchy was originally elective, citing one of the earliest recorded events in the history of Hattusas which tells of the elders' dissatisfaction with King Labernas and their nomination of a rival king to replace him (Gurney 2004 [1952]: 61). The struggle between the elders and the king seems to have resurfaced many times, particularly when a king passed away and his heir had been appointed without the legal approval of the elders, therefore rendering the appointment invalid.

Beyond the power of the elders, a more general assembly seems to have convened irregularly throughout Hittite history. Perhaps because this council was made up of the higher echelons of the state's bureaucracy, it appears to have wielded enormous power as a judicial body. Much like the Babylonian assemblies before them, these gatherings at Hattusas dealt with the more complex cases and had the power to convict even the most influential citizens (including the king) and condemn the guilty to death. However, the kings gradually set about establishing hereditary succession as the principal way of garnering authority against this backdrop of consensus and collective action. Although the nobility remained and the general assemblies of the bureaucracy still convened to preside over important cases, the authority of the king was not subject to the election or approval of the elders, eventually leading to a succession of despotic dynasties in Hattusas (Beckman 1982: 441–2, Gurney 2004 [1952]: 61–2, 66–7).

Examples of early forms of democracy can also be found amongst the ancient Israelites. Here, as E. Theodore Mullen Jnr. has illustrated, there is a clear lineage between the ancient Mesopotamian postulations regarding the Assembly of the Gods and those found in early Canaanite and Hebrew literature. Thus, in methods paralleling earlier Sumerian developments, the book of 'Exodus' reveals that Israelite leaders such as Moses were nominated via a mandate direct from God which was confirmed by the assembly of elders (Schultz 1981: 146–8). Later, various councils and bodies of elders are evident throughout several of the key books of the Old Testament,[6] an era which witnessed the emergence of the Judges' authority (around 1400–1020 BCE), the eventual ascendency of the Hebrew monarchy under the leadership of Saul, David and Solomon (1020–931 BCE) and, later, the division of the kingdom into two separate enclaves: Israel in the north and Judah in the south (931–722 BCE). In introducing his study into the democratic practices of ancient Israel, C. Umhau Wolf notes that 'In the Old Testament certain terms and relationships appear which suggest that democracy, in the broadest definition of the term … was prevalent in the earliest times and that vestiges of democratic procedures may be discerned in both political and religious concepts throughout the later periods of Israelite history' (Wolf 1947: 98).

As with many of the earlier examples, the entire free male population of the community constituted the people's assembly where each individual had the right to speak openly about the issues at hand. These councils appear to have been convened for both religious and political purposes and assembled at the city gate or at the door of the tabernacle. Within the assemblies the more elderly, experienced or gifted rhetoricians amongst them tended to be widely respected and thereby dominated much of the proceedings (Schultz 1981: 146). When the deliberations came to a close, a proclamation was made that reiterated the key decisions and announced the people's consent. Later, during the times of the monarchy, such assemblies continued to wield 'at least strong advisory powers, if not full veto power, over the king' (Wolf 1947: 104). The potential for despotism was kept in check by the people's assembly, and the actions of the king required the approval of a complex bureaucratic hierarchy of temple officials, prophets, priests, courtiers and, in some cases, the entire body of citizens. The ascension to the throne itself required neither blood lineage nor divine right, but the consent of the majority who 'had the power to reject any candidate for the kingship, even the heir apparent' (Wolf 1947: 105). Here, the story of Rehoboam (933–916 BCE), the son of Solomon, is particularly instructive. In his aspirations for kingship, Rehoboam was 'forced to confront the full assembly of Israel, an open democratic forum' as well as 'the old men who worked for his father and the young men who had grown up with him' (Martin and Snell 2005: 399–400). While Rehoboam's

---

6 Including 'Joshua', 'Judges', 'Samuel I' and 'II', and 'Kings I' and 'II'.

campaign was ultimately unsuccessful, it indicates that Israelite leadership which 'was not only averse to violence and autocracy, but also encouraged broad degrees of consultation and consensus' (Martin and Snell 2005: 400).

On the north-western border of ancient Israel resided the citizens of Phoenicia. The had lived in the Levant since as far back as the third millennium BCE. However, it wasn't until 1100 BCE that they emerged as a significant cultural and political force and, from the ninth to the sixth centuries BCE, the Phoenicians became vigorous sailors and traders, establishing colonies across much of the Mediterranean, including Cyprus, Italy, North Africa and as far west as Spain. In this way, the Phoenicians came to act as cultural middlemen, disseminating 'ideas, myths, and knowledge from the powerful Assyrian and Babylonian worlds in what is now Syria and Iraq to their contacts in the Aegean. Those ideas helped spark a cultural revival in Greece, one which led to the Greeks' golden Age and hence the birth of Western civilization' (Gore 2004: 36–7).

One such idea – that has since become regarded as quintessentially Western – is that of democratic governance. Throughout the few early Phoenician documents extant are references to an assembly of elders with which the king consults regarding the important matters of state (Goedicke 1975, Moran, 1992). Later, in a treaty between the kings of Assyria and Phoenicia dated to the seventh-century BCE, this council appears to govern alongside the monarch. It is precisely because these councils were made up of the wealthy merchants who had gained their fortune and subsequent status from their extensive trade networks that stretched from Mesopotamia to Western Europe, that they garnered such municipal power and authority. However, power was not simply vested in the king and the wealthy. As with the developments discussed in detail above, the ancient Phoenician texts also recount the existence of a 'people's assembly' found on the mainland and constituted of the entire free male citizenry.

In the outlying colonies established by the Phoenicians across North Africa and the Mediterranean, are found even more sophisticated democratic practices. Essentially, these settlements were governed by two chief magistrates, or 'Suffetes', who supervised both the senate and the people's assembly. Here, the senate was made up of thirty-plus key members who readied and collated details of foreign policy matters, such as declarations of war or proposals to resolve external conflict, before presenting them to the elected body of one hundred officials. Even in these remote settlements, the power of the senate was mitigated by the people's assembly which not only elected its members, but also withheld the right to deliberate and debate over the decisions reached by this higher body (Markoe 2005: 101–5). In *Black Athena Writes Back*, Martin Bernal not only illustrates that these sophisticated models of Phoenician democracy were influenced by the long traditions of collective governance found throughout the ancient Middle East, but that they also had a specific impact on the rise of the Athenian *polis* (Bernal 2001: 345–70). As Stephen Stockwell has concluded:

> The Phoenicians brought more than just trade into the Greek sphere; they also brought the experience of people governing themselves and, clearly in the case of Sparta and on the balance of probabilities in other cities, the Phoenicians had a formative influence on the rise of democratic political institutions ... the Athenian contribution was based on powerful ideas that were already circulating among Greeks who had contact with the Phoenicians (Stockwell 2011a: 47–8).

In this way, the narrative of Western democracy and its supposed origins in ancient Greece can, at the very least, be problematized by the fact that the Phoenicians – an Oriental people – were responsible for perhaps the earliest forms of collective and egalitarian governance in the Occident.

A later example that is particularly demonstrative of ancient Middle Eastern concerns about democratic principles such as the freedom and equality of the citizen can be found in the Persian Empire of Achamenid (550–330 BCE). At its greatest extent, this empire, founded by Cyrus the Great, spanned across three continents (Asia, Africa and Europe) and had a lasting influence on the region, including in Iraq. At the time of Cyrus' expansion into Mesopotamia, the Neo-Babylonian Empire was run by an allegedly incompetent, cruel and unholy king known as Nabonidus. 'He continually did evil against his city', by taking many of the free citizens of Babylon into slavery and forcing them to work against their will, 'Daily, [without interruption], he [imposed] the corvée upon its inhabitants unrelentingly, ruining them all'. When Cyrus conquered the city, however, perhaps without fighting a single battle, he was determined to re-establish the basic rights of the individual and to encourage both religious tolerance and personal freedom. Because of their former oppression, 'All the people of Babylon, all the land of Sumer and Akkad ... rejoiced at his kingship and their faces shone ... amidst rejoicing and happiness'. Cyrus was careful not to 'permit anyone to frighten (the people of) [Sumer] and Akkad' but instead set about restoring social justice and the 'welfare of the city of Babylon and all its sacred centres'. As for the citizens of Babylon 'upon whom he [Nabonidus] imposed a corvée which was not the god's will and not befitting them' Cyrus 'relieved their weariness and freed them from their service' (Cogan 2003: II.124). The Persians even permitted the ancient Babylonian assemblies to continue under their auspices which 'still adjudicated in property litigations and crimes of a local nature' (Dandamayev 1995: 25). More broadly, the Achamenids sought to decentralize power by separating the state from religion and by setting up autonomous satrapies governed by regional ethnic minorities.

The various wars between the Assyrian and Babylonian empires as well as the Persian and Macedonian conquests did not bring to an end the antediluvian assemblies of ancient Iraq which maintained jurisdiction over local disputes and crimes and continued throughout much of the first millennium BCE. Muhammad Dandamayev lists various examples of civil, legal, administrative, private and temple-related cases presided over by the popular assemblies. These cases included murder, theft, rent and tenancy issues, paternity cases, prison escape attempts, disputes between civil officials and temple administrators, debts, complex contractual arrangements, business arrangements, slave ownership and inheritance issues. As with the earlier examples, these assemblies were made up of the free male population of the city who were both permanent residents and property owners, with the more esteemed citizens such as high-ranking officials, temple representatives and wealthy merchants playing a more dominant role. Specifically, one particular assembly consisted of 24 elders who presided over a congregation of 291 ordinary men, including archers, gold and silver smiths, beer brewers, shepherds, farmers, cooks, temple staff and bureaucrats (Dandamayev 1995: 23–8). Dandamayev also documents the last known reference to the ancient Mesopotamian tradition of democracy, bringing to an end almost 3,000 years of collective governance across ancient Iraq. Occurring long after the democratic impetus of Athens had been subjugated by the militarily superior Macedonians in 322 BCE, the city of Cutha (modern Tell Ibrahim, Iraq) convened in a temple assembly as late as 187 BCE. In concluding his paper on this particular era of Mesopotamian politics, Dandamayev states,

> On the whole, the Babylonian popular assemblies were stable bodies which outlived the empires of the Sumerian, Babylonian, Assyrian, Persian, and Macedonian kings. The final disappearance of the popular assemblies, perhaps at the beginning of the Christian era, marked both the loss of civil rights by the inhabitants of Babylonian cities and the end of ancient Mesopotamian tradition (Dandamayev 1995: 29).

Conclusion

The democratic history of Iraq can be seen to have a lineage tracing back as far as civilization itself. Its ancestry lies in the ancient myths recounted by the early Mesopotamians as the region developed its first sophisticated human settlements and systems of governance. These systems evolved as the region witnessed the birth of early city-states that eventually gave way to grand empires. They not only pre-empted Greek developments and the birth of the discourse of Western democracy, but outlasted the much lauded Athenian *polis*, with Mesopotamian councils continuing to convene until at least as late as 187 BCE.

However, the notion that democracy existed in ancient Mesopotamia is not only useful in terms of understanding it as a precursor to the development of the Greek *polis*, but it is also particularly apposite when viewed in relation to the broader project being conducted here. In scrutinizing the presuppositions that have for so long informed Western understandings of the Orient's incompatibility with democracy, these ancient Mesopotamian examples serve to foreground an alternative history of the region. It reveals that collective models of governance and a lively political culture existed across the broader region at various junctures. While it would be unwise here to over-state the extent of these political developments or their influence, they nonetheless indicate just how long the will towards democracy has been alive in Iraq.

Beyond this, the ancient Mesopotamian democracies have particular significance for contemporary Iraq and its ongoing struggle from despotism to democracy. It should be remembered here that ancient Mesopotamia is not a distant, unknown past to the Iraqi populace; it is instead a rich cultural motif which has been frequently appropriated and worked into political, educational, sociological and literary discourses which have long underpinned notions of national unity and cultural pride amongst the Iraqis (Al-Musawi 2006, Baram 1983, 1991, 1994). It is precisely because of this familiarity with Iraq's ancient Mesopotamian heritage that this epoch's democracies could serve as a powerful historical memory in the process of building and legitimating democratic governance in Iraq today. Where modern Western democracies recall with admiration the Athenian *polis* and Roman Republic, Iraqi citizens may engage ancient Mesopotamian democracy as their own indigenous example of democracy.

Chapter 3
Islam and Democracy in Iraq

[I]t is clear that Muslims are not willing simply to adopt Western democratic models. The period of unquestioningly borrowing techniques and concepts from the Western experience has passed (if it ever took place), and now the effort is to establish authentically Islamic democratic systems. This effort is not inherently anti-Western, but it contains a recognition that there are significant problems with Western-style democracy ... [and that] major concepts in Western democracy have their analogues someplace in the Islamic tradition.

Esposito and Voll 1996: 30–1

Islam and Democracy?

The next historical epoch that must be addressed in any thorough analysis of the political history of Iraq is that which began with the founding of the Islamic religion in the seventh century and concluded with the fall of the Ottomans – the last great Islamic empire – at the beginning of the twentieth. For a significant portion of this same period, Europe wallowed in the so-called 'Dark Ages', caught between the past achievements of the Greco-Roman world and the future accomplishments of the continent after the Renaissance. While much recent scholarship has indicated that parts of Europe, such as Venice, the Nordic countries and the teachings of the Catholic church were practising or preaching at least quasi-democratic systems of governance (Byock 2002, Hittinger 2003, Kilcullen 1999, Stockwell 2011b, 2012), mostly the medieval period is known for the rise of European monarchs who insisted on the legitimacy and divinity of their hereditary regimes.

During this same period however the various Islamic empires not only ruled vast swathes of land across Eurasia and North Africa, they also became the epicentre of human civilization, the benchmark of scholarship and the hub of culture and creativity. Scholars of linguistics worked tirelessly to translate key texts from Greek, Hindu, Pahlavi and Syriac into Arabic and Latin; historians, geographers and travel writers compiled significant volumes that documented the natural world, its people and their past; artists and writers brought new life to the poetic beauty of Arabic as a language and composed great works of literature; philosophers and legal thinkers expounded on both religious and secular questions, developing influential centres of learning and schools of law; scientists introduced key innovations and methodologies in fields such as medicine, mathematics, chemistry and astronomy; various schools and strands of Islam emerged which encouraged free thought and a robust exchange of ideas; and non-Muslims were accorded significant rights and freedoms with many working alongside their Muslim counterparts and achieving degrees of success and influence within the Islamic world (Hourani 2005 [1991], Lombard 1975, Saliba 2007, Watt 1972, 1987 [1962]).

This string of cultural, religious and artistic accomplishments has been – and continues to be – a significant thread in the socio-political fabric of Iraq. Islam is not only the majority religion in Iraq (making up about 95 per cent of the population), it is also a fundamental characteristic of the myriad ways in which Iraqis have imagined themselves. It informs a rich array of cultural practices, is embedded into civil and political discourse, expressed in vibrant artistic motifs and is central to the practices of day-to-day life. Historically, from its earliest encroachment into Iraq during the seventh century and up until today, Islam has played a fundamental role in Iraqi national identity and the historical memory on which it is based. As we shall see in Chapter 4, in the 1920s the British installed Faisal, a Hashemite and the son of Sharif Hussayn, the Sharif of Mecca, as the first modern king of Iraq. Intrinsic to the subsequent reign of the Hashemite monarchy was their ability to harness their own cultural history and their ancestral connection to the Prophet Muhammad, and thereby legitimate their claim of being the rightful legatees of the Arab lands.

More recently, while Iraq under the Baath remained an ostensibly secular state, the Baath were nonetheless keen to re-engineer Iraq's classical Islamic past in ways similar to that of its Mesopotamian heritage. Most notably, as part of his own surreal cult of personality, Hussein also increasingly likened himself to a handful of key figures from Iraq's Islamic past. He routinely celebrated the achievements of the Abbasid caliph Al-Mansour, who had built the original round city of Baghdad during the 8th century, with the Baathist propaganda machine frequently asserting 'Al-Mansour Mansuran' ('There are two Al-Mansours', literally, 'There are two victors') (Lassner 2000: 94). Another example can be found in Hussein's 'official' genealogy which 'proves' he was a direct descendant of the Prophet Muhammad's nephew, Ali, who is revered by the Sunni as one of the first four caliphs and especially by the Shia who continue to emphasize the legitimacy of Ali's line (Bengio 1998: 80). Hussein also frequently invoked the famous military general, Saladin, who was conveniently born in Hussein's hometown of Tikrit and was most famous for defeating the Christian crusaders and restoring Muslim dominion over Jerusalem. The creation of a connection between these historical figures and Hussein was very carefully constructed in order to cross ethno-religious sectarian divides: Al-Mansour was a Sunni Arab, Ali a Shia Arab and Saladin a Kurd. Further, these celebrations of Iraq's Islamic past carried with them strong Baathist undertones and were specifically engineered to demand loyalty to the regime.

However, neither the Hashemite monarchy nor the Baath genuinely wanted to engage with Islamic teachings on politics as this would pose a direct threat to authoritarian forms of power and advocate a more inclusive and democratic system of government. Instead, they both sought to connect the great achievements of the nation's Islamic past to the centralization of power. They ignored the teachings and practices of Islam which have emphasized diversity and debate among the polity and thus contributed substantially to the notion that Islam is simply anathema to democracy.

This sat well with Western analysts. As we have seen in Chapter 1, from at least as far back as the turn of the eighth century, Islam had been viewed pejoratively in Europe, and had been used to explain away any perceived or real failures in the region. This is also true of studies of Iraq, such as that of the British administrator and scholar Stephen Longrigg who had first gone into Iraq at the beginning of the First World War and remained until 1931. In his sweeping account of *Four Centuries of Modern Iraq* Longrigg examines in detail the evolution of the social and political landscape of Iraq from the Ottoman conquest (1534) through to the conclusion of the nineteenth century. It is worth quoting a lengthy section from his conclusion as an example:

> The country passed from the nineteenth century [a] little less wild and ignorant, as unfitted for self-government, and not less corrupt, than it had entered the sixteenth; nor had its standards of material life outstripped its standards of mind and character ... Government's essential duty of leading tribe and town together in the way of progress had scarcely been recognized, barely begun, when our period closes; in the yet clearer task of securing liberty and rights to the governed (however backward), it had failed more signally perhaps than any government of the time called civilized ... A harsh sentence on this seeming crime of neglected opportunities, of perverse backwardness, may be mitigated by several pleas. No Islamic state in modern times has reached the first rank among nations. The conservatism into which the tenets of that great religion are interpreted has proved incompatible with progress as it is ordinarily judged: and in the very air and aspect of the East there seems to lie an acquiescence, a lack of the forward impulse, which critics of an Eastern state should not ignore (Longrigg 2002 [1925]: 321–2).

In Longrigg's typically Orientalist account, we find the very hallmarks of Oriental despotism, applied as it is to Iraq and blamed on the religion of Islam. For Longrigg, Iraq is wild and ignorant, corrupt, and deficient in every measure of material, intellectual and cultural life. In terms of Iraq being incapable of democracy, Longrigg is even clearer: the nation was simply unfit for self-government. The government that did exist, at that time a British installed and controlled democracy (see Chapter 4), had abjectly failed to secure the rights and liberties of the governed, the Iraqi people – who Longrigg refers to as 'backward'. But this was not the fault of the British, nor the ruling elite they brought to power, it was due to the fact that Iraq was a majority Islamic state. The 'perverse backwardness' of Iraq was caused by the 'conservatism' of Islam; it had 'proved incompatible with progress' and to foster 'an acquiescence, a lack of the forward impulse'.

While such Colonial-era discourses concerning the futility of bringing democracy to Iraq because of the nature of Islam are clearly disconcerting they are indicative of an epoch in which intellectual production in Europe concerning the East was built within an Orientalist framework. Indicative of the pervasive and insidious nature of such discourse, it is little wonder that such sentiments have been reiterated by various Western commentators in their discussion of the effort to bring democracy to Iraq following the invasion and occupation of 2003. To cite just one example, Diana West argued that the fundamental problem facing democracy in Iraq is Islam itself. She urges the US to acknowledge that the

> failure to establish liberty and justice for all in Iraq – namely, freedom of conscience and equality before the law – is due to the nature of Islamic culture, not to the efficacy of American efforts. If, five years after September 11, we finally faced the fact that liberty in Islam – defined, literally, as 'freedom from unbelief' – has nothing to do with liberty in the West, we could finally understand why an Iraqi constitution enshrining sharia is wholly incompatible with everything our own democracy stands for, and is thus not something worth dying for (West 2006).

In counteracting such Islamaphobic media discourse, recent decades have seen several notable studies which have argued that, at various times and in various ways, the religion of Islam, its various empires and its civilization, have utilized political systems strikingly similar to what we have come to term democracy (Esposito and Voll 1996, Sachedina 2001, Soroush 2000). This chapter therefore builds on this literature to analyse the collective forms of government and egalitarian social movements found throughout both the history and doctrine of Islam. From the life of the Prophet through to the Ottoman era, the history of various Islamic empires and the teachings of its clerics and scholars reveal a picture very much at odds with the overwhelming consensus in the West that the religion of Islam is antithetical to democracy and works against inclusion, diversity and debate. Well before the advent of modern representative democracy in Europe, Islam enabled various forms of participatory governance and put in place certain power-monitoring institutions. Focusing the bulk of its attention on Iraq, this chapter also documents the fundamental role that Baghdad played in promoting the democratic ethos via an active public sphere of learned scholars, great theologians and schools of jurisprudence. It concludes by noting that the re-examination of Iraqi Islamic history and politics not only raises a specific challenge to the received dichotomy between Western democracy and Oriental despotism, it also reveals new and exciting ways of thinking about democracy in Iraq today.

Democracy in Early Islam: The Prophet Muhammad and the Rashidun Caliphs

Amid the harsh mountains and the dry gorge of Mecca, a man by the name of Muhammad ibn Abdallah was born into the Quraysh tribe in or around 570 CE.[1] In his youth, Muhammad came to prefer solitude and prayer over what he saw as the increasingly decadent and brutal world of the Arabs. Every year, around the month of Ramadan, Muhammad would retreat to a cave at Mount Hira, perched on the rocky steppes that surrounded his home city, where he would meditate and fast, sometimes for as long as several weeks at a time. On one such retreat toward the end of Ramadan in 610, Muhammad is believed to have been visited by the Archangel Gabriel in the form of a man who served as a conduit for God's divine revelations. The first of these revelations began with the Angel asking Muhammad to 'Recite!' and he replied: 'I am not a reciter'. This continued and after the third time the Angel recited to Muhammad the first five verses of the *Quran* (96.1–5). Initially, when Muhammad began to speak of his experiences publically he was overwhelmingly rejected, but over the next 21 years, the messages he received from God (*Allah*) through the Archangel Gabriel attracted an enormous following across Arabia. These divine messages were recounted to his brethren from memory and either transcribed or memorized by his followers, and were eventually collated into the *Quran* (the recitation). These revelations were accompanied by the Prophet's commentary on day to day issues, and the example he set for his followers, which went on to become the *Hadith* (the traditions).

At the centre of Muhammad's teachings, and a major theme of the *Quran*, was the concept of *tawheed*, belief in the one all-powerful God. Also at the heart of Islam was the notion that the Islamic community (*ummah*) would practise a form of social justice in which Muslims were expected to create a pious community founded on the principles of virtue, compassion, justice and the fair distribution of wealth (*Quran* 3.105). The *Quran* recognizes equality and condemns discrimination and prejudice based on tribe, race, gender or religion (*Quran* 49.13). Jews and Christians (*dhimmis*) were not forced to convert and were accorded high degrees of both civil and religious liberties, for the *Quran* maintained that all children of Adam are honourable, regardless of faith, colour, gender or race (*Quran* 3.113–4, 199; 5.69;

---

1   There are many accounts of the life and times of the Prophet Muhammad. As with many historical figures, particularly those who come to be revered by religious orders, even the best of these accounts relies heavily on anecdotes and oral narratives purposefully constructed to lionize the Prophet and promote the new religion, while the worst are little more than fanciful and idealistic tomes. Although they are therefore difficult to rely on with any degree of certainty, they do hold certain things in common and these commonalities provide a relatively reliable and accurate picture of the man and his undertakings. Perhaps one of the best and earliest accounts of the life of the Prophet Muhammad is Ibn Ishaq's *The Life of Muhammad: Apostle of Allah* (Ishaq 2003 [725]), but for a more recent account, see Martin Lings's *Muhammad: His Life Based on the Earliest Sources* (Lings 1983).

17.70; 29.46). Similarly, Islam brought great respect and rights to women, enabling them to inherit property, divorce disrespectful husbands and play an active role in the social and political life of their communities. Women are described as playing many forthright roles in the earliest days of Islam; they fought alongside men in battle and do not appear to have experienced Islam as an oppressive religion.

Beyond notions of social justice, however, were Islam's specifically political ordinances. One driving principle of Islamic governance – and indeed of Islamic law – is that of *shura* (consultation). The *Quran* frequently asserts that all political decisions need to be made in consultation with the *ummah*. For example, the Prophet Muhammad was regularly instructed to 'Take counsel with them [the community] in the conduct of affairs' (*Quran* 3.159) and the community itself was asked to 'conduct their affairs by mutual consent' (*Quran* 42.38). Such consultative practises were, as we shall see, repeatedly put into practise by the Prophet who sought the counsel of men and women, elite and commoner, Muslim and non-Muslim, Arab and foreigner.

In 622, following years of persecution at the hands of the elite of Mecca, the Prophet and his followers migrated to the nearby city of Medina (*Yathrib*), whose people had already embraced the new faith and offered Muhammad and his followers sanctuary. This move to Medina is known as the *hijra* (migration) and can be seen as a decisive moment in Islamic history, effectively starting the Islamic calendar and cementing the popularity and strength of the new religion. Medina was a sprawling series of hamlets that housed three main Arab-Jewish tribes, as well as two main Arab-Muslim tribes. They had no centralized leadership, with each of the tribes subject to the authority of their own chieftain hierarchy, and the city had been locked in the grip of various tribal feuds.

One of the main reasons that Muhammad had been invited to Medina was the hope that he would be able to bring peace to the community. He was able to do so via a document that has come to be named the 'Constitution of Medina' which was based on the central principles of Islam as highlighted in the *Quran*. It is worth citing at length here:

> This is a covenant given by Muhammad to the believers [i.e. non-Muslim monotheists, mostly the Jewish tribes of Medina] and Muslims of Quraysh, Yathrib [Medina], and those who followed them, joined them, and fought with them. They constitute one Ummah ... All pious believers shall rise as one man against whosoever rebels or seeks to commit injustice, aggression, sin, or spread mutual enmity between the believers, even though he may be one of their sons ... Any Jew who follows us is entitled to our assistance and the same rights as any one of us, without injustice or partisanship. This *Pax Islamica* is one and indivisible ... The Jews have their religion and the Muslims theirs. Both enjoy the security of their own populace and clients except the unjust and the criminal among them ... Each shall assist the other against any violator of this covenant. Their relationship shall be one of mutual advice and consultation, and mutual assistance and charity rather than harm and aggression ... The town of Yathrib

shall constitute a sanctuary for the parties of this covenant … To every smaller group belongs the share which is their due as members of the larger group which is party to this covenant (cited in Haykal 1976: 180–3).

Here, and throughout the remainder of the document, the Prophet created a formal covenant between all of the significant tribes and families of Medina, who each recognized him as their new political leader. It outlines the rights and procedures for conflict resolution and community action, it also guarantees each citizen their civil and religious rights and allows them equal participation in the daily life of the state. Throughout its forty-eight clauses, the document frequently asserts that the new community is to be governed by the principles of freedom, justice, equality and peace. It is adamant against despotism and demands that the community should not be governed by those who commit crime, practise corruption or injustice, or act with aggression and intolerance. It asserts instead that politics should be conducted according to the principles of 'mutual advice and consultation, and mutual assistance and charity'. It even argues that such consultation is to be used in negotiations with foreign states, that the representatives of all parties should be present and that no negotiation should be conducted unilaterally. The significance of the Constitution of Medina is clear in terms of its democratic nature, its importance for the earliest Muslims and its relevance today. It also has specific relevance to the history of democracy, as it pre-dates both the *Magna Carta* and the *Declaration of Independence*.

The Constitution of Medina, along with the egalitarian message of the *Quran* and Muhammad's undeniable talents as a diplomat, not only brought peace and prestige to Medina, but also brought a democratic impetus that was to serve as the basis for the politics practised by the Islamic community. This is demonstrated in the prelude to Islam's first major battle, the 'Battle of Badr' in which the powerful Meccan elite retaliated against Muslim raids in 624 by cornering Muhammad's forces at a watering hole. Prior to the battle, the Prophet initially sought the advice of his most senior companions who advised him to maintain a siege within the walls of Medina and not leave the city to fight. Muhammad was not convinced that this was the best course of action however, and decided instead to convene an assembly of the entire Muslim community and seek their advice and opinion (Istanbuli 2001: 37). Less conservative in their views and more determined to fight, the community advised Muhammad to march out against the enemy (Lings 1983: 174). Not only did the Prophet accept their advice, but the Muslims went on to seize their first military victory despite the overwhelming odds in favour of the Meccans. As with the *Epic of Gilgamesh* discussed in the preceding chapter, Muhammad's desire to submit major decisions of war and peace to the entire community not only constitutes a major democratic achievement in its own right, it also parallels traditional Grecian or Roman assemblies of the arms-bearing men during times of war.

Another example of the democratic nature of early Islamic politics comes shortly after the Muslims conquered Mecca in 630 when the Prophet received a delegation representing the Christians of Najran (a small town in the south-west of the Arabian Peninsula). They had come to negotiate a peace treaty with the Muslims. Instead of demanding their conversion, the Prophet signed a peace treaty with Najran that demonstrates Islam's central ideals of religious freedom and civil liberties. It reads:

> To the Najranites, and to those living among them, the protection of God, and the pledge of Muhammed, the Prophet and the Apostle of God, is conferred upon them their faith, their land and their properties, upon those who are absent or present, upon their caravans, their sanctuaries and their sacred possessions ... If anyone among them raises a claim for a right, then justice and equality will be asserted. No oppressed there will be or oppressors in Najran (cited in Istanbuli 2001: 45).

Shortly after conquering Mecca, Muhammad returned to Medina and fell gravely ill, passing away in 632 at the age of 63. In the course of one lifetime, Muhammad ibn Abdallah had successfully brought Islam into the world, a religion centred on the concept of one true God and notions of social justice, religious law and piety. This provided the framework through which he was able to unite the warring factions of much of the Arabian peninsula into a single polity, adhering to a very specific set of legal, social, moral, military and political norms. Such norms also included fundamental ideals of human equality and the need for consultative and deliberative mechanisms in governance. From his recitation of the *Quran*, the Constitution of Medina, the various peace treaties he implemented and his practical and personal examples emerged a pragmatic framework for the equitable conduct of human affairs. In turn, this created an entirely new civilization that would come to control much of the known world, to make unprecedented advances in military, cultural and scientific endeavours and leave behind a democratic legacy that is rarely acknowledged today.

The death of Muhammad brought with it a question of deep concern to the *ummah*: who would lead the followers of Islam now? A series of complex political deliberations ensued, particularly in Mecca and Medina, with a number of competing factions jostling for power and control. It was Abu Bakr (632–4), the Prophet's closest friend and father-in-law, who, in a demonstration of the democratic nature of the early Islamic period, was eventually elected by the majority of votes to be the first *Caliph* (Steward) of the growing Islamic community. The election was also ratified by the community itself as they congregated in the mosque and swore allegiance to him. Abu Bakr's incumbency marks the first of four leaders, collectively known as the *Rashidun Caliphate* (Rightly-Guided Caliphs), who were all early converts to Islam as well as being close friends or family of the Prophet. Despite the fact that Abu Bakr was in office for only two years, he dealt with a very tumultuous era in Islamic politics, including the *Ridda Wars* (Wars of Apostasy) which quelled various rebellions from across the *ummah*. What is particularly interesting is that while such military campaigns, like those of all expanding empires, were often bloody and destructive, the campaigns themselves were guided by nominally democratic virtues. Abu Bakr issued several pieces of advice to the leaders of the army, including the fair treatment of enemy soldiers, how best to receive envoys, and the use of consultation in military strategy: 'If you consulted the others, be truthful to them, so you may get from them the true counsel' (cited in Istanbuli 2001: 59).

Such military strategy was to prove crucial to the campaigns against the Sassanid and Byzantine Empires that were conducted under the leadership of Abu Bakr's key advisor and successor, Umar ibn Al-Khattab (634–44). Although Umar was appointed by Abu Bakr, his authority was endorsed by an assembly of the Islamic community in Mecca. Perhaps Umar's most well-known achievement was the expansion of the Islamic empire beyond the Arabian Peninsula.[2] Included in this, was Islam's first real encroachment into today's Iraq where the Muslims defeated the Sassanids at the Battle of Qadisiyya (637), famously leading to the capture of Ctesiphon, and in time, the collapse of the entire Sassanid Empire. As with his predecessor, Umar's management of the Islamic military was conducted according to relatively democratic principles. In one particular letter concerning military issues, for example, Umar points out that his decisions are not only based on his interpretations of the teachings of Islam, but that he 'consulted, too, the companions of the Prophet, who, each one of them has voiced his opinion' (cited in Istanbuli 2001: 60).

Before his untimely death, Umar nominated an administrative body composed of six of his most prominent companions and entrusted them with choosing his successor from among themselves. In this way, Uthman ibn Affan (644–56) was eventually elected to the position of *caliph*, following the approval of the community. Uthman had been among the first converts to Islam and is perhaps best known for ordering the compilation of the *Quran* as a written text. However, Uthman often privileged his fellow Umayyad family members for senior positions over perhaps more deserving candidates; he gave the important post of the governor of Syria to an Umayyad of rising power and prestige, Muawiyyah. Such nepotism further eroded the confidence of the majority of Muslims in Uthman's leadership and his rivals murdered him in 656 in Medina.

A congregation in the Prophet's Mosque then elected the Prophet's cousin, Ali bin Abi Talib (656–61), to become the fourth and final of the Rashidun caliphs. He believed, as had his predecessors, that such a decision was only valid if the majority of his immediate community endorsed the decision, which they did by freely pledging their loyalty to him. This is not surprising given the fact that Ali was a devout Muslim and believed in the Islamic principles of justice and the importance of being compassionate towards the subject peoples of the empire. Ali was also the only one of the *Rashidun caliphs* to have been a blood relative of Muhammad and the descendants of this prestigious blood line have been highly revered by the Shia sect of Islam ever since in their belief that only a descendant of Muhammad should lead the *ummah*. Despite his esteemed lineage, Ali's leadership was fraught with problems from the outset. When Ali sought to challenge the growing power

---

2   For a detailed account of the Arab conquests in these early days as well as later successes, see Hugh Kennedy's recent *The Great Arab Conquests* (Kennedy 2008).

of the Umayyads in their Syrian stronghold of Siffin (today's Ar-Raqqah in Syria) in 657, the two forces reached a stalemate (Istanbuli 2001: 74–81). A council of arbitration was set up, and charged with the duty of deciding who should lead the *ummah* on the basis of the *Quran* (Wellhausen 1975 [1901]: 1–7). This did not work in Ali's favour and the Islamic world was temporarily split into two: Ali controlled Iraq and Arabia while Muawiyyah ruled Syria and Egypt. This further eroded Muslim confidence in Ali and he was eventually murdered in 661.

Aside from the time of the Prophet, the era of the Rashidun caliphs represents the most significant epoch of Islamic history. This is as true for the Sunni majority, who revere the governance of all four of the Rashidun caliphs, as it is for the Shia minority who continue to emphasize the legitimacy of Ali's line. This era not only saw the rapid expansion of Islam and its territories, but also saw the democratic ideals laid down by the Prophet put into action. As Noah Feldman has pointed out, the Rashidun caliphs 'were understood to be selected by people, not God; they were subject to God's law as described in the *Quran* and the sayings of the Prophet; and they were expected to engage in some sort of consultation with the community they governed' (Feldman 2003: 52). The Rashidun were not the Oriental despots that Muslim leaders are so often assumed to be, but ruled in accordance with the notions of social justice and equality that underpinned Islam and had become normative amongst the *ummah* of their time.

Islamic Bureaucracy, Theology and Philosophy in Iraq

With Ali out of his way, Muawiyyah (661–80) seized the opportunity to establish his own *caliphate* out of the stronghold of Damascus. This was the beginning of the Umayyad dynasty which was to last for a little under one hundred years (661–750) and was to see the lands of Islam transformed into a unified empire with a common identity and ideology. It is often assumed that Muawiyyah was able to achieve such unity because he was the first leader of the Muslims to declare himself king. There is no denying that the leadership of the Muslim community had not only shifted physically from its traditional heartland in Mecca and Medina, but had transformed ideologically with many of the Umayyads ruling in a much more secular and autocratic fashion than their predecessors. However, the Umayyads still had to govern traditional Arab Muslims, many of whom lionized the days of the Prophet and the Rashidun. The Umayyads therefore sought to balance their move towards autocracy with traditional methods of Arab governance such as consultation, popular elections and public ratification. They were known to adopt

> several institutions of Beduin democracy – such as the Wufud, deputations from provinces and the principal tribes – to consult the views of such assemblies on as many occasions as possible, [and] to associate them openly with public business by recognizing their right to remonstrate (Houtsma, Wensinck, Gibb, and Heffening 1993: 620).

While later Umayyad caliphs like Umar II (717–20) were elected by a wide franchise and had the people's overwhelming support, the Umayyad period also saw a number of morally weak, cowardly and murderous individuals assume the head of the empire. By the time Marwan II (744–50) had taken control of the empire, anti-Umayyad sentiment was rife and he was forced to spend much of his incumbency desperately trying to maintain power.

Harnessing popular resentment of the Umayyads, particularly among the Arab Shia and the non-Arab converts to Islam (*mawalis*) who were often not treated equally, was a group of Arabs who had been garnering political momentum since around 715. They claimed to be the descendants of one of the uncles of the Prophet, Abbas ibn Abd Al-Muttalib,[3] and they emanated from Kufa in Iraq. By 743 the movement, known as the Abbasids, had attained an almost messianic momentum across Persia and in 747 the black banners of the Abbasids were first raised around Merv (in today's Turkmenistan). In 749 the Abbasids openly controlled Kufa and the following year they won a decisive victory against the Umayyads at the Battle of the Zab in Iraq (Kennedy 2005: 1–10). This saw the instalment of the Abbasid dynasty which was to maintain official power over much of the *ummah* for the next five hundred years (750–1258). 'Broadly speaking', as Amira Bennison puts it, 'the appeal of the Abbasid revolution was … it offered a fairer Islamic order in which Muslims, whatever their origin, would be able to participate on equal terms' (Bennison 2009: 24).

Despite its promise, the Abbasid dynasty began with Abu Al-Abbas Al-Saffah (750–4), who became known by the unfortunate but apt sobriquet of 'the blood-shedder' due to his brutal massacre of the Umayyads and their supporters. Such blood-thirsty politics continued under the reign of his brother, Abu Jafar Al-Mansur (754–75) who murdered all of the Shia leaders that he considered a credible threat to his leadership. This cruelty aside, Al-Mansur is perhaps best remembered for the fact that he ordered the building of the Abbasid's new capital, the round city of Baghdad, in 758. Due to its strategic location on the banks of the Tigris and its connection to various trade routes, Baghdad was quickly transformed into a cultural and economic hub, eventually becoming a bustling metropolis that hundreds of thousands of people called home. The creation of Baghdad was a turning point in the history of Iraq. Already home to the garrison towns of Kufa

---

3   It is from the name Abbas ibn Abd Al-Muttalib that the Abbasids got their name. Abbas had been the paternal uncle of the Prophet Muhammad and he had played an important role in Muhammad's family, even going as far as protecting the Prophet against his enemies in the earliest years of Islam. However, claiming the lineage of Abbas was nowhere near as significant as being a descendent of Ali, as Abbas was neither a descendent of the Prophet nor a Muslim (Kennedy 2005: 3–4). Despite this, as Hugh Kennedy has pointed out elsewhere, the Abbasid claim to the caliphate would have been strong given the broad understanding of 'family' in the eighth century and the reverence held for all relations of the Prophet (Kennedy 1986: 124–5).

and Basra, Iraq soon became the centre of the Muslim world and the bastion of Islamic civilization.

From his new capital Al-Mansur was able to enact a series of revolutionary changes to the government of the *ummah*. This included his own personal style of governance which was refreshingly concerned with the needs of the people. He was widely known for his piety, but also for his political insight, his sharp wit and his great public oratory. Following the Friday prayers in the newly erected mosque of central Baghdad, the caliph would stand before a large audience ranging from the wealthy elite to the everyday commoner. He would deliver powerful political speeches and encourage people to question and debate openly his policies and agendas. As Hugh Kennedy notes, 'He had a ready response to the hecklers who occasionally dared to challenge him … in Mansur's time the caliph could be seen and heard by anyone who came to Friday prayers in the great mosque of the capital' (Kennedy 2005: 14).

Beyond his willingness to engage with his subjects, Al-Mansur also set in place a series of bureaucratic changes that further developed and refined those of the Umayyads. Under Al-Mansur, an egalitarian bureaucracy emerged in which any man of adequate ability could ascend the hierarchy of the court and administration. Foremost in this hierarchy were the powerful chief viziers of the Barmakid family who descended from Persian aristocracy and held enormous sway over the Abbasids. There were also the military elite and key strategists whose opinions were regularly sought in matters both soldierly and civilian. Other courtiers of more humble origins include the office of the *khatib* (secretary), which was held by a highly intelligent commoner responsible for managing the details of provincial finances. Such a sophisticated political scene suggests that Al-Mansur was not a tyrant. The caliph was enveloped within a deeply complex political environ in which various stakeholders competed, often on behalf of the people, to promote various agendas, policies and reforms.

This system was to continue under the leadership of later caliphs like Muhammad ibn Mansur Al-Mahdi (775–85), Musa Al-Hadi (785–6), and then perhaps the Abbasid dynasties most well-known caliph, Harun Al-Rashid (786–809). It is widely understood that Harun ruled as an absolute monarch and claimed himself the 'Shadow of God on Earth', living an opulent lifestyle and leaving many of the affairs of the state to his courtiers and viziers. Yet Harun was also an avid patron of both cultural and scientific endeavours who utilized his enormous wealth and power to encourage the pursuit of knowledge and the practise of varied artistic forms. Perhaps his most well known accomplishment was the foundation of the *Bayt Al-Hikmah* (The House of Wisdom), an intellectual institution later run by his son, Abu Jafar Al-Mamun (813–33).

The early Abbasid period also witnessed the formation of the *Mazalim* (court of complaint) and other mechanisms and institutions which enabled citizens to bring grievances about injustices or maladministration to the caliphal representative (Kennedy 2005: 34). One such representative was the famous Barmakid vizier, Yahya, who would find a line of petitioners at his front door every morning and who would work long into the night to make sure that all of their grievances were heard and the most amicable solutions found (Kennedy, 2005: 43). In addition, the Barmakid salons which were scattered across Baghdad, served as 'a forum in which ideas could be discussed with a freedom not possible in the more circumscribed surroundings of the caliph's own audience' (Kennedy 2005: 65). Further evidence of this culture of debate and difference can be found in an excerpt from a letter sent by Hashimi, a cousin of the caliph Al-Mamun, to an opponent. He writes:

> bring forward all the arguments you wish and say whatever you please and speak your mind freely. Now that you are safe and free to say whatever you please appoint some arbitrator who will impartially judge between us and lean only towards the truth and be free from the empery of passion, and that arbitrator shall be Reason, whereby God makes us responsible for our own rewards and punishments. Herein I have dealt justly with you and have given you full security and am ready to accept whatever decision Reason may give for me or against me (Hashim cited in Arnold 1961 [1913]).

Perhaps the best indication of the ongoing democratic legacy within Islam in the Abbasid epoch is not found among the highest echelons of the state, but among the clergy and the scholars. Despite the common misconception in the West that Islam has never enabled a distinction between 'church' and 'state', there is wide consensus among scholars of the early Abbasid period (750–833) that it was constituted by a distinct separation between the *ulama* (religious scholars) and the caliph. Because the caliph failed to live up to the theocratic virtues of the early leaders of the community, the devout looked increasingly to the rising power of the *ulama* for both spiritual and political guidance rather than to the court of the caliph (Lapidus 1973, 1975). In this way, the *ulama* came to form an alternative pillar of power and authority to the Abbasid state many centuries before similar European developments and, just as in later Europe, the 'church' served as not only a moral compass for the people, but also as an effective check on the political power of the state (Lapidus 1975).

For their part, the *ulama* held the responsibility of producing the definitive guide to Islamic thought and life, the *Shariah* (Islamic law). To do this, they drew not only on the *Quran* and *Hadith*, but also on Quaranic ideals (*fiqh*) in the hope that they would develop a better understanding of God and his desire for the *ummah*. From here, the *Shariah* developed into a complex code of legal prescriptions in which 'local rulers and judges were called upon to make many decisions within the general framework of the developing understanding of the fundamentals of Islam in diverse contexts' (Esposito and Voll 1996: 44). Much to the chagrin of the caliphs however, the *Shariah* became a benchmark of religious, political and juridical virtue that generally opposed the authoritarian and decadent nature of the state. As Karen Armstrong has noted,

The Shariah totally rejected the aristocratic, sophisticated ethos of the court. It restricted the power of the caliph, stressed that he did not have the same role as the Prophet or the *rashidun*, but that he was only permitted to administer the sacred law. Courtly culture was thus tacitly condemned as un-Islamic. The ethos of the Shariah, like that of the Quran, was egalitarian. There were special provisions to protect the weak, and no institution, such as the caliphate or the court, had any power to interfere with the personal decisions and beliefs of the individual. Each Muslim had a unique responsibility to obey God's commands, and no religious authority, no institution (such as 'The Church') and no specialized group of 'clergy' could come between God and the individual Muslim. All Muslims were on the same footing; there was to be no clerical elite or priesthood acting as an intermediary (Armstrong 2000: 52).

It is within this atmosphere that the *ulama* began to further refine the machinations of *shura*, stipulating that Muslim leaders must consult with their subordinates and acquire their consent (Hassouna 2001: 50). In theory, this posited that a consultative council should be elected by the people whose support the leader legally required in order to administer the affairs of the state (Choudhury 1990: 45). In larger states, the *shura* would take the form of a *Majlis Al-Shura* (national assembly) which was designed to be truly representative of the entire community and 'therefore the members of the *majlis* must be elected by means of the widest possible suffrage, including both men and women' (M. Asad 1980 [1961]: 45). At the very least, the *shura* was intended to secure 'the people's right to choose their government freely, openly and fearlessly from among themselves at all levels from the lowest to the highest' (Pasha 1993: 70–1). Further to this, Islamic law of this time also prescribed several other concepts analogous to the fundamentals of democracy such as *Ijma* (consensus), *Ijtihad* (independent interpretive judgement) and the concurrent condemnation of *Fitnah* (civil disorder) matched with the tolerance of *Ikhtilaf* (disagreement). In addition, Syed Pasha notes that, under Islamic law, *Al-Naas* (the people) also have the right to life and property, to choose their beliefs and behaviour, to know, to read, to write, to speak, to have power and – most importantly – the right to choose their government (Pasha 1993: 67–71).

Paralleling the clergy's development of the *Shariah* was the work of the scholars of this time. Al-Mamun was himself a Mutazilite and therefore believed that theoretical reason and rationalism were the arbiters of revelation. Under his leadership, the *Bayt Al-Hikma* attracted scholars, artists, philosophers and scientists who travelled from across the Muslim world to visit and work in the library. They also convened in public assemblies, presided over by Al-Mamun, in which theological, political and philosophical debates over the most radical ideas of the time – even including questions about the legitimacy or style of Al-Mamun's reign – were conducted in a collegial environment that upheld strict rules of intellectual candour (Fakhry 2004 [1970]: 10). Later, during the reign of another Abbasid caliph, Al-Mutawakkil (847–61), this atmosphere continued as scholars worked tirelessly to translate key philosophical and scientific texts from Greek, Persian and Syriac (Saliba 2007).

After the death of Al-Mamun in 833, however, the socio-political landscape of the Abbasid Empire, and indeed the Islamic world, began to change dramatically. Among the myriad reasons for these changes, was the fact that an ever increasing number of people converted to Islam. As they converted, the citizens of the provinces 'demanded to be admitted to the political process as full members of the Muslim community. In this way the provinces came to be dominated by men whose roots and family were entirely local' (Kennedy 1986: 202–3). Although they were Muslims, their loyalty to a caliph which could be thousands of miles away and in a land they had never visited was difficult to earn and maintain. While the Abbasids were to remain the official figureheads of most of the Islamic world for centuries to come, their power and influence waned substantially from the late ninth century onwards and would never re-gather its strength. Instead, political plurality became the norm as important regions such as Central Asia, North Africa, Iran, Egypt, as well as parts of Syria, developed their own systems of governance and paid little more than token homage to the Abbasid caliphs, with some going so far as to directly challenge their claim to authority.

One very substantial challenge to the power of the Abbasids came during the so-called 'Shia century' which saw the Buyids (945–1055) extend their influence out from their stronghold in Iran to conquer much of Iran, Iraq and the surrounding areas. The Buyids occupied Baghdad in 945 but they did not overthrow the Abbasid caliph because they reasoned that a Shia toppling of the Sunni elite might cause a popular revolt among their mostly Sunni subjects (Jiwa 1992: 64–5). Among their many notable achievements, the Buyids are credited with ushering in what Adam Mez has famously termed 'The Renaissance of Islam' (Mez 1937). This renaissance saw a renewed cultural florescence as the patronage of the arts, philosophy, sciences and theology were no longer solely the province of the state, but spread outwards to a wider circle of wealthy or influential people interested in fostering achievement. In Joel Kraemer's study of the Buyid period he notes that it

> witnessed a powerful assertion of individualism, a burst of personal expression, in the domains of literary creativity and political action. It thrived in a remarkably cosmopolitan atmosphere. Baghdad … [was] the rendezvous of scholars from far and wide, of diverse cultural and religious backgrounds. Philosophers belonged to a class of their own, transcending particular loyalties, united by the pursuit of wisdom, the love of reason … [Baghdad] was permeated by a spirit of scepticism and secularism. Rebellion against convention, characteristic of free-spirited poets, was often accompanied by libertinism (Kraemer 1992 [1986]: vii).

Because of this spirit of individualism, cosmopolitanism and secularism, the philosophers, poets, artisans and scholars of this period added an additional and very important layer to the complex social-strata of Baghdad. Like the *ulama*, they came to wield significant power in part because of their enormous popularity and in part because their ideas served as an alternative voice to both the clergy and the state. This meant that, in addition to the mosque and the court, scholarly discussion of socio-political issues now took place in independent schools, arcades, city-squares, gardens, markets, and bathhouses. Such discussions were also very heterogeneous, with debates common between Arabs and Persians, Jews and Christians, Sunni and Shia, Sufi and atheist, poet and philosopher. Many of the more successful scholars and poets had their own schools and delivered lectures to huge crowds. According to Kraemer, 'On special occasions, large assemblies were convened for discussion' where 'a question was initially proposed and then theses and antitheses stated in turn' (Kraemer 1992 [1986]: 56).

Central to this cultural renaissance was the intellectual legacy of Greek antiquity. Although, as mentioned earlier, the translation and transmission of Grecian texts had begun during earlier Abbasid times, by the time of the Buyids, Islamic scholars had thoroughly studied the works of antiquity. Aside from Greek scholars such as Euclid, Galen, Ptolemy and Socrates, scholars of the Buyid epoch had a particular penchant for Plato and especially Aristotle, whom they nicknamed 'The First Teacher' (Vagelpohl 2008). At the tenth-century school of Aristolian studies in Baghdad, for example, students and scholars had access to Aristotle's complete *oeuvre* (Kraemer 1992 [1986]: xx, xxiii). Neoplatonic and Aristotelian thought dominated their investigations into natural philosophy, their reflections on ethics and their rich debates on politics.

This Grecian-inspired Islamic renaissance has several important dimensions that must be spelled out here. First, it had an immediate effect on various religious scholars who attempted to reconcile the pagan beliefs and erudite philosophies of the Greeks with their Islamic religiosity (Alon 1991). This brought about a form of religious disputation known as the *Kalam*, where 'The arguments put forward ... were expected to conform to the Aristotelian pattern, that is to say to be intellectual in conception and dialectical in form' (Rice 1961: 115). Second, given the fact that the Islamic world now stretched from Spain to the borders of India, the knowledge of the ancient Greeks was spread further and wider than it had ever been in antiquity, reaching new and diverse audiences. As they translated and added important developments to Grecian works on science and philosophy, the Islamic world transmitted ancient knowledge across much of the known world, including into Europe.

Finally, what is also significant about the Islamic exposure to Grecian thought is that it would have included Greek musings on political matters and models. Islamic scholars were particularly fond of the Aristotelian dictum that 'man is naturally a political animal' (Kraemer 1992 [1986]: 18). Clearly the Islamic scholars of the Buyid dynasty had access to works such as Plato's *Republic* and *Laws* and Aristotle's *Politics* which concern themselves with the Grecian experiment with *demokratia* (Aristotle 1943 [350 BCE], Plato 1975 [360 BCE], 1975 [380 BCE]). This is certainly true of the Persian born Shia philosopher Abu Nasr Al-Farabi (Alpharabius in Latin, 870–950) who, whilst working in Buyid Baghdad, wrote expositions on *The Philosophy of Plato and Aristotle* and penned important works such as the *Book of Political Science* and *The Virtuous City* (Al-Farabi 1962 [935]-b, 1996 [948], 2001 [930–45]). Al-Farabi not only laid the 'foundation of logic, metaphysics and politics in the world of Islam' he also came to be known as 'the "Second Master", the first master being Aristotle' (Campanini 2008 [2004]: 10). Of particular relevance here is the connection that Al-Farabi drew between happiness and politics in *The Virtuous City* in which he argued that

> man cannot attain the perfection, for the sake of which his inborn nature has been given to him, unless many (societies of) people who co-operate come together who each supply everybody else with some particular need of his, so that as a result of the contribution of the whole community all the things are brought together which everybody needs in order to preserve himself and to attain perfection (Al-Farabi 1996 [948]: 205).

This connection between happiness and politics is further elaborated in his *Attainment of Happiness* in which Al-Farabi argues that 'The human things through which nations and citizens of cities attain earthly happiness in this life and supreme happiness in the life beyond are of four kinds: theoretical virtues, deliberative virtues, moral virtues and practical arts' (Al-Farabi 1962 [935]-a: 13). In other words, the attainment of human perfection not only involves an appreciation of science, religion and the arts, it also requires man to deliberate; to be happy, people must co-operate with their fellow citizens in order to reach collective decision towards the common good. Al-Farabi also proposed a radical reform of the politics of the Arab caliphate premised on Aristotelian and Platonian philosophy. While he did not go as far as advocating a re-birth of the Grecian form of *demokratia*, he did argue that the caliph – as successor of the Prophet – must conform to the principles of good governance as espoused by the ancient Greeks (Walzer 2007: 166).

These ideas had a profound influence on many successive generations of Islamic intellectuals, from Abu Ali Al-Husayn Sina (Avicenna, 980–1037) to Ibn Khaldun (1332–1406) (Khaldun 1967 [1377]; Sina 1973 [1012]). One particular Sunni philosopher is worth mentioning here, Abu Al-Walid Muhammad Ibn Rushd (Averroes, 1126–98) who followed Plato's critique of Greece to argue that Islamic regimes such as the Almohads were too democratic (Rushd 1974 [1165]). For Averroes,

> Democracy is the system in which people, feeling free from bonds and constraints, abandon themselves to pleasures and desires. In a democracy, the heart of society and the very real goal for which the state exists is the family; there are laws, but a powerful majority betrays the multitude and a state of war and violence, stimulated by human passions, gains the upper hand (Campanini 2008 [2004]: 157).

Averroes thought that such messy and bellicose democracies therefore created the need for an aristocratic elite who were forced to rule tyrannically over the people.

Such a situation was unjust and therefore the antithesis of the model both Plato and Averroes preferred: that of a virtuous state ruled by a wise and benevolent ruler, what Plato referred to as the philosopher-king. The notion that Islamic philosophers like Al-Farabi and the later Averroes were familiar with, and added to, the Grecian literature on democracy is a widely under-recognized aspect of the history of democracy. While such Islamic philosophers may not have explicitly argued in favour of democracy, they did understand its central principles and did not argue against it because of some fundamental contradiction with Islam.

Returning to Iraq, it is important to note that the Buyids eventually succumbed to a band of Turks from northern Khorasan, the Seljuks (1035–1194) who despised the Buyid Shia influence over Baghdad and sought to replace it with their own Sufi-inspired Sunni faith. Like the Buyids, the Seljuks recognized the significance of the Abbasid caliph to the wider *ummah* and left him on the throne even though he became increasingly isolated from the real business of government. Politically, the Seljuk *sultanate* (rulers) continued the tradition of plurality in political life and allowed many autonomous states to exist within its jurisdiction (Bennison 2009: 47). The Seljuks derived their power from the local councils and institutions that thrived across their empire. Each of these provincial outposts had their own civil official who acted on behalf of the *sultan* and served as a link between the central government and the people, often representing the latter to the former. Generally speaking, the appointment of a local official was not in the hands of the state or its representatives, but occurred via local political mechanisms, which included elections by popular vote (Bulliet 1978: 47).

The central government was made up of a number of civil administrators inherited from Abbasid and Buyid times. However, the Seljuks expanded the state bureaucracy into a complex machine governed by five major *diwans* (ministerial departments) including that of finance, diplomacy, court affairs, the army, and the ministry of the vizierate which oversaw the others (Klausner 1973: 16–8). Although the vizier remained the most powerful civil official of the state, the Seljuks saw the rise of state institutions which mitigated any moves towards empery. An indication of its egalitarian nature, was that even the most lowly scribe could ascend the hierarchy to the rank of vizier, as long as he held the required experience, education and savvy (Klausner 1973: 19). To become a minister, the candidate underwent the procedure of being brought before the assembly of the *sultan* and his court and made to deliver key policy speeches to win over their support before being elected to the post (Rice 1961: 90).

With a Sunni authority regaining control of the *ummah*, the *ulama* also re-emerged as a significant political force during the time of the Seljuks. The *madrasa*s (religious schools) also expanded in their role, bringing with them certain prestige and power to Sunni Islamic knowledge. As Carla Klausner has noted, the religious classes 'played a significant role in preserving the balance of power between the temporal and spiritual authorities' they 'often acted in a more public capacity as envoys and mediators' and 'in general were often the spokesmen of and on behalf of the people' (Klausner 1973: 23). Although this role gradually weakened as a number of the *ulama* became assimilated into the state bureaucracy, the Seljuk epoch still maintained a determined separation between religion and politics.

This separation continued centuries later when, after 1534, Iraq came under the rule of the Ottoman Empire (1299–923). Part of the reason for the Ottoman Empire's endurance and success was its shrewd understanding of the systems of power and local governance that existed throughout its extensive and multitudinous regions. Generally speaking, the Ottomans believed that a strong, civilized state was a cosmopolitan one. They were therefore very tolerant of the region's many minority groups, such as the myriad of Jewish and Christian communities, even going as far as allowing these communities to be governed by Halakhan or Canon law respectively, under the *millet* (nation) system. Beyond the freedoms accorded to religious minorities, the Ottoman Empire also encouraged a relatively robust civil society in which secondary structures such as tribal organizations, village councils and trade guilds not only thrived, but also wielded significant power over policy formation and governance (Gibb and Bowen, 1950). This democratic culture extended out into the many coffee houses of Istanbul and other cities like Baghdad where lively and scholarly debate often focused on the machinations of state politics and the pertinent political issues of the time (Arjomand 2004). There were also a number of formal limits on the *sultan*'s ability to be autocratic, including the convening of several ad-hoc consultative assemblies made up of dignitaries which convened 'at times of serious international emergencies', where 'the right to express opinion was free' and the 'emergent consensus in such assemblies had a bearing on the *sultan*'s subsequent decisions' (Gerber 2002: 79). In summarizing his work on the democratic impetus within various bureaucratic mechanisms and informal practices of the Ottoman Empire, Haim Gerber concludes that 'there is ample evidence that Ottoman society featured several institutions that worked on the basis of autonomous powers and initiatives' which were able to express 'the entire gamut of relations between the Ottoman government and the populace' (Gerber 2002: 80).

In addition to such complex and egalitarian politics, the Ottomans were also a decidedly Sunni Islamic Empire and even the *sultan* was subject to the legal prescriptions of *Shariah* law. As they had in earlier centuries, the *ulama* wielded significant power over the government. They formed a sphere of influence separate to the state, held the government to account via their religious credibility, and exercised important administrative, juridical and even economic judgements (Nieuwenhuis 1982: 27–8). They had the right to veto any decision or law made by the state if they deemed it to be in conflict with Islamic law (Shaw 1976: 134–9). Beyond this, the most senior member of the *ulama*, the *Shaykh Al-Islam*, could actually depose the *sultan* if he violated the *Shariah*, a power which was used in the usurpation of Sultans Ibrahim (1648), Mehmed IV (1687), Ahmed III (1730), and Selim III (1807) (Esposito and Voll 1996: 48).

In the region now known as Iraq, the Ottomans at first tried to rule directly by installing their own representatives to positions of power (Nieuwenhuis 1982: 25). However, in time, and in line with their *millet* policy of regional and religious autonomy, the Ottomans issued relative independence to the Mamluk *pashas* (governors) in Baghdad and Basra, the prominent Kurdish families in and around Mosul and the various tribal orders and principalities that scattered the rural areas of Iraq (Preston 2003: 24–5, 107, Tripp 2007 [2000]: 8–10). As with other parts of the Ottoman Empire, although these regional governments officially came under the auspices of Istanbul, they retained considerable autonomy (Hechter and Kabiri 2004: 8). This is especially true of the Mamluks, who were Georgian Christian soldiers taken from their families at childhood and converted to Islam. The Ottomans installed them in Baghdad as both administrative and military minions but under the leadership of Hasan Pasha (1704–23) they began to assert their dominance and became increasingly independent of their Ottoman overlords. The Mamluks went on to hold formal power over most of Iraq (1747–831) and were preferred by most Iraqis, especially in Baghdad, because they suppressed tribal revolts, restored order, introduced a programme of modernization and transformed the region's crippling economy and under-achieving agricultural sphere.

In Tom Nieuwenhuis' study of the Mamluk period in Iraq he brings to light a number of important details about the political landscape of the time. Mamluk government can be characterized by two key *diwans* (executive administrative councils) that served as the administrative nucleus of the state. The first, the administrative *diwan*, was ostensibly controlled by the Mamluks, but the second, the consultative *diwan*, was made up of a much broader array of citizens including religious, tribal and military representatives. It served as an advisory council, playing a significant role in both deliberating over the key issues and informing the officials of the administrative *diwan*. In addition, even a lowly clerk of the consultative *diwan* could, in theory, and with the *pasha's* blessing, ascend the hierarchy to become a *pasha* himself, as was the case of Ali Pasha (1762–4) who was from a humble Persian background (Nieuwenhuis 1982: 15, 28). Outside of the official coterie in Baghdad, traditional Shia centres such as Najaf and Karbala, and Kurdish and Turkomen centres like Kirkuk and Mosul not only enjoyed religious and political freedom but the elite of these towns came to wield significant influence. This is particularly true of the Shia clergy whose loyal following meant that the local *pasha* could rarely implement policy without first consulting with the seminaries and gaining their approval. The Shia elite became so powerful in the holy city of Najaf that, in 1815, they rebelled against their governor and declared themselves independent. Although this did not last long, Najaf's independence also saw the formation of two political parties, *zurqurt* (the poor) and *shumurd* (the rich). The former, led by Abbas Al-Haddad, undertook a number of important public works projects including important irrigation and agricultural projects and the fortification of the town (Nieuwenhuis 1982: 31–2).

The rule of the Mamluks came to an abrupt end in the middle of the nineteenth century when, in reaction to a series of important regional and global events, including the rising power of European nation-states, the Ottomans sought to consolidate their authority over centres like Iraq. In 1831 they captured the Mamluk *pashas* of Baghdad, Basra and Mosul and the three provinces returned to Ottoman control (Tripp 2007 [2000]: 14). Despite their increased control over regions such as Iraq, the Ottomans also enacted a number of significant democratic changes. Its fledgling press sector began to expand following the legalization of printing in both Turkish and Arabic and the opening of the first Turkish printing press in 1727 (Kinross 2003 [1977]: 364, Lewis 1961: 50).

In Iraq, the progressive Ottoman *Vali* (Governor), Midhat Pasha, took the post of Baghdad in 1869 and among his many achievements was the founding of the weekly newspaper, *Al-Zawra* ('the Curved [City]', a popular soubriquet for Baghdad) (Ayalon 1995: 25). In the 1870s journalists across the Ottoman Empire were responsible for stimulating much of the discussion surrounding controversial ideas like constitutionalism and the legitimate rights of the everyday man (Mardin 1969: 276). For Toby Dodge, this collection of reforms implemented by the Ottomans clearly 'point towards a much more balanced, integrated and negotiated relationship between state and society in Ottoman Iraq than the discourse of Oriental Despotism allows' (Dodge 2005 [2003]: 50).

Such changes also fostered a rich scholarly scene across the Ottoman Empire in which various Muslim intellectuals – both men and women – began to engage with the contemporary political ideas and events of Europe, including the emergence of representative democracy (Gandolfo 2011). Many of these Muslim intellectuals were not only inspired by events in Europe, but were also deeply critical of their own governments and saw no direct contradiction between the fundamentals of Islam and the practice of modern representative democracy. As just one example, the Egyptian scholar Muhammad Abduh writing in the second half of the nineteenth century argued that Muslims did not so much need to look to Western civilization for democratic inspiration, as they did to the doctrine of Islam itself. He claimed that

> If despotism is not Islamic, then all means, excuses and devices that lead to despotism are themselves not Islamic. If freedom, justice, equality and human rights are Islamic, then all means and devices that lead to liberty, justice, equality, fraternity, and human rights are themselves Islamically valid (Khatab and Bouma 2007: 49).

The increasingly democratic impetus in the work of various Muslim intellectuals and the expansion and liberalization of the press sector converged to form another significant development in this era of Ottoman politics, namely the First Constitutional Period of the late 1870s. Here, the Ottomans requested the various provincial councils scattered across the empire elect representatives who would form a national parliament. This parliament was then given the task of writing the Ottoman constitution and an electoral law that was to be utilized in not only guaranteeing the rights of the citizen but in ensuring an ongoing process of empire-wide elections that would enable a modern representative democracy to emerge. Specifically, the constitution stipulated that the Ottoman Empire should be governed by a *Heyet-I Ayan* (nominated senate) and a *Heyet-I Mebusan* (elected chamber of deputies) (Kayali 1995: 267).

This climate of reform led to what has come to be called the 'Young Turk' movement which successfully challenged the Ottoman Empire in 1908 and set about re-establishing constitutional government and restoring measures of autonomy to the various national-cultural entities within their governance (Shmuelevitz 2004: 28). They also went on to establish secular schools and liberalized the publications sector. In Iraq, this included not only papers in support of the ruling party in Istanbul such as *Al-Zawra*, but also opposition papers including *Bayn Al-Nahrayn* ('Mesopotamia') (Ayalon 1995: 66). Iraqis also had access to newspapers from Syria and Lebanon as well as those from Istanbul, including anti-Young Turk papers like *Volkan* ('Volcano') and Zionist papers published by the Jewish community such as the weekly *Hamevasser* ('Herald') (Shmuelevitz 2004). Many of these newspapers and magazines of the Young Turk period were filled with long editorials praising the new era of tolerance and press freedom.

The Young Turk movement also brought with it another very significant development in terms of the unfolding story of democracy in Iraq. In 1908, the Young Turks orchestrated provincial elections in which citizens across the empire, including those in Iraq, were asked to vote for their chosen representative to the Ottoman Chamber of Representatives. In the lead-up to the polls, the empire was divided into electorates in which there was one representative for every 50,000 male citizens. Enfranchisement extended to all men over the age of 25 who paid taxes and all reports indicate that the election was free and fair with only minimal complaints of coercion or fraud (Kayali 1995: 269–71). The significance and legacy of this election are clear in that they

> provided precedents and standards that are yet to be equalled in the Middle East and many other parts of the world; introduced the Middle Easterners to fundamental norms of political participation and mobilization; and defined the main contours of political contestation that have endured long after the end of the empire (Kayali 1995: 265).

This brought with it a strong augmentation of Iraq's culture of public debate and criticism as is best evidenced by the atmosphere surrounding Iraq's 1912 election. By all accounts, these elections were even better than the ones of 1908; a resounding success for democracy, they were 'outstanding elections' that involved 'spirited contestation' and had 'significant implications' for the political landscape of the Ottoman empire (Kayali 1995: 273). This is especially true because they were very fiercely contested, particularly in highly politicized regions like Syria and Lebanon which saw a vast array of candidates engaged in a series of rich and complex policy debates (Khalidi 1984). The foremost success of these elections was their enormous contribution to the public sphere of the region in which an engagement with politics became central to the lives and needs of many normal citizens. As Hasan Kayali summarizes,

Electioneering occurred both on public platforms and in the press. Campaigning went beyond the confines of clubs and halls to large mass rallies. The press, both in the capital and in the provinces, not only covered the campaign but became an integral part of it by contributing to the political agenda. The number of petitions from individuals and local groups arriving in various government agencies increased dramatically (Kayali 1995: 273).

What is also particularly interesting about the 1912 elections is their Islamic dimension. Rising trends towards secularism amongst the literate classes of the Ottoman Empire prompted religious groups to demand that political parties make clear their theological position. Far from stifling debate, this meant that the negotiation between modern representative democracy and traditional Islamic principles once again came to the fore. For many political factions Islamic symbols and motifs as well as religious rhetoric formed a central pillar of their election campaigns. This brought another unintended consequence, the votes of the Arab provinces – whose inhabitants were generally less educated and less secular than those in Anatolia – became of central importance to political parties who had hitherto campaigned mostly to the Ottoman elite. This meant that political parties increasingly adapted their campaigns and policy to the needs and beliefs of the Arab regions and saw no conflict between Arab political culture or Islamic doctrine and democracy (Kayali 1995: 273). While it is important not to overstate the role that these elections, newspapers and political parties played in developing a public sphere in the Ottoman-controlled regions which later became the nation of Iraq, they nonetheless indicate just how far back discourse and debate on democratic issues were evident across the region. In this way, Ottoman Iraq played a fundamental role in establishing and informing the nascent civil movements that, as we shall see in the following chapter, came to play such a crucial, diverse and oppositional role in twentieth century Iraqi politics.

Conclusion

What is evident here is that from the very earliest days of Islam the religion contained a democratic ethos that sought to bring a more equitable and egalitarian system of governance to the people. These sentiments were brought into Iraq and fostered under the various Islamic empires that ruled over it. Beyond the fact that the highest echelons of the state waxed and waned in their commitment to the Islamic doctrines and to democracy, lies the even more important – and more Islamic – legacy of the *ulama* who provide for us important insights into the ongoing struggle of the *ummah* towards democracy. Later, Iraq's democracy continued to flourish with the holding of free and fair elections, and the development of various Iraqi newspapers and political parties that continued to agitate towards greater diversity, debate and discourse. Islam, in Iraq as much as anywhere else, is far from antithetical to democracy and should not be viewed either now or in the past as a determining cause for any failures in Iraqi politics. Instead, Islam must be acknowledged for having preserved and spread both the ethic and practice of democracy perhaps further and wider than had heretofore been the case.

What is most significant about Iraq's Islamic democratic history is that this heritage remains so much a part of the socio-political landscape of Iraq today. As we shall see in Chapter 6, the democratic history of Islamic Iraq has been central to the nation's fledgling democracy as a wide collection of senior Islamic scholars and clergymen called upon the faithful to vote, to campaign, to protest, and generally to become more involved in politics. Islam is a key part of Iraq's constitution with Article 2 not only stating that 'Islam is the official religion of the State and is a foundational source of legislation' but also that no law may be enacted which contradicts 'the established provisions of Islam' nor the 'principles of democracy', including religious freedom (*The Constitution of Iraq* 2010 [2005]: 308). It is by no means the case that Iraq is emerging from a history dominated by a despotic Islam that fostered oppression but instead that, both historically and today, Islam and democracy can be seen to hold key virtues and practices in common. To be a Muslim is to bring you no closer, or take you no further away, from being a democrat.

Chapter 4
Discourses of Democracy in Colonial Iraq

Personnel sent from across the British Empire to build the new [Iraqi] state interacted with the remnants of the Ottoman Empire on the basis of popular imaginative constructions influential in British and wider European society ... This European vision of the world the British staff confronted was sustained by two central tenets. First, the Ottoman Empire in Iraq was conceived as an Oriental Despotism. Under this rubric it was unchanging and unable to escape the constraints of its inherent superstitions, violence and corruption. Secondly, Iraq was perceived as fundamentally divided ... The Iraqi state constructed by the British was to be an occidental one, operating in a balanced and harmonious way with the Iraqi people. It was to be defined in absolute ideological contrast to the Ottoman state, seen as despotic, inefficient and tyrannical.

Dodge 2005 [2003]: 43–4

Beyond Colonial Discourse

It was the impact of the First World War (1914–18) and the subsequent Arab Revolt which brought about the ultimate demise of the Ottoman Empire and their rule over the Arab lands. These events ushered in the emergence of the modern nation-states of the Middle East under the auspices of European powers such as Britain and France who moved into much of what is now Iraq, Syria, Jordan and Israel, carving up the region into two zones of influence under the clandestine Sykes-Picot agreement (Preston 2003: 164–72). Craving the rich oil reserves of the Gulf region to fuel its expanding military machine, the British occupied Basra from the start of the war and the rest of Iraq by the end of 1918 (Kent 1976, Majd 2006, Stivers 1982). This era of Iraqi history, referred to here as Colonial Iraq (1921–58),[1] saw the British play both an overt and covert role in Iraqi politics until the Revolution of 1958.

On the whole, the British occupation revealed a condescending, ill-informed and inexperienced administration that was widely unpopular in Iraq. The British invaded

---

1 In some accounts, the Colonial era in Iraq is understood to have concluded with the signing of the Anglo-Iraqi treaty in 1930 and the formal end of Britain's mandate over Iraq in 1932. However, the latter date of 1958 has been used here because, until the Revolution of that year, Britain maintained a strong presence in and influence over Iraq. This included a military presence as well as a collection of 'advisors' who functioned behind the scenes, often demanding that the monarchs kowtowed to British interests. Britain also maintained veto powers over various military and bureaucratic mechanisms of the state and tightly controlled the country's foreign relations. As Peter Sluglett has so succinctly put it 'British influence was not removed [in 1932], simply employed more covertly and less directly ... from behind the scenes' (Sluglett 2007: 210).

Iraq 'not only with army and armour' as Muhsin Al-Musawi puts it, but with 'an Orientalist legacy that spoke for and of the colonized' (Al-Musawi 2006: 58). In Iraq, this 'Orientalist legacy' had the effect of dividing up the Mesopotamian region

> between cities supposedly 'corrupted' by the 'despotism' of the Ottoman Empire and a countryside which was believed to be the preserve of the 'true Iraqi' who was, nonetheless, backward, even prelapsarian, and irrational. This simple-minded and offensive dualism ensured that indigenous voices would not be listened to and indigenous agency denied (Gregory 2004: 148).

The evidence of such simple-mindedness is found in even the most cursory analysis of Colonial-era literature written about Iraq. It reveals a catalogue of tropes underpinned by conceptions of Iraq and its people as incapable of democracy. In the correspondence he kept with the British Foreign Office, Sir Arnold Wilson, the Colonial Administrator of Iraq from 1918–20, argued that to 'install a real Arab Government in Mesopotamia is impossible, and, if we attempt it, we shall abandon the Middle East to anarchy' (Wilson 1919). Similarly, David Samuel Margoliouth, who was not only part of the British Administration in Iraq from 1919 but also a renowned and authoritative British scholar of the Middle East, attempted to connect Iraq's ancient past with its subjugation under British control, arguing that 'Iraq is used to foreign rule since ancient times, for it was ruled by the Mongols, the Turks and the Iranians, as it cannot rule itself. Thus, the Iraqis should choose the British to rule them, or to be under their mandatory rule and protection' (Margoliouth 1919).

Another example can be found in the writing of British explorer Freya Stark who spent much of the late 1920s and 1930s travelling the Middle East and compiling important records for those back home. In one of her many letters, this one to Sir Henry Lawrence and dated 6 March 1930, Stark offers her opinions on Iraqi democracy by arguing that, 'The whole show here is run by a few rather disgusting local politicians: they don't represent anything except themselves' (Stark 1951: 127). 'Everyone agrees', she continues, 'that Iraq is not fit to govern itself … I think the Iraqis themselves agree in this: the difference is that they don't care so frightfully much about being well governed' (Stark 1951: 128). In a classically Orientalist way, Stark moves forward from here to separate out British interests from Iraqi politics, stating that

> I don't know why one should bother so much about how Iraq is governed. The matter of importance to us is to safeguard our own affairs. It is only because we assume that the two are bound together that we give so much weight to the local politics. It seems to me that the one only vital problem is to find out how things we are interested in can be made safe independently of native politics. If this was solved, all the rest would follow – including as much Arab freedom as their geography allows: for I imagine no one would wish to stay here for the mere pleasure of doing good to people who don't want it (Stark 1951: 129).

This kind of discourse also extended to the media debates that were going on in the United Kingdom during the Colonial period (J. Bernstein 2008). In a letter to the editor published in the *London Times* on 21 June 1920 the author argues:

> Eastern peoples as a rule detest efficiency and sanitation, and although the Arab welcomed us when we were beating the Turk ... I doubt if he wishes to be civilized in a hurry, and certainly he resents excessive control and taxation ... therefore the new system [of democracy] is not likely to be acceptable to the Arab community ... [and may require] an army of occupation for many years until the people have become civilized and accepted our form of administration (*London Times*, 1920).

However, this kind of Orientalist vision of Iraqi politics is not confined to the annals of Colonial history, it is also evident in more recent scholarship which has sought to examine the Colonial era in Iraq. Elie Kedourie completely ignores the positive developments of the era, instead focusing on the region's tendency towards violence, barbarism and despotism. In one instance, Kedourie concludes that the politics of the Colonial period of Iraqi history are constituted by 'a wretched political architecture and constitutional jerry-building of the flimsiest and most dangerous kind' (Kedourie 1970: 239). This is reinforced in his later *Democracy and Arab Political Culture*, which details several democratic experiments that were conducted under the auspices of the British and French across the Middle East throughout the first half of the twentieth century (namely Iraq 1921–38, Egypt 1923–52, Lebanon 1926–75 and Syria 1928–49). According to Kedourie the main reason these attempts at introducing constitutional rule to the Middle East failed is the fact that the people of the region have historically been accustomed to 'autocracy and passive obedience' (Kedourie 1994: 103).

Despite this overwhelmingly negative picture of Iraqi politics throughout the Colonial epoch, some recent studies have attempted to challenge the received wisdom by asserting counter-histories and counter-narratives. For several notable scholars, it was not that the British had confronted despotism in Iraq, but that they had introduced it. The failures of the British in terms of their extensive nation building project and their modest attempt to bring Westminster-style democracy to Iraq sowed the seeds of the authoritarian and tyrannical regimes that were to flower in later decades (Dodge 2005 [2003]: 43–61). For Hana Batatu, the British and the French were the first to have both the technological capability and experience to obliterate the existing social order and create in its place the economic and cultural conditions necessary for authoritarianism to emerge (Batatu 1982 [1978]). Along these same lines, Gareth Stansfield has recently stated that 'The rise of authoritarianism in Iraq can be traced to the tensions caused by the legacies of British Colonial involvement in the formation of civilian governments that were more often than not perceived to be corrupt and inefficient' (Stansfield 2007: 81).

Despite the abject failures of the British and the authoritarianism which emerged as a result of their occupation, other scholars have been keen to point out that the Colonial period nonetheless saw a complex political landscape in Iraq which promoted varied debate and discourse as well as calls for genuine democratic reform (Al-Musawi 2006, Bashkin 2009, Davis 2005b, Dawisha 2009). Despite the many differences among such a diverse range of civil and political movements, what they (mostly) held in common was the call for an end to foreign occupation and the formation of an independent and democratic Iraq. As Orit Bashkin has explained, many Iraqis of this time

> did theorize about the nature of their political regime, and some strove to maintain a democratic system. Moreover, the writing about democracy was symptomatic of a larger phenomenon within Hashemite Iraq: the creation of a pluralistic public sphere ... Exploring aspects of heterogeneity in Iraqi society demonstrates how the fluid nature of groupings in Iraq created a space in which the views of numerous groups coexisted and enriched each other (Bashkin 2009: 17).

An examination of the complexities of Colonial Iraq reveals myriad political parties, media outlets[2] and protest movements and their complex role in promoting and upholding sophisticated and diverse discourses of democracy. This chapter documents the debates that circulated in the Iraqi press at the time of the British occupation and Hashemite monarchy and details their role in fostering vitriolic critique of the incumbent regime, in mobilizing the public to protest and in serving as the people's watchdog over the elite. It is precisely the egalitarian and democratic tendencies found throughout the media/political nexus of Colonial Iraq that provide for us a new vision of Iraqi history that is directly at odds with traditional views of Iraqi and Middle Eastern political culture. This chapter also exposes the contradiction between Britain's rhetoric as a harbinger of democracy and its contemporaneous attempts to quell Iraq's free press and to curtail democratic reform.

A Fledgling Public Sphere

After the First World War, the British were at first welcomed by most of Iraq's numerous clergymen, intellectuals and poets who took at face value the promise to deliver the 'complete and definitive liberation of the peoples so long oppressed by the Turks' and 'the establishment of national Governments and Administrations drawing their authority from the initiative and free choice of indigenous populations' ('The Anglo-French Declaration' 1918: 21). This honeymoon period was short-lived, however, as it became increasingly evident that such promises would go unfulfilled and that 'the British neither intended to cede control of Iraq to an

---

2   It should be noted here that earlier work by the author has included a set of detailed tables that document the most significant media outlets of Colonial, Post-Colonial, and Re-Colonial Iraq (Isakhan 2009a: 247–75). While such media outlets and their respective political parties are discussed in great length throughout Chapters 4, 5 and 6, much of the initial detail compiled in these tables has been necessarily excluded.

indigenous government nor planned to support Arab nationalist demands' (Davis 2005b: 44). Reasoning that the Iraqis were incapable of governing themselves, the British went to great lengths to abolish the Ottoman governing institutions, which included the elected provincial councils, and installed their own political officers in a system of direct Colonial rule (Tripp 2007 [2000]: 38). Unsurprisingly, such moves were widely resisted by the people and remained highly contentious across Iraq.

Perhaps the first example of such resistance came from a subsidiary of the earlier Istanbul-based political party *Al-Ahd*, known as *Al-Ahd Al-Iraqi* ('The Iraqi Covenant'), which effectively stood as the first political group to call for Iraqi independence from the British at the very earliest days of its hegemony in 1918 (Stansfield 2007: 41). It was this group that was to provide several of the key figures of twentieth century Iraqi politics, some staunch opponents to the British and their installed monarchy, and others who went on to wield significant power within the state apparatus (Tripp 2007 [2000]: 36). Early calls for Iraqi independence, such as those issued by *Al-Ahd Al-Iraqi*, grew substantially when the British were awarded a mandate over Iraq in 1920 by the League of Nations. This development, which pre-empted the establishment of ongoing British rule over Iraq, produced the political climate in which the Great Iraqi Revolution took place in 1920 (Tripp 2007 [2000]: 39–44). Having been preceded by a brief Kurdish rebellion in 1919, the following year saw the tribesman, religious leaders and secular nationalists of the central Euphrates region band together in an armed nationalist-inspired insurgency against the British occupation. The presence of a common enemy meant that the Shiites and the Sunnis came together, holding joint religio-political meetings which culminated 'in patriotic oratory and poetic thundering against the English' (Batatu 1982 [1978]: 23). The role of poets, intellectuals and religious figures from across the many ethnic and spiritual divides in Iraq was central to mobilizing the people to action (Al-Musawi 2006: 49–51, 95–9).

This collective action promulgated a new sense of solidarity inside Iraq and prompted strong calls for a democratic state. Although the uprising was ultimately defeated by the British, the Iraqis were able to secure a number of the religiously significant southern cities for short periods of time. The political vacuum created by the withdrawal of Ottoman authority and then the temporary defeat of the British, resulted in the establishment of several civil and administrative organizations that functioned like local councils, particularly across the south. As they had done during the time of the Mamluks, the Shia clergy of Najaf made several democratic advances. Most notably, they agreed on the creation of a complex legislative and executive council, the members of which were determined by votes placed in ballot boxes at the entrance to the many open markets that scattered the city. As Dawisha notes, 'this election was a remarkable feat as the impulse emerged spontaneously from the people themselves' indicating the ability of the Iraqi people to practise the very fundamentals of democracy, autonomous of Western tutelage, was strong (Dawisha 2009: 49).

Although these enclaves of autonomous democratic governance were relatively short-lived and were quashed by the British, they are not the only indicators of a fledgling civil society in Iraq at this time. This same period also witnessed a dramatic upsurge in budding journalists with strong ties to various, particularly nationalist, political parties (Davis 2005c: 56). These wordsmiths were generally keen to re-ignite the days of the Young Turks and produced a number of both relatively objective and highly partisan papers which not only covered contemporary events and developments but also played a role in inciting people to resist the British occupation. Many of these papers – some of which were the unapologetic mouthpiece for a particular political faction, while others claimed to be independent – asserted that democracy was the most suitable form of government for Iraq's future. Independent newspapers such as *Al-Istiqlal* ('Independence' of Najaf) and *Al-Furat* ('The Euphrates') published a series of editorials that were not only scathing in their criticism of the British occupation, they articulated the discourses of democracy circulating throughout Iraq at the time. *Al-Istiqlal* appeared for the express purpose of responding to 'the occupiers' deception, to disquiet them, to reveal their barbaric misdeeds' (*Al-Istiqlal* cited in Ayalon 1995: 92). Similarly, *Al-Furat* played a critical role in advocating grass-roots political movements in Iraq, arguing that the Iraqi Revolution of 1920 was 'similar to the Irish and Egyptian Revolutions in every detail ... provoked by protest, inflamed by despotism and spread by the loss of liberty' (*Al-Furat* 1920a). The paper also carried stern warnings for the British, asking them to 'Take it easy' because 'The nation which you were against, and where you unleashed the sword, causing so much bloodshed and casualties among its people, in utter hatred and arbitrary rule, regardless of its rights and justice, this nation is to take you to task in the court of history' (*Al-Furat* 1920c).

Building on this rhetoric, another article from the same paper seeks to explain the growing resistance movement in Iraq as a product of the occupation and its control over political dissent. The author writes,

> The nation got impatient as a result of the oppression practised by the occupation authority, especially in these days when Iraq's complaints are everywhere in line with the principle of 'self-determination and total independence'. The Iraqis realize that legal requests and peaceful demonstrations are useless, as they restore no right. It is especially so because just complaints reach no political circle abroad, as the British are in total control of all media and means of communication (*Al-Furat* 1920b).[3]

Without too much concern for the opinions and attitudes expressed in these papers, Winston Churchill set about hastily designing the nation-states of the modern Middle East at the Cairo Conference of 1921, attended by regional experts such as T. E. Lawrence, Sir Percy Cox and Gertrude Bell. It was their advice which saw

---

3   The translations of *Al-Furat* cited here are taken from Mushin Al-Musawi's chapter and later book on the politics of Iraqi literature and journalism (Al-Musawi 1991: 206–7; 2006: 97–8).

the British unite the three previously autonomous regions, or *vilayets*, of Baghdad, Basra and Mosul and install Faisal I to the position of the first modern king of Iraq (Catherwood 2004: 127–60). Faisal was the son of Sharif Hussayn of Mecca who had declared himself the Caliph of all Muslims and had orchestrated the Arab Revolt against the Ottoman Empire during the First World War. Initially, Faisal was installed as the king of Syria in 1920 but when the French exiled him, the British gave him a second chance, this time as the ruler of the fledgling Iraq. It was this sequence of events which saw a man who had never before set foot in the lands of Iraq, ascend the throne in a ceremony unbeknown to the vast majority of his subjects while the military band played the eerily symbolic 'God Save the Queen'.

Having appointed Faisal, the British staged the first of modern Iraq's artificial experiments with democracy: a national referendum which garnered an impossible 96 per cent endorsement of his rule (Anderson and Stansfield 2004: 14–5). The local authorities of the various provinces were infuriated and the clerics who had so adamantly called on Faisal to implement a parliament and a national constitution, now delivered *fatwas* ('Religious edicts') banning their loyal followers from participating in the elections for the Constituent Assembly until such time as the monarch yielded to the people's call for democratization, civil liberties and freedom of the press (Dawisha 2005a: 13). One *fatwa* stated bluntly: 'Participation in the elections or anything resembling them which will injure the future prosperity of Iraq is pronounced *haram* by the unanimous verdict of Islam' ('Propaganda and Activities Against Participation in Iraq Elections' 1922).

Sensitive to such calls, Faisal did go on to establish a number of quasi-democratic reforms including nation-building exercises such as the development of a highly patriotic national school curriculum, a new Constitution, an Electoral Law and a Parliament consisting of both a *Majlis Al-Nuwab* ('Chamber of Deputies') and a *Majlis Al-Ayan* ('Senate') in 1924 which lasted until the Revolution of 1958. While these developments certainly had the semblance of genuine democratic reform, the king maintained a number of powers including the ability to veto the parliament and issue independent decrees while the British ruled 'largely behind the scenes through a system of political "advisors" appointed to the major departments of government to ensure that British interests were adequately represented within the system' (Anderson and Stansfield 2004: 14). These steps towards democratization were little more than a façade designed to entrench the hegemony of the Sunni ruling elite and the British. Neither party was particularly interested in truly representative democracy as it would cede power to the majority Shia population and undermine British interests. Faisal also had a tendency to nepotism, favouring those Sunni Iraqi-Ottomans who had supported him in Syria and a small number of loyal and well-educated Jews over members of the Shiite majority or the myriad of other ethno-religious groups which constituted the new Iraq (Zubaida 2002: 211–2).

This bred wide dissatisfaction with authority in Iraq and led to the emergence of several opposition parties. The first of these were The Iraqi National Party (*Al-Hizb Al-Watani Al-Iraqi*) and The Iraqi Renaissance Party (*Hizb Al-Nahda*

Al-Iraqiyya), both of which formed in 1922, made up of a number of citizens who had been active in their resistance to British occupation. These opposition parties quickly set up their own daily newspapers – The Iraqi National Party published *Mufid* ('The one who gives benefit') and The Iraqi Renaissance Party produced *Al-Rafidayn* ('Mesopotamia') – both of which were instrumental in mobilizing more than ten thousand people to demonstrate in front of the King's palace on the first anniversary of his ascension to the throne, demanding a representational government and an end to British interference. Seeing the power these two opposition parties had amassed in such a short period, the British High Commissioner, Sir Percy Cox, seized the opportunity to outlaw both parties, close down their publications and expel their leadership from Iraq (Al-Musawi 2006: 50, Dawisha 2005a: 14, 21).

Despite these rulings, the mid to late 1920s saw the re-emergence of several political parties in Iraq, including those of both the government and of the opposition. The pro-government parties included The Progressive Party (*Hizb Al-Taqaddum*) which was created by Prime Minister Abd Al-Muhsin Al-Sadun in 1925 and was supported by partisan newspapers such as *Al-Alam Al-Arabi* ('The Arabic World') and *Al-Liwa* ('The Standard') as well as its own paper, *Al-Taqaddum* ('The Priority'). In 1930 Nuri Al-Said established The Commitment Party (*Hizb Al-Ahd*) and its paper *Sada Al-Ahd* ('The New Echo'). Al-Said went on to become Iraq's Prime Minister several times and, until the 1958 Revolution, he was arguably the single most powerful person in Iraq outside the royal family (Zubaida 2002: 211).

In terms of opposition parties, both The Iraqi National Party and The Iraqi Renaissance Party re-appeared in the mid- to late-1920s, but their power base had been significantly diminished. Other opposition parties were more successful. In 1924 the nucleus of Iraqi Marxists (who were to later form the Iraqi Communist Party [ICP])[4] began to gather some political momentum with the publication of Iraq's most radical organ, *Al-Sahifa* ('The Page'). Although the paper was shut down after only four months and six editions, it had printed translations of Communist texts from Europe, it had critiqued *Shariah* law for being dated and irrelevant to the modern world and, most radical of all, it had passionately advocated women's rights and sought to free them from oppression in the form of the veil and polygamy (Salucci 2005: 9–10). The following year The People's Party (*Hizb Al-Shab*) was established and supported by its own eponymous newspaper while, half a decade later, The Nationalist Fraternity Party (*Hizb Al-Ikha Al-Watani*, [Ikha]) was formed, producing the highly esteemed *Al-Bilad* ('The Country') newspaper. Published by Christians in Baghdad, *Al-Bilad* changed its name several times throughout the 1930s to avoid censorship and, in the 1940s, regularly reported on civil unrest (Ayalon 1995: 93–4, Dawisha 2005a: 14–15).

---

4   The ICP played a fundamental role in twentieth century Iraqi politics. For a scholarly account of this history, see Tareq Ismael's *The Rise and Fall of the Communist Party of Iraq* (Ismael 2008).

What these opposition groups and their newspapers had in common were their calls for 'immediate independence for Iraq, the evacuation of British troops, and the development of a democratic and participatory Iraqi state' (Davis 2005b: 49).

Despite this unity – or perhaps because of it – the British continued to interfere in Iraq's domestic politics and were particularly hostile to any democratic practices or movements, especially if they challenged British dominion over Iraq. Dawisha discusses their meddling in the Iraqi parliamentary deliberations over signing the Anglo-Iraqi treaty, where the High Commissioner 'stormed into the Royal palace with an ultimatum that the treaty be passed forthwith or the Assembly would be dissolved' (Dawisha 2005a: 19). When the Iraqi elections were staged by the British in 1925, 1928 and 1930, they were designed to provide the semblance of democracy instead of ushering in any real reform. As Ofra Bengio notes of the 1925 election, 'Overall, seventy-four of the ninety-eight "proposed" candidates were elected to the assembly, leaving no doubt that the existing Iraqi government – and, behind it, the British – had interfered in the process' (Bengio 2003: 17).

Such interference and manipulation of the democratic processes and practices of Iraq raise a number of interesting questions about the despotic potential of the West. While the British installed governments, falsified referendums and quashed democratic movements and reforms, the Iraqi people continued their struggle towards a more egalitarian and inclusive political order. Between 1920–29, Iraq witnessed an unprecedented diversity in the nation's print sector, with the establishment of 105 newspapers – many of which advocated radical political perspectives (Davis 2005b: 49). Even in their short lifetime, these partisan papers were able to invigorate the Iraqi public sphere, enabling Habermasian rational-critical debate in both the parliament and the streets of the nation. They served as a diligent watchdog of democracy, carefully detailing instances of corruption and nepotism. Collectively, this era brought with it the very seeds of democratization, 'a spirit of dialogue, a willingness to listen to an opposing view, and an ability to compromise if the situation deemed it' (Dawisha 2005a: 20).

With the signing of the Anglo-Iraqi treaty in 1930 and the expiration of Britain's formal authority in 1932, Iraq became the first of the mandated regions to emerge as an 'independent' nation state (Silverfarb 1994: 11–22). Many Iraqis assumed that the United Kingdom would henceforth play a decreasing role inside Iraq, however, the British continued to interfere in Iraq's domestic politics until the Revolution of 1958. In addition, the democratic and egalitarian steps taken during the 1920s were eased somewhat during the 1930s as Iraq moved through a rather tumultuous decade of politics. This arguably began when the Christian Assyrians of northern Iraq called for complete autonomy within the fledgling nation-state, understandably hopeful that the end of the British mandate might provide the opportunity for them to end their lengthy and broad Diaspora. When the spiritual and political leaders of the Assyrians were not swayed by the central authority in Baghdad and the wider community proved resilient to small military skirmishes, Iraqi General Bakr Sidqi (himself a Kurd from the northern city of

Kirkuk) ordered the 'Simele massacres' which left hundreds of Iraqi Assyrians dead by the end of August 1933 (Husry 1974a, 1974b, Joseph 1975).

Within a month of the attack on the Assyrians, King Faisal I died unexpectedly, leaving his twenty-one year old illiterate and relatively inexperienced son, Ghazi Ibn Faisal, in the position of Iraq's supreme leader (crowned King Ghazi I of Iraq). Despite the fact that Ghazi was opposed to continued British interference and was popular with some nationalists and even early pan-Arabists, his legitimacy as ruler of Iraq and his effectiveness in running the affairs of state were constantly brought into question by many Iraqi intellectuals and politicians (Balfour-Paul 1982: 12, Wein 2006: 9). With his power waning, in 1936 King Ghazi supported the first military *coup d'état* in the Arab world, in which General Bakr Sidqi overthrew the civilian government and replaced it with military rule (Lukitz 1995: 81–90). Within a year, however, much of the national army withdrew their support for Sidqi and he was assassinated at Mosul airport. Three years later, in 1939, Ghazi I died in a mysterious car accident which many believed to be the work of the British (Anderson and Stansfield 2004: 18). By the end of the 1930s Iraq had changed dramatically from the developments of the 1920s; it had witnessed the senseless slaughter of Assyrians, ineffective kings, military coups and assassinations of some of the highest officers of the state. In addition, the 1930s also saw a small circle of the elite seize the opportunity provided by the 'independence' of 1932 to exert itself over the public discourse of Iraq and suppress dissent. This is perhaps most evident in the media sector where a new series of Press Laws imposed limitations such as the censoring of 'criticism of the government or the administration' and the suspension of 'press organs for long and even unlimited periods' (Wien 2006: 54).

However, this is not to say that media and political freedom was completely nullified in the 1930s. Instead, various intellectual organizations, political parties and newspapers were established across Iraq throughout this era, effectively harnessing the emerging public sphere of the time. This included the founding of the Union of Iraqi Artisans' Organizations (*Ittihad Al-Sanaia Al-Iraqiya*) which played an instrumental role in mobilizing the citizenry towards the General Strike of 1931 in order to protest the British proposal of a tax on urban commerce. In terms of actual political parties, in 1931 Iraq witnessed the founding of the Western-inspired social democrats or Ahali Group (*Jamiyat Al-Ahali*, 'The People's Group'). By the mid-1930s Iraq was also home to political parties such as the Iraqi nationalists or Baghdad Club (*Nadi Baghdad*) and the Iraqi Communist Party, as well as the Marxist-leaning Solidarity Club (*Nadi Al-Tadammun*) and the Pan-Arab Al-Muthanna Club (*Nadi Al-Muthanna*) (Bashkin 2009: 52–69, Davis 2005b: 72–5, Tripp 2007 [2000]: 82–5).

Despite the strict press law which had been imposed since 1932, many of these new political parties funded their own papers and sent them out across Iraq in order to propagate their respective political ideologies. Newspapers such as *Al-Ahali* ('The People') gave the Ahali Group considerable influence across Iraq and a voice to many prominent Iraqi intellectuals (Bashkin 2010). Similarly, the Communist party published *Kifah Al-Shab* ('The People's Struggle') and *Al-Inqilab* ('The Revolt'), while the Nationalist Party had *Sada Al-Istiqlal* ('The Echo of Independence'). Aside from these highly partisan journals, other newspapers included *Habezbooz* (a term from Iraqi folklore), a Baghdad paper that used satire to criticize the British occupation (Daragahi 2003: 50, Wein 2006: 55) and, perhaps Iraq's most successful, professional and well-respected paper of this era, *Al-Zaman* ('Time'), published by an Iraqi Christian. It is worth noting here that while many of these papers of the 1930s tended to change their party affiliations and ideological adherences according to the 'personal interests and sympathies of their owners' they nonetheless provided 'a lively debate on nationalist issues ... [and] debates also related to cultural questions beyond the daily affairs' (Wein 2006: 53).

Aside from fostering debate on democracy in their newspapers, the political parties of this time also competed in national elections. Ikha took part in the 1933 elections, reasoning that it had an opportunity to win seats and implement reform. Although the results indicated only a slight change in the Parliament, the party managed to secure a significant minority of 15 seats and went on to criticize the government and the monarchy in the national parliament. According to one source, 'the Ikha members violently attacked the Cabinet's programme as devoid of any measures which would transform the administration created under the mandatory regime into one fit for a truly independent country' (Khadduri 1960 [1951]: 37). In a twist of fate, the dominant bloc that controlled the Parliament and largely supported the monarchy dissolved in a matter of days and Ikha unexpectedly held the balance of power. They promptly sought to nullify the 1930 treaty between Britain and Iraq and called for complete independence. A crisis emerged in the Cabinet before King Faisal intervened and a new Government was formed with Ikha members assuming the prominent post of Prime Minister as well as important portfolios like finance and the interior. Ikha lost much of its credibility, however, for acquiescing to monarchical control and reneging on its demands to rescind the 1930 treaty. Although it did win 12 of 88 seats in the 1934 election and held credible influence through 1935, Ikha were usurped in the coup of 1936 (Khadduri 1960 [1951]: 36–67).

Following the tumultuous but short-lived reign of the military, new elections were held in 1937 and again in 1939. These elections were more tightly controlled in order to produce a Cabinet favourable to the monarchy and less critical of the British (Khadduri 1960 [1951]: 101–2, 143). Despite this, British academic Philip Ireland, writing in 1937 and well ahead of his time, argued that putting aside all its deficiencies, the Iraqi parliament

> has fulfilled an important function in the political life of Iraq. It has attracted the most agile brains in the country; it has reflected although imperfectly, public opinion; and it has served as a brake on legislation which might otherwise have been forced on the country ... It has served to curb the attempts of individual Ministers to assume a dictatorial attitude. Its right of interrogation ... has also served to reveal irregularities in administration. It has, moreover, furnished an outlet for Shia aspirations for participation in the Government and has given tribal

opinion a limited means of expression through the tribal representatives ... The
Chamber, together with the conservative Senate of twenty appointed notables, has,
notwithstanding its many deficiencies, laid the foundations upon which democratic
government, if it is to come to Iraq, must be built (Ireland 1970 [1937]: 433).

Not long after this, however, the Second World War (1939–45) broke out. When
the fighting began, the government of Iraq placed the newspapers and magazines
of the nation under tight censorship laws in an attempt to curtail anti-British
sentiment. This, coupled with the severe economic conditions which prevailed
during the war, had implications for Iraqi civil society and the free press, with
many of the smaller papers across the region folding. Politically, the death of
King Ghazi I in 1939 had left Iraq with his three-year-old son, King Faisal II, as
the official head of state. Being too young to rule, Faisal II's power defaulted to
his uncle, the immensely unpopular and fiercely pro-British regent, Prince Abd
Al-Ilah. However, the regent's power was mitigated by the anti-British and Pan-
Arab views of Iraq's four leading colonels, led by Salah Al-Din Al-Sabbagh and
otherwise known as the 'Golden Square'. In 1941 the tension between the monarchy
and the army came to a head, with the latter effectively staging a military coup
that saw the young king, the regent and the Prime Minister Nuri Al-Said flee into
exile (Tripp 2007 [2000]: 100–4). The British were not fond of the Pan-Arab anti-
British ideology of the colonels. Despite being already embroiled in the broader
events of World War II, in 1941 the British staged the Anglo-Iraq War which saw
them quickly defeat the Iraqi army (Silverfarb 1986: 131–41, 1994: 1–7). The four
colonels were subsequently tried and executed and the triumvirate of the boy king,
the hated regent and the hawkish prime minister were reinstated in Baghdad, their
power propped up by the might of the British but their legitimacy and popularity
now permanently undermined in the eyes of most Iraqis.

Perhaps because of this lack of popularity, the regent used the cessation of
World War Two to announce a return to the political life of the 1920s, lifting
the restrictions on the freedom of the press and calling for the formation or re-
emergence of opposition parties. This brought with it an immediate spike in both the
number and variety of political parties in Iraq, from pro-government, pro-British
parties, to centrist, right- and left-leaning parties, Pan-Arab, Nationalist, and two
Marxist parties as well as a blossoming of labour unions, cultural movements and
artistic/literary associations. This era also witnessed the emergence of two of Iraq's
more influential parties, the nationalist-leaning National Democratic Party (*Hizb
Al-Watani Al-Dimuqrati* – NDP) and the Pan-Arab-leaning Independence Party
(*Hizb Al-Istiqlal*) as well as a credible expansion of the ICP (Tripp 2007 [2000]:
111–15). Once again, many of these parties spawned their own publications. The
NDP controlled 'The Voice of the People' (*Sawt Al-Ahali*) and the Independence
Party had 'The Independent Standard' (*Liwa Al-Istiqlal*), both of which launched
repeated attacks against the Iraqi government, and Prince Abd Al-Ilah, leading
to censorship that forced several name changes. These were joined by the many
papers of the ICP which tended to be nationalist in their persuasion including the

newly added *Al-Qaida* ('The Base'), *Rayat Al-Shaghila* ('The Worker's Flag') and the later *Ittihad Al-Shab* ('The People's Union') (Dawisha 2005a: 15–16, 22–3).

It appears that, on the whole, the newspapers of this era were relatively free to express diverse opinions. In 1945 the opposition paper *Al-Ahali* published an editorial that was vitriolic in its critique of the government's claim that Iraq was a democracy. It sought to remind the Iraqi people that in a democracy the Parliament works on behalf of the people and in their interests, but that in Iraq the parliament worked instead in the interests of the monarchy and the British (Dawisha 2009: 120). It is perhaps because of such open discussions of democracy that the broader Arab press of the post-Second World War era has been compared by one commentator to that of the press which followed the American Revolution in so far as it was dominated by 'the numerous, tiny enterprise, highly partisan, political party press' (McFadden 1953: 36–7). Speaking specifically about Iraq, Charles Tripp has stated that the press of this era was politically significant in that it gave 'voice to trenchant criticism of political and economic conditions and … [outlined] ideas for the future of Iraq which were radical in their implications' (Tripp 2007 [2000]: 112).

This optimism is not unjustified given the role that the press was to play in 1948 in mobilizing the people of Iraq to protest against the proposed revision to the Anglo-Iraqi treaty. When word reached the Iraqi opposition that such amendments would bring Iraq further into line with British interests and extend their hegemony over the nation, they were virulent in their dissent, using their newspapers to encourage massive demonstrations on the streets of Baghdad (Silverfarb 1994: 141–55). Unfortunately this series of relatively peaceful demonstrations (dubbed the *Wathba*, 'Outburst') caused a panic amongst Iraq's political elite who ordered the military to use any means necessary to quell the uprising. As well as arresting, imprisoning and torturing many of the demonstrators, the military also opened fire on the crowds several times (Mackey 2002: 148–9). This crack-down also had ramifications for the Iraqi political and media sphere, with the ruling elite taking the drastic step of banning several newspapers and increasing the levels of censorship. Much of the blame for the demonstrations fell on the ICP, the pro-British government was perpetually suspicious of their political ideology and its popularity among the people. The demonstrations gave the government a justification for targeting the group and authorizing the arrest of the ICP's leaders who were later tried and publicly hanged (Salucci 2005: 27–9).

This series of events did little to quell the many Iraqi opposition and political movements, however, and the execution of several of the ICP's most senior members seemed to spur on the movement. Through the early 1950s several new newspapers were created in southern Iraq, including 'The Voice of Struggle' (*Sawt Al-Kifah* in 1951), 'The Worker's Union' and 'The Peasant's Struggle' (*Ittihad Al-Ummal* and *Nidal Al-Fallah*, both in 1952) and 'The Voice of the Euphrates' (*Sawt Al-Furat* in 1954). Around this time, the ICP also began publishing newspapers that catered to the interests of the expanding number of students (*Kifah Al-Talaba* – 'The Students Struggle') and women (*Huquq Al-Mara*

– 'Women's Rights') who held party membership. Such papers helped to spur on various student demonstrations, rural challenges to landowner authority and industrial strikes. The ICP was able to garner support from across Iraq's complex array of ethno-sectarian and religious divides, including smaller minorities such as Christians and Jews, via its argument that, 'while Iraq was an Arab society, real democracy could only be achieved by recognizing its ethnic, linguistic and confessional diversity' (Davis 1992: 80).

Mounting political pressure, combined with the continuing lack of public support for the Iraqi administration created a situation in which the monarchy had little choice but to allow Iraq's opposition parties to take part in the 1954 election. Here, a well-known member of Iraq's oppositional political scene by the name of Kamil Al-Chadirji[5] had the brilliant idea of bringing together Iraq's divergent opposition groups to form the National Electoral Front (*Al-Jabha Al-Intikhabiya Al-Wataniya*, or NEF). In an unprecedented display of solidarity the various political factions of Iraq heeded the advice of Chadirji, and the NEF soon included a 'Supreme Committee' consisting of members from the NDP, the Independence Party, the emerging Baath Party and the ICP. Serving the Supreme Committee was a second tier made up of a wide base of members from Iraqi opposition groups, including various smaller parties and independents.

The success of this model was instantly recognizable since, despite constant police interference, the message was rapidly disseminated to the broader Iraqi population who came out onto the streets to voice their approval in various campaign rallies. The subsequent elections have been heralded as 'not only the freest but also the most spirited in modern Iraqi history' (Davis 2005b: 102). This success was also felt at the polls where, despite a relatively short campaign period, the falsification of votes and intimidation and interference from government officials, the NEF was able to garner an unprecedented, if paltry, 14 of the 135 seats (Tripp 2007 [2000]: 132). The central government was unnerved by the show of solidarity amongst Iraq's political opposition groups and by the electoral support they received nationwide. The elections not only secured the NEF seats in Baghdad and Mosul (Iraq's two largest cities at the time), they also threatened Nuri Al-Said's parliamentary control. The new parliament met once before being dissolved by a royal decree (Batatu 1982 [1978]: 686–7). The opposition parties, their newspapers and their protests, were suppressed and, with the subsequent elections going ahead uncontested, the hegemony of the ruling elite was restored (Warriner 1962 [1957]: 125). Nuri was then able to conduct a small war 'against any writers, journalists and academics whom he regarded as critical of the status quo', revoking the licences of opposition parties and introducing restrictive legislation to further curtail 'the freedom of the press and the right to hold public meetings and organize demonstrations' (Tripp 2007 [2000]: 133).

---

5   A former member of the National Party and the Ahali Group, Al-Chadirji later founded the NDP and served as the editor of the party's newspaper, Al-Ahali, later renamed Sawt Al-Ahali.

Conclusion

Although the Colonial era of Iraq's history ends with the suppression of media and political freedoms following the 1954 elections, Al-Musawi describes the political climate of the early 1950s in Iraq as running 'opposite to an oppressive but restless political climate, as the educated classes were effectively involved in disseminating a culture of democracy and resistance: democracy for the Iraqis, against martial laws and censorship, and resistance to British virtual control of the many cabinets that spanned the period in question' (Al-Musawi 2006: 115). Al-Musawi's comment might be taken as indicative of the political climate of the entire Colonial period which reveals an alternative Iraqi history, a history in which the nation's public sphere played a pivotal role in mobilizing the people, encouraging democratic participation, stimulating wide debate, coordinating dissent and serving as the watchdog of the elite. More to the point, as Eric Davis has argued, Colonial Iraq also 'established a historical memory to which Iraqi intellectuals can return as an inspiration for a transition to democracy' (Davis 2005b: 85).

However, an examination of Colonial Iraq also raises questions about the discourse of Western democracy. In their occupation of Iraq, Britain – one of the world's strongest advocates of democracy, home of the *Magna Carta*, the modern parliament, the first daily newspaper and the Fourth Estate – can be seen to have all but abandoned the ideals such institutions and documents are said to represent. In their creation and occupation of Iraq, the British not only brought with them the Orientalist legacy common throughout the Colonial period but also installed the nation-state's first Oriental despot in the form of a foreign monarch. They sought to quash democratic movements wherever they found them, they interfered in the nation's parliament and demanded agreement to various suspect treaties. Such actions were not only driven by their desire for Iraq's acquiescence to the will of empire, but also by broader discourses, such as Oriental despotism, which decreed that Iraq was not only unable to govern itself but was also incapable of sophisticated political structures such as democracy. The Colonial period of Iraqi history not only brings to the fore the problematic nature of this widely held assumption, it also reveals the contrapuntal discourses of Western civilization: a force for democracy and human rights on its own soil, a force for despotism and oppression abroad.

Chapter 5
Oppression and Resistance in Post-Colonial Iraq

[T]he artificially-imposed discourses and institutions of constitutional monarchy, elitist ideology, and especially Saddam's brand of Baathism have historically fought so hard to take root in the Iraqi cultural sensibilities that they provoked a heterogeneous counter-culture of resistance.

Al-Musawi 2006: 8

Re-Thinking Post-Colonial Iraq

The Revolution of 1958 marked a fundamental turn in Iraqi politics. It saw the nation proceed from the Colonialism of the British and the hegemony of their installed Hashemite monarchy towards the emergence of a Post-Colonial Iraq (1958–2003). It also saw the emergence of various Post-Colonial political discourses which seemed to carry with them the promise of a new Iraq. Clearly, however, there were a number of competing visions of what this new Iraq should look like. While the events of the revolution and the important political schisms which followed are addressed later in this chapter, it is critical to note here that while Post-Colonial Iraq made many initial steps towards a more equitable and democratic life, most of this period is characterized by the ascension of a number of repressive regimes culminating in the rise of the Baath party and the self-elected presidency of Saddam Hussein.

While the Iraqi people suffered under the weight of these oppressive regimes, in the West the rule of several Iraqi dictators, but especially Saddam Hussein, fitted very neatly with already existing notions of Oriental despotism. This was especially true during times of conflict such as the Gulf War of 1991 during which Saddam was painted as an evil madman, likened to Hitler and compared to the megalomaniacal and bloodthirsty kings of the ancient Near East (Keeble 1998, Philo and McLaughlin 1995, Toth 1992). He was dubbed 'The Beast of Baghdad' as 'Countless stories were needlessly repeated throughout the mainstream media of his brutality ... [while] Tabloid magazines published sensational stories detailing his alleged sexual crimes and perversions' (Kellner 1995: 208). This continued throughout the 1990s, especially when Saddam violated various UN restrictions and Iraq was subsequently subjected to missile strikes by the United States, Britain and France in 1993 and again in 1998 (Richardson 2004: 157–71). By focusing on the desire to punish the Oriental despot, the press were able to evoke 'an imperialist and indeed racist ideology of relations between nations, which contributes to the continuity of imperialist and neo-Colonialist relations in practice' (Fairclough 1995: 102).

While the events of September 11 2001 are not the focus here, it is worth noting that they provided the US Administration with clear evidence that the fundamental paradigm underpinning relations between the West and the Orient was a 'Clash of Civilizations' (Tomanic-Trivundza 2004: 480). This is perhaps best evidenced by US President George W. Bush's declaration of a 'War on Terror' – a clear interpretative framework that enabled him to contrast what he saw as the righteous forces of the West against the terrorizing hordes of the non-Western world. As part of the War on Terror, the US government began building their case to attack Iraq based on two central allegations that were later proven so abjectly false: that Saddam supported terrorism and had links to Al-Qaeda, and that he was harbouring Weapons of Mass Destruction (WMD), which he was likely to use or supply to others. This assertion became especially clear in President Bush's 2003 State of the Union Address, which focused much of its attention on Iraq. Towards the end of the speech, the President claimed that

> Before 11 September 2001, many in the world believed that Saddam Hussein could be contained. But chemical agents and lethal viruses and shadowy terrorist networks are not easily contained. Imagine those 19 hijackers with other weapons, and other plans – this time armed by Saddam Hussein. It would take just one vial, one canister, one crate slipped into this country to bring a day of horror like none we have ever known. We will do everything in our power to make sure that day never comes (Bush 2003d).

The Western mainstream media began beating the drums of war. They painted a typically Orientalist picture of Iraqis as degenerate, primitive and untrustworthy, yet cunning and vicious (Brown 2006: 105). As Said noted in an essay published in the lead up to the war, this one-eyed view of Iraq enabled 'the dehumanization of the hated "other"' by reducing their 'existence to a few insistently repeated simple phrases, images, and concepts. This makes it easier to bomb the enemy without qualm' (Said 2004 [2002]: 217). It also helped to assure Western audiences that the war was legitimate and, more problematically, it 'drew on an imagined and vaguely racist legacy of the way "the West" has historically positioned itself as being responsible for "civilizing the world"' (Richardson 2007: 191).

Central to all of this was the demonization of Saddam. Familiar stories re-emerged as Western media audiences were bombarded with images and articles about his many wives and lovers, his blood-lust and his brutal political strategies. More bizarrely, the media took a peculiar interest in the number of surgically-enhanced body-doubles Saddam apparently had scattered across the country, his sexual perversions, the excessive decadence of his palaces and the endless catacombs and bomb-shelters that would protect him from even the most deadly air raids (Paz and Aviles 2009). The crimes of his sons, Udday and Qusay, were dutifully recounted while others focused on Saddam's alleged tendency to have anyone executed who dared to challenge his authority or question his motives. In this way, the image of Saddam Hussein and his regime fitted well with the age-old discourse of Oriental despotism. Like the excesses and brutality of the Persian kings and other Asiatic despots found in the work of Montesquieu and Chardin for example, Saddam's despotism was that of arbitrary power exerted over an unwilling and terrified populace.

For scholars such as Kanan Makiya, the tyranny of the Baath is indicative of the broader failings of the Iraqi people themselves who, along with all Arabs, had not grasped notions of modernity, liberty, equality and justice (Makiya 1998 [1989]). This is made explicit in his *Cruelty and Silence* in which he claims that

> Men like Saddam Hussein … are indigenous creations of modern Arab political culture, which until now has failed to produce anything better … [Arabs] have failed to evolve a genuinely convincing language of rights in politics … [They] have become fossilized, backward-looking and steeped in a romanticism of 'struggle' which is conducive to violence … [They must] begin to realize that they are overwhelmingly responsible for the deplorable state of their world (Makiya 1993: 282).

Taking such notions even further, Said Aburish opens his work *Saddam Hussein: The Politics of Revenge* by connecting the rule of Saddam to Iraqi history. In a few short pages, he reduces thousands of years of Iraq's complex political past down to a lineage of blood-thirsty and dictatorial regimes. For him, the rise of Saddam

> has to be understood in the context of the history of Iraq … Saddam as an individual may be unique, even demonic, but he is also a true son of Iraq. Even his use of violence to achieve his aims is not a strictly personal characteristic, but rather an unattractive trait of the Iraqi people reinforced by their history … [and] the violence and cruelty which accompanied every change in the governance of the country throughout its history … [Together] the turbulent history, harsh environment and multi-stranded culture of Iraq have produced a complex and unique conglomerate which lacks the ingredients for creating a homogenous country and a commitment to the idea of a national community (Aburish 2000: 1–3).

Aside from their assertion that a culture of unchanging authoritarianism was a product of the failings of the Iraqi people throughout history, such works develop and promulgate a remarkably one-eyed view of the Post-Colonial era in Iraq. It is important to acknowledge from the start that while this chapter does offer a more nuanced view of the Post-Colonial period, it is no way a defence of the tyranny of the Baath and the brutal megalomania of Saddam. Specifically, the first section examines the quashing of Iraq's civil society and the tight restraints exerted over the nation's media throughout the period. It also addresses the ways in which various Post-Colonial regimes, but especially the Baath, were adept at manipulating the discourses of democracy in order to mask their tyranny and coerce people into patriotism. Moving beyond this, however, the second section documents the various clandestine opposition groups that began to emerge across Iraq's divergent ethno-religious and political divides who resisted Baathist oppression and agitated for democratic change. They produced their own media outlets which proved effective in voicing the various frustrations and grievances of Iraqis of all backgrounds and shades of opinion, giving way to a renewed public sphere.[1] The Post-Colonial era, therefore, alternative history of Iraq from the mid-twentieth through to the early twenty-first century in which one finds a sophisticated political culture deeply concerned with the issue of democratic governance.

State Propaganda and the Discourses of Democracy

As far back as 1951 the fledgling Arab Baath Socialist Party (*Hizb Al-Baath Al-Arabi Al-Ishtiraki*)[2] had been gathering momentum in the Iraqi armed forces. Although Baathist ideology developed in Damascus around 1940, it emigrated to Iraq in 1949 and developed a loyal following in Iraq under the leadership of Faud Al-Rikabi, a young Iraqi engineer from Nasiriyya (Baram 1991: 9–13). The early message of the Baath in Iraq was relatively similar to Post-Colonial movements elsewhere: Iraq and the broader Arab region would never reach their potential in the modern world if they continued to suffer the inequities and suppression of foreign occupation. Disseminated via Baathist organs such as *Al-Hurriya* ('The Freedom'), *Al-Afkar* ('The Idea') and, their later subsidiary, *Al-Amal* ('The Labour'), this message understandably appealed to many Iraqis, particularly members of the military and the intelligentsia, who were yet to experience total independence from the British occupation and its installed Hashemite monarchy (Davis 2005b: 96). By 1952 a number of Baathist-leaning cells within the military had emerged, constituting the 'Free Officers' movement, and these were later inspired and somewhat radicalized in a series of major steps taken by Gamal Abdul Nasser in Egypt towards his vision of the 'United Arab Republic' (Stansfield 2007: 92).

Among the more influential converts to the early doctrine of the Baath were two of Iraq's most senior military officers, Brigadier General Abdul Karim Qasim and Colonel Abdus-Salam Arif (Tripp 2000: 144). Together, the forces loyal to these two men had gathered enough momentum to storm Baghdad on 14 July 1958, seizing control of key government buildings, including the national radio station and the royal palace. While Arif used the radio to announce, 'Citizens of Baghdad, the Monarchy is dead! The Republic is here!' (Arif cited in Mackey 2002: 157), his soldiers fulfilled his pronouncement by murdering all but one member of the royal

---

1   Earlier work by the author includes a set of detailed tables that document the most significant media outlets of Post-Colonial Iraq, both those controlled by the state and by the various political and ethno-religious opposition movements (Isakhan 2009a: 251–6).

2   *Baath* translates to mean 'Awakening', 'Renaissance' or 'Renewal' and the party will henceforth be termed the Baath or ABSP.

family. The bodies of the Regent Abd Al-Ilah and the young King Faisal II were promptly sequestered by the angry civilian mob that had followed the military into the palace and dragged through the streets of Baghdad. The next day the body of the newly-deposed Prime Minister, Nuri Al-Said, was seized by another mob after he was discovered trying to flee Iraq dressed as a woman (Dawisha 2009: 171–2).

The revolutionaries were not a homogenous entity, however. They represented a fundamental schism which had long split secular Iraqi political movements into two main camps: those supporting the more left-wing Qasim who had garnered the support of much of the military and the members of the Iraqi Communist Party (ICP) under the loose ideology of Iraqi nationalism; while others followed Arif who adhered to more of a Pan-Arab approach, attracting the orthodox members of the emerging Baathist movement (Fernea and Louis 1991). Given Qasim's superior rank and broader initial support, he was the natural heir to the events of the *coup d'état* and he quickly established a series of lofty goals for his incumbency, including his desire to

> increase and distribute the national wealth … to found a new society and a new democracy, to use this strong, democratic, Arabist Iraq as an instrument to free and elevate other Arabs and Afro-Asians and to assist the destruction of 'imperialism', by which he largely meant British influence in the underdeveloped countries (Curtis 2004: 82).

While such goals were never fully realized, Qasim's leadership did foster the development of a nascent public sphere made up of a myriad of political parties, professional associations, labour movements and intellectual groups who fervently debated the political events and ideologies of their time. Qasim also oversaw the formation of the Sovereignty Council (*Majlis Siyadat Al-Thawra*) and the Iraqi cabinet and he took unprecedented steps to counter Iraqi sectarianism and sexism, including the involvement of Shias, Kurds, other ethnic and religious minorities and women at various levels of government (Davis 2005b: 116–9). This diverse political climate was also reflected in the Iraqi media sector where the heavily partisan newspapers of Iraq generally enjoyed considerable autonomy and popularity. The early 1960s saw an upsurge in newspaper production across Iraq, with over 20 in Baghdad alone. Approximately one-third of these Baghdad papers had pro-Communist tendencies, including the re-launched *Ittihad Al-Ummal* ('The Worker's Union') as *Wahdat Al-Ummal* ('The Worker's Unity') in 1962 and, in 1963, the re-appearance of *Sawt Al-Furat* ('The Voice of the Euphrates') (Batatu,1982 [1978]: 35, Rugh 2004: 46–7). With the arrival of television sets in a number of coffeehouses following the 1958 Revolution, the illiterate and poor Iraqi majority gained a new insight into the machinations of politics, both domestic and international. While Qasim initially used this new medium to broadcast the trials of corrupt members of the former regime, the television later became a format to continue the work of countering sectarianism and to encourage national unity (Tripp 2007: 45).

However, Qasim was ultimately undermined by his inability to form effective alliances with his own power base in the ICP and the NDP, as well as by his failure to realize the importance of Pan-Arab ideology to many Iraqi citizens. This created something of a power vacuum in which the disgruntled members of the ABSP were able to gather significant momentum with their vision of a strong Iraq as the leader of a new Pan-Arab alliance. The ABSP repeatedly tried to assassinate Qasim; in 1959 the first attempt involved a young and relatively unknown Baathist by the name of Saddam Hussein. Eventually, the ABSP was able to once again establish loyal cells in the Iraqi army and on 8 February 1963 they seized Baghdad. General Qasim was executed the following day and the image of his body, lying prostrate in a pool of his own blood, was beamed out across Iraq on state television. It appears that the Baathists had also learned the political power of the television and it was Qasim's final appearance on Iraqi TV which was to be his most memorable.

The first ABSP government of Iraq was thus formed in 1963 under the leadership of Prime Minister Hasan Al-Bakr with Qasim's partner in the 1958 coup, Colonel Arif, installed as President. In events that served as something of a preamble to the tyrannical rule of Saddam Hussein, the Baath Party promptly set about utilizing their newfound powers to imprison, torture and execute what was left of Iraq's nascent opposition movements, especially their long-time foes in the ICP (Stansfield 2007: 93–4). The power of the ABSP was short-lived, however. By the end of the same year, Arif had arrested many of the senior members of the Baath and announced that the military would henceforth be administering the affairs of the state (Goode 1975: 107). In terms of political developments, the events of 1963 – the violent disposal of Qasim, the purge of Iraqi opposition by the Baath and the ascension of the military under Arif – signified the real beginning of authoritarianism in Iraq (Haj, 1997). This trend was to continue after Arif was killed in a helicopter accident in 1966 and his brother, Abdur-Rahman Arif, succeeded him (Batatu 1982 [1978]: 1027–72). Throughout their reign, the Arif brothers also enacted a series of restrictive press laws including Press Law No. 53 which imposed heavy censorship on the press and the tight control of media licences.

The political climate fostered under the consecutive regimes of the Arif brothers did little to encourage the establishment of moderate and legitimate political movements and arguably paved the way for the violent military *coup d'etat* in which the ABSP ascended to authority in 1968 (Dawisha 2009: 183–9). This time Hasan Al-Bakr (now installed as President) made sure that once the military had served its purpose in overthrowing Arif, it would be purged of any potential threats to the new regime (Stansfield 2007: 94–5). A brief struggle for power between the two allies in the coup – the military and the Baath – broke out, with each of these bodies controlling one of the two major newspapers in Iraq at that time, *Al-Thawra* ('The Revolution') and *Al-Jumhuriyya* ('The Republic'), respectively. This struggle for power was promptly decided in favour of the Baath, and served as another valuable lesson for the party regarding the power of the press.

They acted quickly. One of the Baath party's first acts was to jail, charge and then execute Aziz Abdel Barakat who was both the head of the Journalist's Union and the publisher of the independent *Al-Manar* ('The Lighthouse'), one of the most professionally run and widely distributed dailies in Iraq at the time. Following this, in 1969 the Baath Party established a publications law which effectively made the media the fourth branch of the newly established government. This saw the Iraqi media industry quickly transform into one that was 'more controlled, monolithic, mobilized and almost completely stripped of any critical approach' (Bengio 2004: 110). This meant that by the early 1970s Iraq had only five daily newspapers, each of which was heavily influenced, if not completely controlled by the state. In addition to their own paper, *Al-Jumhuriyah*, they took control of *Al-Thawrah* and the English-language *Baghdad Observer*, and added the Kurdish language *Taakhi* ('Brotherhood') in 1969 and *Tariq al Shab* ('The Path of the People') in 1973 (Rugh 1979: 32).

In terms of the Baath's actual views on democracy, the proceedings of the Eighth National Conference of the ABSP in 1965, are particularly instructive. The party declared that:

> Popular democracy, as understood by the Baath, rises on complete voluntary mutual responsiveness that can materialize between the party and the masses once the party maintains an opening with them and abandons all air of superiority … From this it follows that there can be no room for contradictions between the party's concepts and the concepts of the masses, but rather harmony and concurrence (*Program of the Arab Baath Socialist Party* 1965: III).

Here, the Baath cleverly invoked the notion of popular democracy while maintaining that such democracy can only work as long as it does not contradict the party's agenda. To make sure that no such contradiction emerges, the conference proceedings state further that 'The party might be compelled, especially in the early stages of the revolution, to feign terror and coercive guidance with the object of crushing the enemies of the revolution' (*Program of the Arab Baath Socialist Party* 1965: III). In terms of the freedom of the Iraqi public sphere to criticize the party, the Baath warn that while 'the masses [have] the right of constructive criticism within the limits of the nation's progressive line of destiny' such criticism 'cannot become an end in itself, nor can it be allowed to proceed unchecked to the limit of undermining the nationalist socialist line itself' (*Program of the Arab Baath Socialist Party* 1965: III).[3]

These ideas continued after the 1968 coup. From the very beginning of their ascendency the Baath sought to construct themselves as a force for democratic change in Iraq, their 1968 constitution claiming the nation was now a 'popular democratic state' (*Al-Jumhuriyya* 1968). As far as Baathist official policy was concerned, their message to the people was that Baathist democracy was

---

3   These translations are taken from Roy E. Thoman's *Iraq Under Baathist Rule* (Thoman 1972: 32).

something far greater than Western models as it was not only more stable, but more in tune with Arab sentiment. This is particularly evident in the state press, where newspapers like *Al-Thawra* dutifully ran editorials that reinforced the Baathist vision of democracy, claiming that 'the assumption that democracy means freedom of speech seems ridiculous to Iraqis' (*Al-Thawra*, 1969). The same editorial goes on to claim that the interpretation of democracy to mean 'the freedom of forming parties' was a 'bourgeois assumption' and that 'The socialist revolution and the rule of the one socialist party [the Baath] have made nonsense of this unbalanced assumption' (*Al-Thawra* 1969).[4] The Baath regularly used the media to wage attacks on Western liberal democracies while providing little in the way of rational critique or viable political alternatives. The Baath also utilized the press to differentiate themselves from their predecessors, employing the rhetoric of Oriental despotism to explain away the dictatorships of Qasim and the Arif brothers and contrasting them against an image of the Baath as the people's champion against oppression (Bengio 1998: 64).

Concurrently, the little known Saddam Hussein was fast developing a reputation as a ruthless politician and cunning strategist that belied his quiet and aloof nature and his humble rural background. Having played a relatively small but quite strategic role in the ascension of the ABSP to power in 1968, Saddam now dutifully laboured behind the scenes, brilliantly transforming the Baath from a nominal party to a nation-wide phenomenon (Tripp 2000: 195–9). It is now well known that Saddam's rise to power was marked by terror and coercion, that he went on to commit grievous crimes against his own citizens, especially the many religious and ethnic minorities of Iraq and that he was one of the cruellest and most tyrannical despots of modern times (Cordesman and Hashim 1997: 111–8). What is perhaps less well known is that Saddam was the master of a highly developed and multi-tiered propaganda machine. As has been shown in Chapters 2 and 3, he developed his own particular cult of personality by aligning himself with Iraq's Mesopotamian and Islamic heritage. He also managed to build himself a reputation as a political revolutionary, a brilliant strategist, a paternal figure who cared deeply about his nation and a visionary who could lead Iraq – and indeed the entire Arab world – into a modern and prosperous future. He was a powerful and charismatic politician, wielding a rhetoric that appealed directly to the 'everyday' Iraqi.

In this way, Saddam had garnered his own loyal following and when, in 1979, he pressured Bakr to stand-down Bakr had little choice but to abdicate the Presidency to his young protégé. Having witnessed firsthand the power of the media in the rise of the Baath Party to power a little over a decade earlier, Saddam was all too aware of the utility of the press and quickly set about modelling them after earlier totalitarian examples such as Nazi Germany and the Soviet Union (Bengio 2004: 110). Although the nation retained its five daily newspapers under Saddam's rule, he was quick to quash any lingering notions of freedom of the

---

4   The translations of *Al-Jumhuriyya* and *Al-Thawra* found in this paragraph are from Ofra Bengio's *Saddam's Word* (Bengio 1998: 57, 61).

press by making sure that the entire media industry came under the authority of the government and that every working journalist was an active member of the ABSP. This meant that each of Iraq's papers soon became state-run propaganda machines, dutifully reciting official policy and praising governmental action. He ensured that this occurred through careful and clandestine monitoring of the media as well as more banal and overt practices such as insisting that his photograph be featured daily on page one and that each of his speeches was printed in full. Saddam was also careful to prevent Iraqis from too much exposure to external media by periodically jamming news broadcasts from outside Iraq and imposing a five year prison sentence on anyone owning a satellite dish.

Saddam was also keen to engineer a new image of himself as an enlightened and liberal-minded leader, one familiar with sophisticated political models such as democracy. To do so, in the very earliest days of the regime he began creating an aura of radical political change: he allowed several communist works to be translated into Arabic, he wrote his own neo-Marxist editorials and he courted left-leaning intellectuals and activists, inviting them to play an active role in the new Iraq. By shoring up his revolutionary credentials amongst the left and the broader Iraqi community, Saddam was gradually able to shift debate towards the centralization of power. As he became increasingly powerful and dictatorial, Saddam was able to mirror earlier Baathist attempts to manufacture and manipulate a particular image of democracy that suited his own agenda and garnered support for his rule. To do this, Saddam argued that a forward looking Iraq must be centred around a government of 'democratic centralization', a term ultimately used to describe the increasingly authoritarian nature of the Baath (Dawisha 2009: 228–31). Along these lines, the state media dutifully catalogued Saddam's claim that 'Our party has implemented democracy ... drawing on noble and eternal sources and origins compatible with the conscience of the people' (*Al-Iraq* 1979).[5] In another speech, published in *Al-Thawra* under the headline 'Democracy: A Source of Strength for the Individual and Society', Saddam claimed that

> There is no contradiction between democracy and legitimate power. Let no one among you imagine the democracy weakens him, or robs him of his dignity and legitimate sphere of control. This is not true. According to the well-known balance between democracy and centralism, there is no contradiction between the practise of democracy and legitimate central control. Only those of poor understanding could imagine such a contradiction between guardianship and comradely dealings, or between preservation of role and the position of leadership (*Al-Thawra* 1977).[6]

---

5 As translated in Bengio's *Saddam's Word* (Bengio 1998: 62).

6 This translation is taken from Kanan Makiya's *Republic of Fear* (Makiya 1998 [1989]: 80).

To further promote his democratic credentials in 1980 and again in 1984, Saddam conducted Iraq's first Post-Colonial elections for the National Assembly. These elections were designed to serve several key Baathist purposes. They helped to placate domestic Shia and Kurdish grievances and to provide a modern alternative to the rise of Shia theocratic power in Iran. They were also expressly designed to confirm Saddam's alleged commitment to democratization, to garner consent for his war with Iran and, ultimately, to further re-affirm his empery over the Iraqi people. In his studies of these elections, Amatzia Baram documents the fierce competition that existed among the electoral candidates, who themselves came from a variety of different political and ethnic backgrounds, because winning a seat brought with it significant power, prestige and career prospects (Baram 1981, 1989). As Baram points out, throughout the elections the Iraqi media were critical in promoting the elections, in advocating and closely scrutinizing the policies and platforms of the different candidates and in reporting the results. In the lead up to the elections, around 1500 biographies of the candidates were published in the press, including demographic data as well as details about an individual's revolutionary struggle and their length of membership and allegiance to the Baath.

The results are particularly interesting. In both elections a significant proportion of Shia were elected (43 per cent in 1980 and 46 per cent in 1984), as well as smaller numbers of Kurds and women. This, coupled with the fact that the elected candidates had powers such as the ratification of the budget and international treaties, supervision of certain state institutions, and were apparently free to debate domestic and foreign policy issues, meant that the elections had at least achieved the guise of being democratic. In reality, however, the National Assembly was virtually powerless, being at the mercy of the highly centralized Revolutionary Command Council and serving as little more than a rubber stamp for the policies of the state. In addition, Shia, Kurdish and female representatives rarely ascended the political ladder. Nonetheless, Saddam took great pride in these quasi-democratic moments, even appearing on Iraqi state television on the evening of the 1980 election making spontaneous visits to the homes of poor Iraqi families 'to inquire whether they had voted in that day's parliamentary elections' (Davis 2005b: 237).

Immediately after the Iran-Iraq War, however, Saddam was faced with thousands of men who, on returning from the frontline, found few employment opportunities awaiting them. Many of these citizens – particularly the already disenfranchised Shia and Kurds – began to revolt against Saddam's authority and called for democratic reforms (Keeble 1997: 12). Surprisingly, Saddam reacted by co-ordinating further parliamentary elections in 1989, seemingly because he believed that some form of public debate over democracy would enable his citizens to voice their grievances without overwhelming his authority. Not taking any chances, however, Saddam implemented even tighter restrictions over these elections than their predecessors, requiring 'all candidates to have contributed to the war against Iran and to believe that it had resounded to the glory of Iraq' (Bengio 1998: 68). These elections enabled Saddam to label himself 'the engineer of democracy' or 'the shepherd of democracy' and to make public statements such as 'All democracy to the people, all liberty to the people, all rights to the people' (*Al-Thawra* 1989). [7]

Due to the economic cost (not to mention the military and civilian cost) incurred by the Iran-Iraq War, Saddam urgently needed funds. On 2 August 1990 he decided to invade Iraq's oil-rich neighbour, Kuwait, which had long been viewed as little more than an outpost of Basra, unfairly cut off from Iraq first by the Ottomans and then by the British on the basis of its important strategic value as an East-West trading port (Rahman 1997). During the ensuing Gulf War, the lip-service that Saddam had paid to democratization in the 1980s were promptly sidelined and the first anniversary of the Gulf War gave *Al-Qadisiyya* ample opportunity to attack the United States for having misunderstood Iraq's rich history, complex culture and unique politics. It asserted that 'We have Saddam Hussein and they have their democracy … Let them enjoy their democracy … but we are content to have an Arab leader, a Muslim seeker of justice' (*Al-Qadisiyya* 1992). [8]

Immediately following the first Gulf War, the Baath came under intense pressure, both from the heavy international sanctions placed upon it by the international community and by a number of internal rebellions which posed a significant challenge to the embattled and weakened regime. As will be discussed later in this chapter, in the north the Kurds mounted a *Rapareen* ('Uprising', in Kurdish) while in the south the Shia launched a parallel *Intifada* ('Uprising', in Arabic) of their own. In response to these rebellions, Saddam wrote and published a series of seven articles that appeared in *Al-Thawra* between April 3 and 14, 1991. The articles included discussions of Shia and Kurdish roles within Iraqi society and directly addressed some of their grievances. He was forced, for the first time, to acknowledge and confront Iraq's ethnic diversity and to discuss it in an open and public fashion; he was also forced to make at least token references to the need for democracy and dialogue. In Eric Davis' extended discussion of these articles he points out that

> A significant, albeit implicit, admission in the articles is that Iraq is characterized by an authoritarian and repressive state. Saddam justifies this authoritarianism by arguing that any nation-state undergoing a material and cultural renaissance must pass through a transitional period characterized by violence and ill-defined citizen rights. According to Saddam, Western countries confronted this situation during their own development into prosperous and stable nation-states (Davis 2005b: 245).

The implications of such admissions were remarkable. For the first time, Saddam not only acknowledged various problems within Iraq, but also admitted that the Baathist state was not the ultimate form of Iraqi government. Instead, the Baath were a necessary – if chaotic, authoritarian and repressive – stage of transition towards a more open and tolerant society. Iraq was not yet a stable and robust

---

7   As translated in Bengio's *Saddam's Word* (Bengio 1998: 62).
8   As translated in Bengio's *Saddam's Word* (Bengio 1998: 69).

nation and to get there, Iraqis were encouraged to continue the struggle for liberty, equality and democracy.

Despite such promising rhetoric, Saddam sought to tighten his grip on the Iraqi media by promoting his eldest son, Udday Hussein, to the position of the Head of the Iraqi Journalists' Union,[9] leaving him responsible for the censorship and management of most of the nation's media (Daragahi 2003: 47). Specifically, there were six official daily newspapers which all came under the jurisdiction of the newly appointed Udday: *Al-Jumhuriya*, *Al-Thawra*, *The Baghdad Observer*, the military paper *Al-Qadisiyya*, *Al-Iraq* ('The Iraq', a renamed version of the earlier Kurdish run newspaper, *Al-Taakhi*), and Udday Hussein's own personal paper *Babil* which was established in 1990. Udday's influence also extended over several official weekly papers and radio stations, as well as a handful of television channels, all of which were tightly controlled by the state (Hooglund 1990: 199–200, Hurrat and Leidig 1994: 98–9, Rugh 1979: 32, 2004: 30).[10] The result of having his son in such a prestigious position was that Saddam could continue to manipulate the media at will.

In 1995, once again under increasing domestic pressure to democratize, Saddam conducted Iraq's first Presidential elections since the revolution of 1958. Only one candidate, Saddam Hussein, stood for election, however, and the poll took the form of a nation-wide referendum in which his constituents were asked the simple question: 'Do you agree that Saddam Hussein should be the president of the Republic of Iraq for another seven years?' (cited in Y. M. Ibrahim 1995). As with earlier elections, these were little more than a cursory nod to democracy, a carefully constructed mask designed to obfuscate growing Baathist authoritarianism. The campaign involved endless glorification of Saddam and, although he never appeared publicly prior to the election, he paid an army of supporters to march through the streets declaring '*Na'am, Na'am, Saddam*' ('Yes, Yes, Saddam') (cited in Y. M. Ibrahim 1995). On election day, Baathist loyalists rounded up and drove voters directly to the polling booths that were themselves covered in colourful pro-Saddam propaganda. Saddam won 99.96 per cent of the 8.4 million votes cast. Immediately after the elections, Iraqi state television screened a grand ceremony in which the triumphant leader was sworn in for another term. The Baath party celebrated the victory, with the Deputy Leader of the Revolutionary Command Council, Izzat Ibrahim declaring:

> It is an immortal day in the history of Arabism and Islam ... It is a blow to
> the states that have harboured enmity toward Iraq and raised unjustified doubts

---

9   In 2000, the Iraqi Journalists' Union awarded Udday Hussein the rather suspect honour of 'Journalist of the Century' (Tabor 2002).

10   It should be noted here that, although Udday took control of most of Iraq's media in the 1990s, the result of the international sanctions against Iraq meant that much of it eroded dramatically. This is especially true of newspapers, with their quality dropping both in terms of journalistic style, the number of pages and even the paper on which they were printed.

about the legitimacy of its regime or the right of its people to choose the form of government they like (Ibrahim cited in *New York Times* 1995).

Following the events of September 11 and the onset of the 'War on Terror', Saddam staged another sham Iraqi election in 2002, this time trumping his own personal best and winning 100 per cent of the vote. Here, *New York Times* journalist John F. Burns reported on a number of 'small but remarkable' protests that broke out across Baghdad. He claimed that the protests were 'the most visible sign of a new and potentially seismic trend: a willingness among ordinary people to speak up' (Burns 2002). Despite this, the official state media welcomed the result: *Al-Thawra* claimed it as a sure sign of Iraqi unity behind the authority of their leader (*Al-Thawra* 2002); *Iraq Daily* claimed it a better example of democracy than the bungled 2001 US election which brought President Bush to power (*Iraq Daily* 2002); while one journalist at *Babil* opined that 'this pure and mature democratic practice in a besieged country, which is exposed to aggression every day, is the best proof of the ability, vitality and courage of this people' (*Babil* 2002).

Along these same lines, the official Iraqi press continued in its absolute and unwavering support for Saddam in the lead up to the Iraq War of 2003. When, in 2002, President Bush offered Saddam the ultimatum of complying with UN weapons inspectors or facing the consequences, *Al-Thawra* accused Bush of exploiting 'the international body as a tool serving and giving legitimacy to his aggressive schemes against Iraq' (*Al-Thawra* 2002). The invective continued as the war got closer. In January 2003, *Al-Iraq* claimed that the 'Zionists Rumsfeld, Colin Powell and Condoleezza Rice' were 'stupidly and arrogantly continu[ing] to make statements they have learned off by heart' (*Al-Iraq* 2003c). When Bush issued Saddam with his final ultimatum on 17 March 2003, commentators on *Iraqi TV* taunted the US President, calling him an 'idiot', a 'failure' and 'foolish', and critiquing his speech as being premised on 'false assumptions' and an 'incoherent argument' (*Iraq TV* 2003a).

During the combat phase of the war itself, the state-run Iraqi media used a variety of rhetorical techniques to garner wide support for the Iraqi army, to instil confidence in the populace and to undermine the coalition troops. These included: converting the conflict into a religious war and emphasizing that the Iraqi people were protected by God; invoking history to illustrate the wonders of Iraqi civilization and its ability to withstand attacks from invading forces; constructing the war in true ABSP fashion as a 'people's war' and claiming that the Iraqi forces were not only ready for the coalition forces but that they would turn the invasion into a blood-bath despite the odds (*Al-Iraq* 2003b, *Al-Thawra* 2003, *Iraq TV* 2003b, 2003c). One particularly scathing article in *Al-Iraq* drew parallels between the looming US invasion and that of the British nearly a century earlier. It blamed the British for deceiving the Arabs and exploiting their revolution against the Ottoman empire, after promising them help to free their lands and set up a unified Arab state ... Britain, instead, issued an ill-fated document providing for the fragmentation of the Arab homeland into small states under a British mandate ... history shows that in Iraq, tyrants and Colonialists dug their own graves ... Our historic witness is the graves of the English Colonialists. Does the meek lackey [UK Prime Minister Tony] Blair remember this, in order to bring it back to the mind of his master Little Bush, at a time when they are tasting defeat at the hands of the Iraqis (*Al-Iraq* 2003a).

Despite such bravado, by the end of March most of the Iraqi media had begun to struggle under the constant bombing of their facilities. By early April, the Iraqi Satellite TV channel had ceased broadcasting, but many of Iraq's domestic TV and radio stations remained on air, playing patriotic music and broadcasting religious sermons, images of people chanting pro-Saddam slogans and extracts from speeches by Saddam Hussein and other senior Baath members. Finally, with the fall of Baghdad on 9 April 2003, Saddam Hussein's reign over Iraq came to an end, the last of his loyal media now silenced as the coalition forces toppled his statue in Firdos square and took control of the country.

Counter Discourse and Clandestine Opposition

At the official level, Saddam's leadership effectively eroded much of Iraq's long established civil society. The ranks of the nation's numerous opposition movements began to thin as strict punishments, including execution, were handed out to those affiliated with political parties other than the ABSP. The Baathist state also utilized the media not only to promote and maintain its incumbency but to generate a complex matrix of discourses that served to obfuscate state tyranny. Despite their control and manipulation of the nation's media sector, most Iraqis remained cynically aware of state doctrine and learned to maintain a veneer of Baathist loyalty while either 'reading between the lines' or rejecting outright the propaganda they were so routinely fed. Further, the years of ABSP hegemony also saw various ethnic and religious political factions begin to gather momentum. While Saddam's regime can be seen to have been both brutal and despotic, there was also a strong culture of clandestine dissent and opposition. A variety of counter-discourses emerged, characterized by diverse debates, passionate critiques of the regime and the advocacy of a more open and democratic Iraq.

Perhaps the most subtle and nuanced of these counter discourses emanated from within Iraq. Despite the fact that many Iraqi academics, journalists, artists and poets were commandeered by the state to write about and promote Baathist ideology, some managed to utilize subtle imagery, clever analogies, allegory or double entendres to expose the authoritarian and repressive culture of the Baath and force their fellow Iraqis to ponder alternatives such as democratic rule. This was especially true in the 1980s during the Iran-Iraq War when articles began to appear in papers such as *Al-Iraq* and *Al-Qadisiyya* which delicately but deliberately criticized life under Saddam, postulated on the merits of democratic governance, and called for free and fair elections (*Al-Iraq* 1989c, *Al-Jumhuriyya* 1980). In the mid- to late-1980s articles by Iraqi scholar and neo-Marxist, Aziz Al-Sayyid Jassim attacked the Baathist bureaucracy and the sham heroes and revolutionaries it had brought to the fore, sowing the seeds of dissent (Al-Musawi 2006: 85–7). Another Iraqi writer and critic, Muhammad Mubrarak, went as far as arguing that the *Hadith* 'Differing opinions among my nation are a grace [of God]' should become the epithet of all those who wanted to 'build a genuine democracy' in Iraq (*Al-Iraq* 1989a). Other journalists at *Al-Iraq* argued that democracy was 'vital for the progress of the people and for establishing law and justice in their midst' (*Al-Iraq* 1989b). While *Al-Qadisiyya* maintained that 'only backward peoples were afraid of freedom; not so the Iraqis, who were entitled to full democratic freedom' (*Al-Qadisiyya* 1989: 5).[11]

In the 1990s, following the defeat of Iraq in Kuwait, some journalists began to push the envelope even further. At *Nab Al-Shabab* ('The Youth'), the weekly Udday-controlled newspaper of the Youth Union, journalists got away with candidly criticising Deputy Prime Minister Tariq Aziz and promoting opposition figures such as Ahmad Chalabi. As one writer for the paper, Mohamed Bedewi Al-Shamari, commented years later, 'We criticized the government's behaviour … We criticized the checkpoints, the limited freedoms of the people, the actions of the Baathist security officers. We called on the government to respect the people's rights' (Al-Shamari cited in Daragahi 2003: 47).

Aside from the subtle critiques offered by journalists working for the state, the Baathist period also saw the emergence and strengthening of various political parties from across the vast number of religious and ethnic divides. For example, the Kurds were politically active in Iraq from as early as 1946 when famed guerrilla leader Mulla Mustafa Barzani established the first Iraqi political party based purely on ethnicity: the Kurdistan Democratic Party (KDP) (Stansfield 2003: 66–7). It was not until 1970 that the Kurds were able to gain semi-autonomy from the Baathist government, however, and in 1974 the Baath passed an autonomy law which would see the region governed by an elected legislative council (McDowell 2000 [1996]: 327–37). Realising that the law would set a dangerous precedent by allowing free and fair elections in Iraq, the Baath quickly amended it to clarify that the elections were in fact nominations, to be held under full Baathist supervision with all candidates to be approved by the central government. During the early 1970s, the KDP mouthpiece, *Al-Taakhi* ('Brotherhood'), wrote critically on several social and political topics making it understandably popular across Iraq. *Al-Taakhi* was especially vocal when it came to Kurdish nationalism, arguing that 'The Kurdish movement in Iraq is the movement of Kurds anywhere. It is a national

---

11　These translations are taken from Bengio's *Saddam's Word* (Bengio 1998: 39–40, 62–4).

movement, not any different from the national movements of other peoples' (*Al-Taakhi* 1972).[12] Such rhetoric put the Baath in the uncomfortable position of having to enter debates they would normally choose to avoid and they frequently used their own newspapers to rebuke and rebuff the rebellious northern Kurds.

When the KDP was defeated by the Iraqi army in 1975, the left-leaning urban members of the party had formed their own political organization, the Patriotic Union of Kurdistan (PUK) with Jalal Talabani[13] as their leader. However, the KDP quickly re-grouped under the leadership of Barzani's son, Massoud Barzani[14] and the rivalry between the two factions re-ignited (Stansfield 2007: 67–8, 79–86). During the Iran-Iraq War, the Kurds were caught in the cross-fire with Iran supplying sporadic military assistance and, by 1987, the Kurds again controlled much of northern Iraq. The Baath, fearing the re-emergence of an autonomous Kurdish region, waged a brutal attack on Kurdistan known as the *Al-Anfal* ('The Spoils of War'). The campaign saw an estimated 100,000 non-combatant Kurds killed, including, in 1988, Saddam's infamous authorization of the use of chemical weapons for the purpose of genocide, killing some 5,000 Kurdish civilians and maiming a further 7,000 in Halabja (Rose and Baravi 1998). Despite such egregious acts, the resolve of the Kurds remained strong and, when Iraq was defeated in Kuwait in 1991, the Kurds waged a *Rapareen* ('Uprising' in Kurdish) against the central government that resulted in many Kurdish deaths but also gave the people limited autonomy within the Iraqi state (Tripp 2000: 253–9). This newfound autonomy brought with it several elections, an independent parliament and the establishment of the Kurdish Regional Government (KRG) in 1992 (Anderson and Stansfield 2004: 155–83).

The following era in Kurdish history – from the end of the Gulf War in 1991 to the Iraq War of 2003 – saw Iraqi Kurdistan not only wrest autonomy from the central ABSP government, but also develop a significantly active public sphere. The region was home to a gamut of non-official political parties aside from the KDP and PUK including the Iraqi Kurdistan Toilers Party, the Kurdistan Socialist Democratic Party and the Communist Party of Iraqi Kurdistan. All of these parties controlled their own partisan media outlets and the media landscape swelled to include approximately 200 newspapers and magazines, two satellite TV stations, 20 local TV stations and 10 Radio stations. These media outlets, ranging from the sophisticated efforts of the KDP and PUK through to the tawdry ventures of smaller parties, were not only highly critical of Saddam and his Baghdad-based government, but also often asserted an alternate vision of Iraq that advocated democracy. Foremost among these were the newspapers *Brayati* ('Fraternity', run by the KDP), *Al-Ittihad* ('The United', PUK) and the regions first independent newspaper, *Hawlati* ('Citizen'), which was widely esteemed for its objectivity and

---

12   This translation is taken from Bengio's *Saddam's Word* (Bengio 1998: 116).

13   Jalal Talabani remains the leader of the PUK today and also serves as the State President of Iraq.

14   Today, Massoud Barzani is both the President of the Kurdish Regional Government (KRG) and he remains the leader of the KDP.

for its unreserved criticism of various Kurdish authority figures (Osman 2002). Iraqi Kurds also enjoyed unfettered access to satellite TV, while internet access was readily available at the region's three university campuses and the many internet cafés that dotted the cities. Collectively, the Kurdish public sphere from 1991 onwards was relatively free to debate Kurdish issues, to promote Kurdish history and culture, and to foster various civil society movements.

Despite the fact they have always been the majority in modern Iraq, the Shia have long been marginalized by the central Sunni-led government and consequently produced a number of active opposition movements. This arguably began with something of a Shia political renaissance that occurred in Iraq around the 1950s under the leadership of Grand Ayatollah Muhammad Baqr Al-Sadr who founded the enormously popular *Hizb Al-Dawah Islamiyya* ('The Islamic Calling', or more commonly referred to as *Dawah*, the 'Calling')[15] in 1957. Although Baqr Al-Sadr called for the establishment of an Islamic Republic, his vision was of a state ruled not by clerics, but by the combination of *Shariah* (Islamic law) and *Shura* (consultation), an important distinction which has long divided many Iraqi Shia scholars from their contemporaries in Iran (Abdul-Jabar 2002, Litvak 1998, Nakash 2003 [1994]). This line of thinking was to have a substantial impact on the Shia politics of the second half of the twentieth century. For its part, Dawah repeatedly challenged the central government, with several assassination attempts on Saddam Hussein and other senior ABSP members. Saddam banned the organization and, in 1980, he ordered the arrest, torture and execution of Baqr Al-Sadr for having supported the Shia-led Islamic Revolution in Iran (Anderson and Stansfield 2004: 124–7).

The persecution of Dawah by the Baathist state had several important consequences for Shia politics in Iraq, all of which have become very significant in the politics of the Re-Colonial era. During the Iran-Iraq War of the 1980s, many senior members of the party fled to Tehran and in 1982 formed the Supreme Council for the Islamic Revolution in Iraq (SCIRI)[16] under the leadership of senior Iraqi cleric, Ayatollah Mohammad Bakir Al-Hakim (Baram 1998: 52). From the safety of Iran, SCIRI was free to express their grievances with Saddam, setting up a number of radio stations that broadcast into Iraq and which spoke directly to the Iraqi Shia population, advocating the overthrow of the secular Baathist regime. They also reasoned rightly that a more democratic order in Iraq would provide considerable power to the majority Shia population.

As with the Kurds in the north, the southern Shia population also waged a considerable *Intifada* ('Uprising' in Arabic) at the conclusion of the Gulf War,

---

15   The Dawah party is currently led by former Iraqi Prime Minister, Ibrahim Al-Jaafari and its Secretary-General, Nuri Al-Maliki, is also the current Prime Minister of Iraq.

16   The SCIRI changed its name to the Supreme Islamic Iraqi Council (SIIC) in 2007 and is currently led by Sayyid Ammar Al-Hakim. Due to the fact that this study mostly concerns the period prior to the name change of SCIRI to SIIC, the party will be referred to as SCIRI throughout.

beginning with a series of anti-Baathist demonstrations that saw several party members killed in Basra (Bengio 1992: 7–8). Eventually, both the Dawah and SCIRI parties joined the fractured revolt and made the error of attempting to galvanize the mostly secular and leftist resistance behind their religious vision. This meant that the Shia uprising lost much of its initial impetus and when Saddam turned his forces against the rebels they were soon vanquished (Tripp 2000: 253–9). Nonetheless, both the SCIRI and Dawah parties continued to wield significant power across the Shia south. During the 1990s, the Dawah movement continued under the authority of Baqr Al-Sadr's brother-in-law, Grand Ayatollah Mohammad Sadiq Al-Sadr, a charismatic and militant leader who sought to revitalize the Shia and engage them in political agitation against the state. Saddam reacted predictably and had Sadiq Al-Sadr assassinated in 1999 (Ehrenberg, McSherry, Sanchez, and Sayej 2010: 317). Meanwhile SCIRI continued in Iran under the leadership of Hakim whose writings on democracy qualified SCIRI as a legitimate part of the US approved 'democratic opposition'. A statement issued by the Ayatollah in May 2001 demanded 'the humanitarian and legal rights for all Iraqi people … those rights that the regime has confiscated without distinguishing between the Sunnis and Shiites, and between Arabs and Turkomen, for the regime has usurped all the rights of the Iraqi people' (Al-Hakim 2001: 319).

In addition to the writings of these key religious figures, throughout the 1990s and in the lead up to the 2003 invasion, a number of expatriate Iraqi Shia began calling attention to the widespread suffering of their brothers and sisters in Iraq, especially in the wake of the massacre that followed the intifada of 1991. In July 2002 three prominent Shia expatriates, Mowaffaq Al-Rubaie, Ali Allawi and Shaib Al-Hakim, penned a manifesto entitled the 'Declaration of the Shia of Iraq' which states:

> Iraq's political crisis … is entirely due to the conduct of an overtly sectarian authority determined to pursue a policy of discrimination solely for its own interests of control, a policy that has ultimately led to the total absence of political and cultural liberties and the worse forms of dictatorship (Al-Rubaie, Allawi, and Al-Hakim 2002: 313–4).

It goes on to argue that 'the sectarian issue in Iraq will not be solved by the imposition of a vengeful Shia sectarianism on the state and society' and articulates the Shia's firm commitment to national unity and aversion to the creation of a separate Shia state (Al-Rubaie, et al. 2002: 314). Their demands included: 'The abolition of dictatorship and its replacement with democracy', the 'Creation of a democratic parliamentary constitutional order' with 'Full respect for the national, ethnic, religious, and sectarian identities of all Iraqis,' and the 'Reconstruction of, and support for, the main elements of a civil society' (Al-Rubaie, et al. 2002: 315).

Opposition to Saddam's leadership was not limited to those who resisted him on the basis of their Kurdish ethnicity or Shia religiosity. Many of the dissident ex-Baathists and members of the armed forces began to form various opposition parties of their own, many of which were backed by the US and UK. These include the *Al-*

Wifaq Al-Watani Al-Iraqi ('The Iraqi National Accord' or INA), founded in 1991 and headed by Dr Iyad Allawi[17] and the Iraqi National Congress (INC), founded in 1992 and led by Dr Ahmed Chalabi.[18] Both of these parties controlled a handful of media which issued blatant anti-Saddam, pro-democracy propaganda. They sought to give a common voice to Iraq's divergent opposition groups, to erode Saddam's support from within Iraq, to promote alternative heads of state (Allawi or Chalabi), to work in the favour of US regional interests and to mobilize dissent against the incumbent regime. Their central platform was to usurp the regime and establish respect for 'human rights and rule of law within a constitutional, democratic, and pluralistic Iraq' (Katzman 2000: 2). They both waged a number of successful terrorist attacks on the ABSP before Saddam reacted by having several senior members executed and by all but crushing the rebellion (Baram 1998: 55–7, Stansfield 2007: 145–8).

On a smaller scale, throughout the Baathist period, the once powerful ICP continued to publish their newspaper *Tariq Al-Shab* ('The Way of the People') and their theoretical journal *Al-Thaqafa Al-Jadida* ('The New Culture'). These newspapers enabled them to be very critical of the regime, even criticizing it for the 'total lack of democratic freedom within Iraq' (Salucci 2005: 61). Several important pieces appeared in *Al-Thaqafa Al-Jadida* in 1992, including one by Ali Ibrahim which argued that, for Iraqis, democracy was no longer 'an abstract term but a specific political structure expressed in a supremacy of the law, a multi-party system, parliamentary life and organization, press and party freedoms' (A. Ibrahim 1992: 17). For Sad Salih, democracy was central to the ICP's broader agenda of 'mobilizing the mutual cooperation among the party's political, cultural and popular organizations in the Arab world for the cause of democracy and the respect of human rights' (Salih 1992: 20). Lutfi Hatim agreed; for him 'democracy should be the most important component of the Party' and

> When the time comes, the pragmatic position of the Iraqi Communist Party today will give the Iraqi democratic movement the position of being an active Arab force for the creation of a democratic Arab solidarity which will restore self-confidence to the Arab citizen ... and which will increase the demand for democratic rule and peace, based on the rejection of military aggression, respect of neighbours, and destruction of military bases (Hatim 1992: 74).[19]

---

17   Allawi was a member of the US-installed Iraqi Interim Governing Council from 2003 and later served as Interim Prime Minister from June 2004 until April 2005. More recently, Allawi's secular nationalist *Al-Iraqiyya* list won the most seats in Iraq's 2010 elections but he was not able to form a government.

18   Chalabi supplied suspect information to the Bush administration regarding Iraq's alleged stockpile of WMD (J. Klein 2005: 25). He later served as Iraq's Deputy Prime Minister throughout much of 2005, but failed to win a single seat following the December 2005 election.

19   The translations of *Al-Thaqafa Al-Jadida* found in this paragraph are from Tareq Ismael's *The Rise and Fall of the Communist Party of Iraq* (Ismael 2008: 279–80).

There is a final category of counter discourse that was critical in resisting and critiquing the Baathist regime, that from among the large expatriate Iraqi community. While this is not the place for a thorough discussion of the varying locations and complex politics of the Iraqi Diaspora, it is worth mentioning that many of Iraq's most noted activists, poets, writers, artists and intellectuals fled Iraq during the Baathist epoch. From the safety of exile, they found new and larger audiences within Iraq, across the Arab world and among the international community. They felt free to criticize Saddam and to advocate democracy and a whole collection of cross-sectarian, cross-political and cross-religious political opinions emerged.

Arguably the epicentre of Iraqi dissident opposition was London, where several important expatriate papers were produced including the organ of the Union of Iraqi Democrats, *Al-Dimuqrati* ('The Democracy') and the Shia-run *Al-Tayyar Al-Jadid* ('The New Movement'). Another important paper was the highly esteemed independent pan-Arab daily, *Azzaman* ('The Times') which was founded in London in 1997 by Saad Bazzaz[20] and quickly grew to include international editions issued from Bahrain and North Africa (Zengerle 2002). Many Iraqi expatriates and dissidents also chose to write for other journals such as the London-based Pan-Arab daily of record, *Al-Hayat* ('The Life'). In the months leading up to the invasion of Iraq in 2003, many Iraqis spoke with renewed confidence about the tyranny of the Baath and began to discuss the options facing the nation beyond his oppression. One such Iraqi writer, Jabbar Yassin, felt free enough to air his grievances with the 'bloody political machine' of Saddam Hussein and 'the cultural genocide being carried out in Iraq' (Yassin 2002). He also raised pertinent questions about the future of Iraq and the role of Iraqi intellectuals in the formation of 'a republic of tolerance' (Yassin 2002). Another Iraqi dissident, Bahr Al Uloom claimed that the re-building of Iraq from the ruins of the Baath regime would require a robust and egalitarian democracy premised on a constitution that included respect and rights for all of Iraq's diverse peoples, free and fair elections, and the adoption of an appropriate legislative and constitutional framework. He concluded by stating that, while all Iraqis have common interest in seeing 'the demise of Saddam Hussein's regime and the establish[ment of] a democratic system', it is Iraqis which 'hold the ultimate responsibility for building their own country' (Al-Uloom 2002).

One particularly prominent Iraqi expatriate was Ghassan Al-Atiyyah who had once served as a Professor of Politics at Baghdad University and had worked for the United Nations. From London, he published the *Malaf Al-Iraqi* ('Iraq File') and wrote several articles for *Al-Hayat* as well as Middle Eastern English-language papers such as Beirut's *The Daily Star*. In one such article, Al-Atiyyah advocated 'democratic change' in Iraq and openly discussed the 'choosing of a post-Saddam

---

20   Saad Bazzaz is the former editor of the Baathist *Al-Jumhuriyya* and later he was the manager of the Iraqi National News Agency and the Ministry of Information, overseeing the production and broadcasting of all Iraqi radio and television (Zengerle 2002).

regime' which would bring about a 'pro-Western and democratic Iraq' (Al-Atiyyah 2002b). In another article, Al-Atiyyah engages with broader questions about Arab democracy arguing that the central problem with it is

> the way Western powers dealt with the region [they directly] cultivated and consolidated undemocratic practices. This not only took place during the Colonial era, but continued even after the Arab states gained independence, when Britain and the United States – the two most influential global players in the Middle East – made fighting communism their number one priority in the region, at the expense of democracy (Al-Atiyyah 2002a).

In another critical article he poses the question, 'What would Iraq be like without Saddam?'. He then moves forward to lambast the Iraqi opposition for its petty divides and rivalries arguing 'that it is precisely because there is no common vision of what a post-Saddam Iraq should look like that the current regime has been able to survive so long' (Al-Atiyyah 2002c). He adds that Iraq's political elites have routinely marginalized the will of ordinary Iraqis in favour of prioritizing their own agenda, that they have failed to draft an appropriate and liberal political framework for post-Saddam Iraq, and that their shortcomings may well pave the way for a new military dictatorship to rise from the ashes of the Baathist era. His searing indictment of Iraqi opposition politics and his insight into the looming political melee in Iraq beyond the US invasion conclude with words that ring painfully true a decade later:

> Achieving democracy requires a readiness to compromise and an acceptance of wide participation. There is an opportunity today for creating a democratic future for Iraq. But this will require that senior opposition figures demonstrate leadership … Waiting for America to establish democracy in Iraq on behalf of the opposition is a dangerous gamble. America wants to have an effective and stable government in power in Baghdad that doesn't threaten its neighbours. Democracy is not an American priority (Al-Atiyyah 2002c).

Conclusion

In discussing Post-Colonial Iraq it is important to note that, despite the withdrawal of the British and the usurpation of the Hashemite monarchy, Iraq did not emerge as a genuine democracy with legitimate opposition parties, a functioning parliament and a free press. While many of Iraq's Post-Colonial regimes promised such institutions, these were generally empty promises designed to gain political advantage rather than broaden participation. Similarly, Iraq's media industry, so often used for authoritarian purposes, served more as the duty-bound propaganda machine of each ensuing regime than the watchdog of a functioning democracy. There can be no defending the hegemony of Arif, Bakr or Saddam, each of whom, in their own way, brought Iraq closer to models of governance aligned with notions of Oriental despotism.

Of all Iraq's Post-Colonial regimes, the Baath was the most adept at manipulating the national discourses of democracy to their advantage. By doing so, however, Saddam effectively created the environ in which a wide range of subversive and clandestine political movements emerged both within and outside Iraq. It is important not to over-determine the extent to which these various opposition groups were democratic by any definition of the term. Similarly, it cannot be ignored that certain Shia, Kurdish and other political parties have proven themselves very capable of utilizing the rhetoric and institutions of democracy in their own quests for power (especially since 2003, see the following chapter). Nonetheless, at the very least this complex web of oppositional politics and their respective media outlets indicates that, to paraphrase Foucault, a complex matrix of intersecting discourses arose in opposition to the centralized power structures and constructed knowledge of the dominant episteme (Foucault 2005 [1969]). Whether premised on ethnicity, religiosity or political dissent, these opposition movements constituted a lively public sphere that asserted alternative visions of a democratic Iraqi state.

Chapter 6

Occupation and Democracy in Re-Colonial Iraq

The images we possess of the current political situation in Iraq are somewhat distorted. To be sure, kidnapping, political violence and sabotage of oil facilities are ongoing and present a serious threat to political stability ... However, there is another reality that has been largely ignored by the Western media. Very little mention has been made of the myriad examples of Iraqis who, since the fall of Saddam and the Baath, have been actively involved in civic life – such as establishing municipal councils, publishing newspapers and journals, and forming artistic organizations – and who are committed to working for democratic change.

Davis 2005a: 241

The Discourses of Democracy and the Re-Colonisation of Iraq

On 17 March 2003, President Bush addressed the United States and the world, offering Saddam Hussein an ultimatum: he and his sons were to leave Iraq within 48 hours or the coalition would launch its 'pre-emptive strike' (Bush 2003a). Despite the fact that by the eve of the war the notion of a military intervention in Iraq was demonstrably unpopular across the globe, Bush fulfilled his promise, stating on 19 March 2003 that

> At this hour, American and coalition forces are in the early stages of military operations to disarm Iraq, to free its people and to defend the world from grave danger. On my orders, coalition forces have begun striking selected targets of military importance to undermine Saddam Hussein's ability to wage war (Bush 2003b).

However, when it was discovered that the initial motives for entering Iraq – Saddam's alleged stockpile of WMD and his links to Al-Qaeda – were grievous intelligence errors, the Bush administration began to spin the war's *rasion d'etre* and redefine the parameters of victory. A central tenet of this approach was to begin speaking about democracy as if it had always been one of the aims of the war itself. In a speech presented before the National Endowment for Democracy in November 2003, President Bush claimed that although bringing democracy to Iraq would be a

> massive and difficult undertaking – it is worth our effort, it is worth our sacrifice, because we know the stakes. The failure of Iraqi democracy would embolden terrorists around the world, increase dangers to the American people, and

extinguish the hopes of millions in the region. Iraqi democracy will succeed – and that success will send forth the news, from Damascus to Teheran – that freedom can be the future of every nation. The establishment of a free Iraq at the heart of the Middle East will be a watershed event in the global democratic revolution (Bush 2003c).

The notion that the US could use its enormous influence and military power to not only pre-emptively attack independent nation-states and overthrow existing regimes, but also to install democratic governments in their place is exclusive to the former administration and has come to be termed the 'Bush doctrine' (Jervis 2003). In addition, the Bush administration also held the overly simplistic view that by installing democracy in Iraq they would enable a 'domino effect' across the region where autocratic regimes would have no choice but to convert to robust democracies. In a sense, the Bush doctrine can be seen to be reminiscent of the Colonial era in that it claims to be a civilizing force aimed at liberating the barbaric non-Western world from Oriental despotism. It also taps into the discourse of Western democracy by asserting that the United States and the broader Western world is the legitimate legatee of democracy and has the right to democratize – under military force and occupation if necessary – the non-Western world.

That Iraq could become a democracy was widely ridiculed by the international news media, however, as well as by prominent academics, senior policy-makers and bureaucrats. Senior civil servants who worked with the Coalition Provisional Authority (CPA) which governed Iraq during the earliest days of the occupation expressed very serious doubts about Iraq as a potential democracy. These included eminent figures such as Rory Stewart, who, in 2003–04, was the deputy coordinator of Maysan and later a senior advisor in Dhi Qar. In his *Occupational Hazards: My Time Governing in Iraq*, Stewart suggests that Iraq is particularly unique in the broader story of human civilization because of its lack of democratic potential. He writes:

> I had never believed that mankind, unless overawed by a strong government, would fall inevitably into violent chaos. Societies were orderly, I thought, because human cultures were orderly … But Maysan made me reconsider. A secure and functioning government was not emerging of its own accord (Stewart 2006: 81).

Here, Stewart seems to suggest that Iraq is a nation predisposed to violence, chaos and despotism and incapable of tolerance, inclusion and peace. The further implication here is that these problems are so unparalleled that one could even question the humanity of the Iraqi people. If 'mankind' or 'human cultures' are orderly and peaceful, and Iraq is naturally violent and disorderly, then the conclusion must be that this is not a human culture at all (Isakhan 2010a).

Similar sentiments emerged in a great deal of scholarly literature that attempted to explain why the establishment of democracy will at least be difficult, if not impossible in Iraq. In 2003 Andreas Wimmer ominously warned that 'the seeds of democracy may have difficulties to germinate in the sandy soils of Iraq' (Wimmer 2003: 111). Others claimed that Iraq has 'little tradition of power-sharing' (Byman 2003a: 57) or 'experience with democracy' (Benomar 2004: 95). There was said to be no 'society in Iraq to turn into a democracy' and that the people had not 'learned democratic practices' (Byman 2003a: 59). Iraq had been a nation of 'uneasy order maintained through rations of oppression and fear' (Benomar 2004: 95). Daniel Byman offered a list of factors that he believed would inhibit the spread of democracy in Iraq including, among others, 'a lack of cohesive identity to unify Iraq's different communities … bellicose elites who pursue adventurism abroad and whip up tension at home, a poorly organized political leadership, and a lack of a history of democracy' (Byman 2003b: 49). What is particularly interesting here is that these scholars chose to use words like 'tradition', 'society', 'identity' and 'history' to suggest that Iraq has long been home to a stagnant culture that is inhospitable to diversity, debate and difference.

Along similar lines, the Western media coverage of the democratization of Iraq not only emphasized the ongoing violence and the disagreements between Iraq's various ethno-religious groups, but also argued that Iraq simply lacked the social and political prerequisites necessary to build towards a democratic form of government (Isakhan 2007b, 2008a). Once again, Iraq was seen as 'a society riven by centuries of religious and ethnic conflicts with little or no experience with representative institutions' (Kissinger and Shultz 2005). Iraqis were 'not used to democracy … [with] little tradition of tolerance' (*Australian* 2006); they were trapped in a barbaric world in which 'violence remains the more pragmatic way to achieve justice and to protect one's interests' (Clemons 2005). This uncritical and careless adoption of Orientalist ideologies is clearly problematic and stems from the notion that even when given democracy and freedom, the people of the Middle East are too backward and barbaric to embrace a future free of tyranny and despotism. Here, any examples of collective forms of government, egalitarian societies or democratic political movements within Iraqi history are all but eschewed in favour of clichés of despotism, ineptitude and violence.

The convergence of such bureaucratic, scholarly and media discourse in the Re-Colonial period is startling in its familiarity. It mirrors and indeed draws upon the vast array of discourses that were employed in the Colonial period in Iraq and elsewhere, utilizing the same language of Oriental backwardness and the need for Western dominance. This is not altogether surprising given that the effort to invade and occupy Iraq cannot be wholly disentangled from a Colonial project which saw the West only begrudgingly relent its subjugation of the non-European world during the last two centuries. Or perhaps the project of Colonialism should be understood not so much as having come to an end (a direct affront to the curious prefix of 'post' in 'post-Colonial studies'), but as having momentarily subsided as Western powers regrouped and devised new economic, military, and ideological mechanisms of power. As several scholars have recently noted, the invasion and occupation of Iraq might best be described as ushering in what is referred to here as Re-Colonial Iraq (2003–11) (Gopal and Lazarus 2006, Gregory 2004,

Lazarus 2006, Spencer 2006). Such theoretical work was pre-empted by Tariq Ali who argued that the invasion and occupation of Iraq not only represents the re-colonisation of this particular sovereign nation-state by Western powers, but also marked a return to the broader Colonial project 'that was disrupted by the twentieth century and is now back on course' (Ali 2003: 185).

As the central aim of the project being undertaken here is to problematize and scrutinize Orientalist discourse via a closer examination of Iraq's history, this chapter seeks to re-interpret the post-Saddam period and the alternative discourses of democracy emanating from within Re-Colonial Iraq. It builds on the preceding chapters by detailing the complex public sphere of the post-Saddam era and points to the inclusive nature of the positive developments that have occurred across the nation since 2003. The first part discusses the post-Saddam media landscape which has played a positive role in covering the nation's difficult transition to democracy. The second part of this chapter documents and examines the Iraqi people's exercise of their democratic right to protest and the influence these protests have had on the politics of the post-Saddam era. The chapter concludes that Iraqi citizens who play an active role in their own governance and participate in democratic mechanisms such as elections and mass demonstrations are helping to create a more robust democracy.

Elections and the Public Sphere

With the fall of Baghdad on 9 April 2003, Iraq's media environment was changed forever. Almost overnight it transformed from being Saddam's tightly controlled propaganda machine to one of the most diverse media environments on earth. By the middle of 2003, Iraq was home to more than 20 radio stations, around 15 Iraqi-owned television stations, with approximately 200 Iraqi-owned and run newspapers published across the country. Even smaller regional towns such as Najaf boasted more than 30 newspapers in a city of only 300,000 people. Most of these new television stations, radio stations and newspapers were started by the seemingly countless political parties, religious factions and/or ethnic groups of post-Saddam Iraq, each of them jostling for support and legitimacy in the nation's struggle from despotism to democracy (Cochrane 2006). As Ibrahim Al-Marashi points out, the Iraqi media sector has witnessed the rise of various ethno-religious sectarian and highly partisan 'media empires' which have evolved into 'quite a pervasive element in Iraq's Fourth Estate' (Al-Marashi 2007: 104). Foremost among these are those controlled by the major Kurdish political parties (the PUK and the KDP) and the Kurdistan Regional Government (KRG), those controlled by the two largest Shia parties, Dawah and SCIRI, and Shia religio-political movements like the Sadr Trend, as well as those owned by key Sunni, Christian, Turkomen and other ethno-religious groups. There are also those controlled by smaller political parties like the ICP, the INA and the INC. These publications have been joined by those which claim to be free of any specific political, religious or sectarian allegiance but which desire to report the news in a professional and objective manner.[1]

Several problems have accompanied Iraq's divergent, ad-hoc and highly volatile media landscape. Although it is beyond the scope of this study to detail each of these, it is worth mentioning that some of the more serious factors include: the absence of an appropriate legal framework; the ongoing dangers faced by journalists whose death toll continues to climb;[2] the uneven quality and dubious professionalism of some media organizations; and the interference in Iraq's media by various regional powers (Saudi Arabia and Iran), the occupying forces (particularly the US and UK), as well as by the Iraqi government and the KRG (Isakhan 2009b). Despite these manifold problems, there are several reasons to be optimistic about the contemporary media landscape of Iraq. First among these is the fact that the Iraqi media can be seen to have played an overwhelmingly positive role – despite their inherent biases – in fostering the emergence of a renewed public sphere in Iraq. They have been instrumental in serving the number of functions that a free press is expected to perform in a nascent democratic order like post-Saddam Iraq.

This role began as far back as February 2004, when the Iraqi media began to offer its views on the Interim Governing Council's (IGC) deliberations over a temporary constitution. In a plethora of opinion pieces and news articles across Iraq's divergent media, the nation's journalists were generally critical of US involvement. This included interference from the head of the CPA, Lewis Paul Bremer, especially his attempt to avoid any reference to Islamic law in the wording of the constitution itself. Others implored the IGC to avoid the temptation to skew the wording of the constitution in favour of their own interests or those of their particular ethno-political group. As Abd-Al-Munim Al-Aasam opined in *Azzaman*,

> All those who have gathered around the conference table to discuss the draft
> interim constitution … would do well to rule out any possibility of coming up
> with anything tailored so as to be in full harmony with their own views. They are
> duty-bound to put aside the unworthy ploy of threatening to rouse the public into
> civil war in a bid to have their own ideas incorporated in the constitution. Any

1   Earlier work by the author includes a more detailed overview of the post-Saddam Iraqi media landscape (Isakhan 2006: 136–46, 2008b, 2009b: 10–2), including a set of detailed tables that document the most significant outlets (Isakhan 2009a: 257–75).

2   Iraq remains one of the most dangerous nations for the press as is demonstrated by the Annual Report of Paris-based *Reporters Sans Frontieres* ('Reporters Without Borders') which designated Iraq as having a 'Very Serious Situation' in terms of press freedom since 2003 until it was downgraded in the 2010 report to a 'Difficult Situation' ('Annual Report and Press Freedom Index' 2009, 2010). As with the death toll of the overall Iraq War, however, the number of Iraqi journalists killed since 2003 increases daily making reliable and up-to-date figures difficult to ascertain. Arguably the best, and certainly the most chilling, accounts of civilian casualties in Iraq also concern the coalition efforts to cover up the carnage (Hil and Wilson 2007, Otterman and Hil 2010).

such practice would run counter to the reality of the political, ethnic, religious
and sectarian diversity that is characteristic of Iraq (Al-Aasam 2004).

When campaigning for the January 2005 election began on 15 December 2004,
information about it almost immediately 'permeated every part of the Iraqi media,
providing at least the show of a nascent democracy in action' (Usher 2005b).
Throughout the campaign period Iraqi radio stations, newspapers, television
channels and websites played a critical role in not only promoting certain political
parties and their stated ideologies and agendas, but also in encouraging Iraqis
to defy the insurgent and terrorist threats and take part in the election (Dawisha
2005b: 38). Throughout the electoral campaign the German government funded
a daily half hour broadcast that covered various aspects of the election. They
selected 25 young Iraqi journalists (all under the age of 30) and provided training
for them in neighbouring Jordan. These young journalists then returned to Iraq to
seek out stories relating to the election which were broadcast on Iraqi stations such
as the independent *Radio Dijla* ('Tigris'), and the KDP's *Voice of Iraqi Kurdistan*,
as well as being made available for download on the internet. Over the course
of the campaign these short broadcasts included profiles of politicians, political
parties and the various coalitions that emerged in post-Saddam Iraq as well as
comment by foreign election observers (Usher 2004). In addition to these half
hour broadcasts *Radio Dijla* also ran its regular programming which encouraged
Iraqis to phone-in and offer their opinion on the elections as well as quiz shows
that posed questions such as: 'Which is better, a pre-set democratic model or one
that is in harmony with Iraq's culture?' (Radio Dijla cited in Usher 2005b).

Iraq's leading television stations, the state-run *Al-Iraqiya*, and the privately
owned *Al-Sharqiya* ('The Eastern One') and *Al-Diyar* ('The Homeland'), led the
domestic television market. They screened campaign advertisements ranging from
the techno-savvy efforts of groups such as Allawi's Iraqi List and the coalition of
Shia groups known as the United Iraqi Alliance, through to the hackneyed efforts
of the smaller parties (Usher 2005b). All three of these channels worked in the
public interest by disseminating information regarding the curfews, restrictions
and security measures that had been placed across the nation in the lead up to the
election. *Al-Iraqiya* aired statements by Iraq's religious leaders urging Iraqis to
vote and provided the kind of access to the political elite rarely seen in even the
most highly esteemed Western media (Misterek 2005). For example, it broadcast
a weekly phone-in programme hosted by the incumbent Iraqi Prime Minister, Iyad
Allawi, who answered unscreened calls from Iraqis keen to discuss various issues
with their leader and air their frustrations (Usher 2005b).

As the election drew closer, Iraq's print media played an increasingly important
role in raising and discussing several key issues related to the forthcoming
election. The independent *Al-Dustour* published a collection of in-depth articles
including those critical of the incumbent Iraqi government, those which provided
details of some of Iraq's various smaller political factions, those which countered
rumours about the election, those which discussed the thorny issue of religion and

politics and those which called for peace and unity (Al-Shaykh 2005a, 2005c, 2005e, 2005f, 2005g, Jamil 2005, Zaydan 2005a, 2005b). On the issue of whether or not the elections should be postponed, a wide range of views and opinions were expressed in papers as diverse *Azzaman*, the INC's *Al-Mutamar*, Iraqi Hezbollah's *Al-Bayynah* ('The Evidence'), the Dawah party's *Al-Bayan* ('The Dispatch' or 'The Manifesto') and the eponymous *Dawah* party paper, *Al-Dawah* (Al-Muqdadi 2005, Al-Pachachi 2005, Al-Raziqi 2005, Al-Shimmari 2005, Al-Ubaydi 2005, Humadi 2005, Khudayyir 2005, Rasul 2005b). Meanwhile, Kurdish papers such as the independent *Hawlati*, the PUK's *Kurdistani Nuwe* ('New Kurdistan') and the KDP's *Xebat* ('Struggle'), ran a collection of stories both before and after the election that detailed the various Kurdish concerns and developments, such as the issue of federation, Kurdish regional elections, unity among the many different people of Kurdistan and the future status of Kirkuk (*Hawlati* 2005a, 2005b, *Kurdistani Nuwe*, 2005a, 2005b, *Xebat* 2005a, 2005b).

The Iraqi press also fostered a lively and diverse discussion on the merits and tenets of democracy. Various Shia backed organs, such as Dawah's *Al-Bayan* and SCIRI's *Al-Adala* ('The Justice'), published several articles that were often unrestrained in their optimism. Of these, the Shia papers are adamant that the Iraqi people must not miss this great opportunity to 'pave the way for the rise of the rule of law, in which democracy, freedom, security, and sovereignty will prevail' (Al-Juwari 2005). As if to capture this enthusiasm and summarize these sentiments, an editorial which appeared just days before the election in *Al-Bayan* stated:

> The countdown has begun for a great, historic day in the life of our people. On this day, the people will master their own destiny and future when they will select their representatives to the constitutional assembly that will draft the permanent constitution and choose an elected government expressing their will and working to achieve their hopes and aspirations. The responsibility for making this election a success does not rest only with the government or the electoral commission that will supervise and ensure a fair vote. Rather, it depends, above all, on our people through their broad participation, with all their sects, ethnic groups, political forces and social categories. We believe the high turnout will be the most telling response to the terrorists and killers who seek to confiscate Iraqi people's will. With it, they will tell those terrorist they are much more stronger than their criminal means (*Al-Bayan* 2005b).

Similar sentiments can be found across the pages of the INC's *Al-Mutamar*, where writers such as Shaykh Ali Abd-Al-Husayn Kammunah implored the citizens of Iraq to take part in the 'great democratic process for which we have waited long and offered dear sacrifices' (Kammunah 2005). Similarly, Nabil Al-Qassab argued that the election would foster Iraqi unity and 'guarantee the rights of all sects, ethnic groups, and nationalities' (Al-Qassab 2005). *Al-Mutamar* seems to have been such a strong advocate of the elections that it appeared to view them as something of a silver bullet, capable of rectifying all of Iraq's complex problems. Consider the words of Salman Al-Shammari who wrote that

> not only are the Iraqi elections a positive step on the path leading to shortening the occupation's life and solving the political problem in Iraq and a positive and good initiative to boost and deepen the principles of democracy, plurality, and rule of law in the country, but they are also the key and main way to get rid of the security and economic crises that Iraq suffers from (Al-Shammari 2005).

The independent press of Iraq seemed to largely follow his line of argument. Much of the coverage in *Al-Dustour* emphasized the need for national unity, with Ibrahim Zaydan opining that 'In order to build a pluralist, democratic Iraq, as we hope, we have to open the doors for participation to everybody because Iraq is home to all Iraqis, rather than to a particular sect, ethnic group, tribe or religion' (Zaydan 2005b). To some degree this was echoed by the chief editor of *Al-Dustour*, Basim Al-Shaykh, who claimed that Iraq needed to seek 'God's help and rise up as one man with their hands united to place the voting card deciding their destiny in the ballot box holding their aspirations for tomorrow' (Al-Shaykh 2005b). However, *Al-Dustour*'s coverage also came with a stern warning to those who would manipulate the Iraqi elections or the broader body politic to suit their own ends. 'Let it be known from now on' begins another piece by Al-Shaykh,

> that the average Iraqi will tolerate no mandate other than that dictated by his own conscience. Advocates of fake heavenly agendas had better steer away from Iraq and Iraqis, for we have had enough at the hands of opportunists touting bright religious and nationalist slogans. Let them seek their fortune elsewhere, for we have made a solemn vow to root out anyone stalking our beloved Iraq, regardless of their race or colour and no matter how dazzlingly bright their banners may be (Al-Shaykh 2005c).

It is not surprising that the various independent papers, as well as those controlled by the Shia and Kurdish parties or the INC and INA were relatively optimistic about the January elections, given that they each had much to gain politically. Less optimistic were the Sunni journals which represented the increasingly disenfranchised minority which had ruled Iraq since its inception in the 1920s. A little over a week before the election, the Sunni organ of the Association of Muslim Scholars, *Al-Basair* ('The Insight'), expressed its concerns regarding the forthcoming election which included the 'insufficient legal and technical preparations, lack of security, the occupation forces' total domination of security, and most important of all, they aim at legitimizing the occupation of Iraq' (*Al-Basair* 2005). This issue is raised in several articles in the same issue of *Al-Basair*. Prominent Iraqi writer Karim Latif Al-Dulaymi referred to the Iraqi elections as 'a poisonous honey' which has been 'given by the US to Iraq in order to legitimize the occupation of the country' (Al-Dulaymi 2005).

In terms of the watch-dog function of the media, the well-respected Kurdish newspaper *Hawlati* took the unrivalled step of publishing the list of candidates on the Democratic Patriotic Alliance of Kurdistan in the lead up to the election itself. What made *Hawlati*'s move significant was that not only had no other media published such a list due to security concerns, but also that about a dozen Kurdish candidates were former Baathists (Glantz 2005). Other newspapers waited until after the election to raise their concerns. In mid-February 2005 Iraq's *Azzaman* published an unofficial list of the candidates elected to the Iraqi National Assembly while several other newspapers continued to publish their concerns about the make-up of the post-election assembly (*Al-Adala* 2005, *Al-Bayan* 2005a, *Al-Mutamar* 2005b, *Azzaman* 2005). Iraq's highbrow independent paper *Al-Mada* ('The View') controversially accused the Iraqi Council of Commissioners of having pre-defined the number of seats and percentages for political entities which would go on to form the National Assembly following the election (*Al-Mada* 2005b).

Despite such serious concerns, immediately following the January election much of Iraq's diverse media landscape expressed almost unanimous praise for the conduct of the elections and their significance for the future of the nation. The jubilance of many Iraqi journalists was splashed across the pages of several important newspapers (*Al-Bayan* 2005d, *Al-Bayynah* 2005, *Al-Mada* 2005a, *Al-Mutamar* 2005a, Al-Sanduq 2005, *Baghdad* 2005). As just one example, *Al-Bayan* printed the following comment on the election,

> It was a historic day in the life of our people. On this day, Iraqis taught the peoples of the region a great lesson in democracy. The first winner and victor in these elections is, beyond any doubt, the Iraqi people. This, in itself, is quite enough for all those who contributed to writing this national epic to feel proud. It is, indeed, a remarkable feat added to Iraqi civilization records (*Al-Bayan* 2005c).

However, it did not take long for the Iraqi press to begin lobbying the newly elected Iraqi government regarding various concerns and issues which it saw as central to the success of the new Iraq (*Al-Bayynah* 2005, Al-Tikriti 2005, Rasul 2005a). What Iraq needed now, according to Rida Al-Zahir of *Tariq Al-Shab*, was 'national accord among the political forces that believe in democracy to build the country' (Al-Zahir 2005). This would not only 'see an end to the US occupation' as Riyadh Abu Mulhim put it in an article published by *Al-Mutamar*, but enable 'the constitutional institutions required to guarantee that Iraqis will get the sort of government they yearn for, free of sectarian bias and representative of the nation's cultural makeup' (Mulhim 2005). Another major concern of Iraqi journalists was that of the culture of corruption that had been pervasive throughout government institutions under the Baathist regime (Al-Baldawi 2005, *Al-Mashriq* 2005, Zaki 2005). On this issue *Al-Dustour*'s Basim Al-Shaykh implored the new administration to 'purge government departments and security offices of the lingering corrupt practices inherited from the past' (Al-Shaykh 2005d).

This close monitoring of Iraqi state politics by the nation's media was to continue at the time of the country-wide referendum which effectively ratified the Iraqi Constitution in October 2005. Not only did the Iraqi media, across its rich array of formats and persuasions, play a critical role in disseminating the draft constitution in the lead up to the referendum, but television stations such as *Al-Sharqiya* also hosted a phone-in programme to discuss the finer details of the document, while various newspapers discussed the constitution's merits and drawbacks (Al-Ansari 2005, *Al-Shahid* 2005). One of Iraq's more influential Islamist papers, *Al-Adala*, also featured an editorial which argued that the ratification of the constitution was itself indicative of the fact that

> Iraqis have defeated their enemies: terrorists, dark forces and those who dream of a return of the unfair equation. What has been achieved for Iraq would not have seen the light of day had it not been for the sacrifices by Iraqis and their friends. The time of coercion and pressure has gone for good, and the time of freedom and democracy has come. Democracy and freedom have been created in Iraq by all the honourable men in the world who have stood by Iraq in its ordeal, offering all that is dear to them (Khlayf 2005).

In December 2005, as Iraqis prepared to nominate a permanent government, Iraq's media landscape once again buzzed with the excitement of the looming election. Newspapers across Iraq were awash with political advertising and long articles explained the complexity of Iraq's various political coalitions as well as providing details of polling stations and how to vote. Iraq's television stations took the unprecedented step of offering free political advertising, which immediately saw a series of non-partisan and well-produced, if rather emotive, short films screened which encouraged Iraqis to participate in the election. Less emotive were the government-funded advertisements which also gave details of how to vote as well as the location of polling booths. The free airtime meant that many of Iraq's smaller minorities and political factions were able to broadcast their own amateur advertisements, although they did complain that they were not given equal airtime and were simply unable to compete with the larger parties and coalitions (Usher 2005a). Despite such complaints, the fact that every legitimate political party in Iraq had access to free airtime on the nation's state-run television channel indicates the degree to which the Iraqi media served as a locus where the general public had ready access to a diverse range of political opinion, policy and debate (Dawisha and Diamond 2006: 97).

Despite the free advertising, most of Iraq's TV stations took a decidedly biased stance in the lead up to the elections. For example, both *Al-Sharqiya* and *Al-Iraqiya*, which had previously been lauded for their professional and objective reporting, were unwavering in their support of the incumbent government of Iyad Allawi and his ministers, repeatedly airing his arty black-and-white commercials (Al-Marashi 2007: 109, Usher 2005a). The SCIRI-owned *Al-Furat* on the other hand, revealed its deeply partisan nature by refusing to offer free airtime or screen paid advertisements from political parties other than the United Iraqi Alliance (which was a reincarnation of the January 2005 Unified Iraqi Coalition) (Al-Marashi 2007: 109, Usher 2005a). The Sunni parties also managed to have a voice in the December elections via their newly established *Baghdad* satellite channel. Having suffered the consequences of boycotting the January election, many of the various Sunni political movements formed the Al-Tawafuq Front in 2005 and quickly set about establishing the channel. In a bid to counter the clearly partisan nature of their rival stations, *Baghdad* only featured advertisements for the Al-Tawafuq Front in the lead up to the December election (Al-Marashi 2007: 111).

Following the December 2005 elections, a six-month political stalemate emerged among the various political entities as to exactly what the new Iraqi government should look like and who should hold the key positions of power. This impasse was eventually resolved with Dawah's little known Nuri Al-Maliki nominated as Prime Minister, his government finally taking office in May 2006. Although the many divisions on the path to forming a government were resolved peacefully, this short period of divisiveness set the tone for political infighting and was a forerunner to the sharp upsurge in ethno-religious motivated sectarianism and violence that was to follow. Over the next two years Iraq descended into a particularly dark and unprecedented period in which ethno-religious factions, who mostly lived in peaceful co-existence, waged bitter and deadly battles against each another (Isakhan 2012c).

Consequently, this became a central concern for the Iraqi press who covered and criticized the unfolding conflict, demonstrating not only journalistic standards of the highest order but also remarkable bravery. As just one example, *Azzaman* was very critical of the mass ethno-religious violence that was tearing Iraq apart, and held to account the Iraqi government, various sectarian politicians and the militias they controlled (Abbas 2007, Al-Shaboot 2007, Maraai 2006a, 2006b). What was most significant about the Iraqi press of this time, however, was the connection so many journalists drew between the violence and the type of democracy that the US had imposed on Iraq. They condemned virtually every aspect of the US occupation: the failure to foster political solutions and reconciliation, the subsequent violence it had fostered, the troop surge of 2007, as well as the merits and drawbacks of a complete US withdrawal (Al-Khafaji 2006, Allo 2007, Sami 2006). Perhaps the most virulent, articulate and consistent criticisms on the pages of *Azzaman*, however, came from its Editor-in-Chief, Dr Fatih Abdulsalam[3] (Abdulsalam 2006b, 2007a, 2007c, 2007e, 2007f). In a nuanced account of post-Saddam Iraq, Abdulsalam reserved much of his critique for the Iraqi government which he viewed as being in complete disarray (Abdulsalam 2006a, 2007b). He denounced Iraq's politicians who he saw as stubborn, ineffective, corrupt and held hostage

---

3 Abdulsalam is an Iraqi author and academic, as well as being the Editor-in-Chief of the International Edition of the London-based Arabic daily newspaper, *Azzaman*. Formerly, Dr Abdulsalam worked in Iraq as a professor of modern Arabic literature and criticism at the University of Mosul.

to religious clerics. For Abdulsalam this was 'an embarrassing situation because none of the influential political factions is ready to compromise despite the fact that the country is imploding' (Abdulsalam 2007d).

While much of 2006 and 2007 was particularly grim, the US troop surge of 2007 and the increasing efficiency of the Iraqi Security Forces (ISF) – among a host of other factors – did see increased stability and security across Iraq by 2008. This meant that the nation was relatively peaceful when Iraqis went to the polls in January 2009 for Iraq's provincial elections in which some 400 parties and 14,500 Iraqi candidates registered to compete. As with the lead up to the 2005 national elections, the Iraqi press went to great lengths to provide details on the various parties and candidates and to encourage the Iraqi people to vote. Among the many Iraqi news outlets, *Aswat Al-Iraq* ('Voices of Iraq') stood out for the quality, objectivity and neutrality of its reporting. Throughout this period *Aswat Al-Iraq* lived up to its name, airing the voices of Iraqis of all backgrounds and shades of opinion. The paper frequently included commentary from experts and analysts of Iraqi politics, representatives of the various political parties, University professors, writers, artists and poets, key figures like Nuri Al-Maliki and Jalal Talabani and everyday 'man on the street' interviews (*Aswat Al-Iraq* 2009c). It also included the voices of the most marginalized Iraqis – women, the disabled, and tiny ethno-religious minorities like the Yazidis (*Aswat Al-Iraq* 2008b, 2009f, 2010c).

Aswat Al-Iraq also did an excellent job of promoting the elections across Iraq. To this end, they focused much of their coverage on the Sunni-dominated parts of Iraq in order to avoid a repeat of the mass Sunni electoral abstinence of 2005 (*Aswat Al-Iraq* 2008a, 2009e). In other parts of Iraq, such as the Shia-dominated south, *Asawt Al-Iraq* interviewed a host of Iraqi poets, authors, artists and intellectuals in Basra who were very positive about the 2009 provincial elections, seeing them as an opportunity for change. Among them, Iraqi author Abdilghafar Al-Itwi argued that

> This electoral round is important, because it would affect the path of democracy ... From now on, being [a] member in the provincial council will not be an easy issue to be achieved, as it would rely on providing services to people (Al-Itwi cited in *Aswat Al-Iraq* 2009b).

Others demonstrated an intimate awareness of the problems plaguing Iraqi politics. One Iraqi political writer, Abdulameer Al-Mijar, pointed out that sectarian politics had created a political elite in Iraq who had failed to adapt to the evolving nature of political consciousness in designing and articulating their key policies and in crafting their rhetoric. As he put it, in the elections of 2005, 'Shiites voted for Shiites, Sunnis for Sunnis, Kurds for Kurds' but today, the Iraqi people 'want parties and entities that serve them, not those that represent part of their identities' (Al-Mijar cited in *Aswat Al-Iraq* 2009d). Along similar lines, Iraqi writer and political analyst, Gomaa Al-Halafi, stated that while 'The coming elections are considered as an important move in the democratic and constitutional life in

Iraq' the 'Big parties which took part in the previous elections still dominate the political life in Iraq and have the money and means, including ways that violate the elections law' (Al-Halafi cited in *Aswat Al-Iraq* 2009a). Such concern was certainly warranted as the elections did see many familiar faces return to power with Nuri Al-Maliki's recently formed State of Law Coalition (SLC) winning a considerable proportion of the votes.

Just over a year after the provincial elections, in March 2010, Iraq held its next round of national polls. Once again, the Iraqi press did an excellent job of covering the lead up to the vote, demonstrating their ability to serve as the Fourth Estate of this fledgling democracy. Beginning in October 2009, journalists discussed a plethora of issues facing Iraqi democracy and did not recoil from writing about some of the harder aspects of the electoral process. Abdallah Al-Sukuti, writing in *Al-Mada*, argued that 'the gruesome massacres we are witnessing' are part of a broader insurgent plot 'to get serious about derailing the approaching Iraqi public elections' (Al-Sukuti 2009). Others blamed the violence on the Iraqi government, with Fatih Abd-Al-Salam of *Azzaman* arguing that the situation has been 'created by a persistent political failure to come up with a vision of the future that can make the necessary shift from the language of liquidation, eradication, assassination' to a democratic culture of the 'open-minded inclusiveness required to salvage Iraq from sinking forever' (Abdulsalam 2009). As Sabah Al-Lami put it in the independent *Al-Mashriq* ('The Arab East'),

> We have to realize that the forthcoming elections … will either save Iraq from the deteriorations of the 2003 invasion and the 2005 elections or turn the country into a graveyard for democracy as a cheap compensation for all its suffering … Iraq's plight is the result of non-existent political stability and lack of ideological wisdom at the levels of both government and opposition (Al-Lami 2009).

As the election drew closer, the Iraqi press continued to host varying opinions about the challenges and prospects of democracy in Iraq. *Aswat Al-Iraq* included opinions by leading experts that were very optimistic about Iraq's elections. The published comments by Kirkuk's deputy governor, Adwar Uraha claimed: 'The increase in the number of electoral lists is a kind of the new democratic practice and … This multiplicity is an indicator of the society's diversity and the development of the citizens' mentality' (Uraha cited in *Aswat Al-Iraq* 2010e). Elsewhere, Bassem Saheb of the Iraqi Communist Party stated that 'The elections were a national occasion to congratulate our people on their success with this great performance. It proved that Iraqis are a civilized people who are able to overcome pain and to reach the rank of democratic country in a short stage' (Saheb cited in *Aswat Al-Iraq* 2010f).

Similarly, in a series of articles published in *PUK Media*, Qubad J. Talabani correctly predicted that 'We will likely see shortly some close outcomes, potentially leading to disputed results … This will create tension within the system and delays will result'. For Talabani, however, this is 'merely the sign of a country continuing the difficult transition from oppression to democracy' (Talabani 2010b). In another article, published shortly after the election, Talabani continued this line of thought by claiming that

> the post-election coalition building will serve as a critical test of Iraq's fragile democracy and will continue to affect more than just the country's political future ... Iraq can take significant strides towards democratic governance if it adheres to the country's constitution ... What cannot be overlooked is what the majority of eligible Iraqi voters want their country to be – a stable, prosperous, federal democracy (Talabani 2010a).

These astute observations proved to be true. On the one hand, the Iraqi people had certainly demonstrated their will towards a democratic future, again risking their lives to vote in Iraq's latest round of elections while on the other hand the obstinacy and incompetence of many of their elected representatives failed to encourage the mutually beneficial dialogue and debate critical to democracy. This saw the nation plummet into nine months of political stalemate. Inevitably, the Iraqi media became very critical of the impasse and of Maliki in particular, urging the various political entities to put their differences aside and make progress (*Aswat Al-Iraq* 2010a). To this end the *PUK Media* published an editorial by Abdul Rahman Al-Rashid in which he offered the following scathing critique of the incumbent Iraqi Prime Minister,

> We do not understand what has afflicted Al-Maliki to cause him to raise all of these obstacles, especially as there is no clear victor that would be able to form a government on their own ... Do not forget that this was an open election that was overseen by bodies that Al-Maliki's government put in place and found acceptable, and th[at] the elections results that did not produce a clear victory was ratified by them. Perhaps a candidate not winning a majority is in the interests of Iraq as this is something that forces the politicians to work together over the next four years as a team and form a government that represents everybody, rather than there being a majority ruler who issues orders. This will be a difficult task for the next Prime Minister of Iraq, but this is a good balance, especially for Iraq at its current stage of political maturation (Al-Rashid 2010).

It is worth noting how Al-Rashid moves from critiquing Maliki and the political stalemate to arguing that the failure to form a majority government could actually serve to improve Iraqi democracy. Other Iraqi commentators have also argued along these lines, suggesting models by which the impasse might be resolved. A particularly popular option of this period was for Iyad Allawi to form a strong opposition party (Amin 2010). Despite such suggestions for the resolution of Iraq's political stalemate, the deadlock continued until early November when an agreement was signed that confirmed Maliki as Prime Minister and paved the way for the formation of a government (Ottaway and Kaysi 2010). The Iraqi press reacted immediately. Sadiq Hussein Al-Rikabi in the independent *Al-Akhbaar*

('God is Great') was grateful that Iraq finally had a government, 'The whole world was watching a unique democratic experiment ... most Iraqis see it as a nice dream that at long last could usher in an era of stability, prosperity and reconstruction' (Al-Rikabi 2010). On the other hand, authors such as Mahdi Qassim of *Sot Al-Iraq* were not nearly as optimistic:

> We are going to have a surreal government, with two leaders who are all too eager to lock horns with each other ... As usual, the victims of this anticipated ram fight are, of course, going to be ordinary, vulnerable and harmless Iraqis ... So congratulations to the people of Iraq on another four bleak years (Qassim 2010).

Civil Rights and Protest Movements

Paralleling this series of free and fair elections and their coverage in the Iraqi press, the Iraqi people frequently exercised their democratic right to protest. Such protests date back to the earliest days of the occupation and were first sparked by American plans to install a puppet government in Baghdad and disavowing the result of grass roots Iraqi elections (Isakhan 2011a). In April 2003, immediately after the fall of Baghdad, Iraq witnessed a series of spontaneous elections not dissimilar to those that followed the end of the First World War. In northern Kurdish cities such as Mosul, in majority Sunni Arab towns like Samarra, in prominent Shia Arab cities such as Hilla and Najaf, and in the capital, Baghdad, religious leaders, tribal elders and secular professionals called town hall meetings where representatives were elected and plans were laid for local reconstruction projects, security operations and the return of basic infrastructure. These initiatives were initially supported by the occupying forces and there are records of US troops playing a facilitating role in the process (N. Klein 2007: 362).

Much like the Colonial period under British occupation, however, the US was quick to quell these Iraqi-led drives towards democratization and to exert its own hegemony over Iraq. Fearing that the Iraqi people would elect certain 'undesirables' such as military strongmen or political Islamists, Bremer instead decided that he would appoint the members of the Interim Iraqi Government (IIG). Consequently, by the end of June, he had ordered that all local and regional elections be stopped immediately (N. Klein 2007: 363–5). This effectively meant that any decisions made by local councils were revoked and the mayors and governors who had been elected by their own constituents were replaced by hand-picked representatives including former Baathists (Booth 2003, Booth and Chandrasekaran 2003).

Such moves were widely unpopular across Iraq. In the Shia holy city of Najaf, hundreds of peaceful protestors took to the streets demanding that their installed mayor be removed and replaced by an elected representative. Several protestors carried placards reading 'Cancelled elections are evidence of bad intentions' and 'O America, where are promises of freedom, elections and democracy?' (cited in Booth and Chandrasekaran 2003). Much larger demonstrations were conducted in Baghdad and Basra where thousands banded together to chant the words, 'Yes, yes, elections. No, no selections' (cited in Hendawi 2003).

These early protests were but a precursor to a movement – particularly among the Shia Arab population of Iraq – that gathered enormous momentum over the ensuing months. Senior religious figures such as Grand Ayatollah Ali Al-Sistani[4] were able to mobilize thousands of Iraqis in protests that called for a general election prior to the drafting of the Iraqi constitution. Al-Sistani, a member of the quietist branch of the Shia faith took the unprecedented step of issuing a politically-motivated *fatwa* (edict) in June 2003 which argued that the US lacked the appropriate authority to install a government in Iraq and demanded that they hold national elections so that the Iraqi people could nominate their own representatives. The *fatwa* read:

> Those [US] forces have no jurisdiction whatsoever to appoint members of the Constitution preparation assembly. Also there is no guarantee either that this assembly will prepare a constitution that serves the best interests of the Iraqi people or express their national identity whose backbone is sound Islamic religion and noble social values. The said plan is unacceptable from the outset. First of all there must be a general election so that every Iraqi citizen who is eligible to vote can choose someone to represent him in a foundational Constitution preparation assembly. Then the drafted Constitution can be put to a referendum. All believers must insist on the accomplishment of this crucial matter and contribute to achieving it in the best way possible (Al-Sistani cited in Feldman 2005: 6).

Although the Coalition Provisional Authority at first underestimated the importance of such a *fatwa*, it ultimately had a profound effect on US plans for post-Saddam Iraq, as they were now forced to appease Sistani's demands. The US put in place an unelected transitional assembly with no guarantee of lasting power in Iraq and no power to write the constitution. Instead, the assembly would pave the way for national elections in January 2005 which would in turn see an elected body responsible for drafting the Iraqi constitution. Although this was a significant compromise for the world's last remaining superpower to make to a religious figure in Najaf, it was not enough for Sistani who demanded that the US seek UN approval for their plan. Incredibly, even though the entire world – including pleas from America's closest ally, the UK – had been unable to bring the US before the United Nations, Sistani succeeded (Feldman 2005: 7–8).

This was still not enough for Sistani, however, who wanted guarantees that the US would not further delay or manipulate Iraqi democracy. To bolster his argument and demonstrate its popularity among the Iraqi Shia majority, in mid-January 2004 the cleric called for the faithful to protest. More than 100,000 Shia marched

---

4   The Iranian-born Grand Ayatollah Ali Al-Sistani, is the pre-eminent Shia cleric or *marja* in Iraq and has been since 1992.

through Baghdad while a further 30,000 took to the streets of Basra to demand democracy (Walker 2005). They called on the US occupation forces to conduct free and fair national elections that would enable the people of Iraq to nominate an Iraqi legislature. They waved flags and chanted, 'Yes, yes to unification! Yes, yes to voting! Yes, yes to elections! No, no to occupation!' (cited in Jamail 2004). Some carried banners with slogans such as 'We refuse any constitution that is not elected by the Iraqi people', while one protestor told reporters that 'If America won't give us the democracy they promised, we will make it for ourselves' (cited in Jamail 2004). Demonstrating the power of the cleric these protests remained peaceful according to his instructions and when he announced that he had agreed to wait for a UN Fact-finding Team to study the situation, the protestors disbanded as quickly as they had assembled (Finn 2004).

Sistani's pro-democracy campaign continued in the lead up to the January 2005 elections for a transitional government. This time, Sistani issued another series of politically-motivated *fatwa*s urging his clergymen to get involved in local politics and encouraging the faithful, including women, to protest key decisions and vote in elections (Al-Rahim 2005: 50). Sistani also played a critical role in uniting the divergent political factions of the Iraqi Shia population – including Sadr, ISCI and Dawah – under the banner of the United Iraqi Alliance (UIA). Reasoning that a greater involvement of the Shia Arab majority in Iraqi politics would rectify the power imbalance that had swung in favour of the Sunni Arab minority since the inception of the state in 1921, Sistani understood that bringing the varying Shia factions together would enable them to wield significant power (Duss and Juul 2009: 11).

Paralleling the pro-democracy movements of Al-Sistani were those of the younger, more radical, Moqtada Al-Sadr[5] who was to gain both notoriety and political influence following the invasion. Arguably this began when the CPA forced the closure of two newspapers produced by Al-Sadr, prompting thousands of protestors to gather at the paper's office in central Baghdad. The protestors chanted slogans such as 'No, no, America!' and 'Where is democracy now?', and vowed to avenge *Al-Hawza*'s closure (Al-Shaykh 2004, Gettleman 2004). In an ironic twist, it was the forced closure of *Al-Hawza*, rather than anything printed across its pages, which ultimately garnered a renewed reverence for Al-Sadr among his followers and arguably incited his *Mahdi Army* to violence (Al-Marashi 2007: 132).

Throughout 2004 Al-Sadr led several military uprisings against the occupation forces and Sunni insurgents. His fire-brand rhetoric and military action quickly earned him immense popularity among the poor, the dispossessed and the devout Shia underclasses, particularly in Baghdad. They helped refine his mastery of anti-occupation political rhetoric and distinguished him against Al-Sistani as a strong militant religious leader who had both the strength and courage to take on the United States. As Patrick Cockburn puts it Al-Sadr 'is the Messianic leader of the

5   Moqtada Al-Sadr has no formal religious training, his popularity comes from the fact that he is the son of Grand Ayatollah Mohamad Sadiq Al-Sadr, who was assassinated by the Baath in 1999.

religious and political movement of the impoverished Shia underclass whose lives were ruined by a quarter of a century of war, repression, and sanctions' (Cockburn 2008: 199). When his military campaigns consistently failed, however, Al-Sadr employed a new set of weapons in his struggle against the occupation from 2005 onwards. These included a dramatic shift in approach from armed resistance to (mostly) non-violent political struggle, an evolution in rhetoric that saw him change from fire-brand pro-Shia Islamism to one who called for tolerance, national unity and social inclusion, and the effective transformation of the *Mahdi Army* from a militia to a social welfare organization (Yaphe 2008: 3). In Sadr city, the political arm of his organization, the Sadr Trend (or Sadrist Movement), began to organize their own religious courts, conduct law enforcement operations, set up prisons and initiate a range of social services including the supply of potable water, health care and food distribution.

As part of this shift, Al-Sadr, following in the footsteps of Al-Sistani, began to capitalize on his enormous support base, which he regularly mobilized in co-ordinated protests across Iraq. On the second anniversary of the invasion of Iraq (April 2005), Al-Sadr orchestrated massive protests in Baghdad. His supporters marched the five kilometres from Sadr city to Firdos square where, in 2003, the US had torn down the giant bronze statue of Saddam in an attempt to look like the liberators and not the invaders of Iraq. Thousands travelled from all over the nation to attend these peaceful protests making them one of the largest political rallies in Iraqi history (Jasim 2005). They chanted anti-occupation slogans while a statement read on behalf of Al-Sadr claimed, 'We want a stable Iraq and this will only happen through independence ... There will be no security and stability unless the occupiers leave ... The occupiers must leave my country' (cited in Al-Khairalla 2005b).

Of particular interest was Al-Sadr orders to his followers to wave only Iraqi flags and not those of the *Mahdi Army* or other Shia Arab organizations. This was a clear attempt to move the protests beyond a pro-Al-Sadr, Shia-backed movement to more of a nationalist struggle against occupation – something which would appeal to Iraqis of all persuasions. Consequently a number of Sunni Arabs and a small contingent of Iraqi Christians also attended the Baghdad protests. In the Sunni city of Ramadi the Association of Muslim Scholars coordinated concurrent protests attended by around 5,000 protestors (Carl 2005). These massive anti-occupation protests, organized by Al-Sadr, have become an ongoing annual event in Iraq with successful and largely peaceful demonstrations being conducted each year since 2005. Al-Sadr's followers have also organized several other demonstrations concerning more pragmatic problems: in the Sunni-dominated city of Samarra hundreds of Al-Sadr's followers have repeatedly demonstrated against the lack of basic infrastructure and public services such as electricity, fuel, potable water, the high cost of ice and the increasingly bleak employment market.

As well as these protests, Al-Sadr has further demonstrated his keen political instincts and acute knowledge of democratic mechanisms. In 2005, he instructed his followers to collect the signatures of one million Iraqis in a petition that asked the US and Coalition troops to leave the country immediately. This continued in

March 2008 when Al-Sadr launched a nation-wide civil disobedience campaign in response to a series of raids targeting the cleric's offices and the subsequent arrest of a number of members of his organization. In several key Baghdad neighbourhoods, including Mahmoudiya and Yusufiya, members of the *Mahdi Army* marched peacefully, while in Abu Disher the streets were emptied, stores closed and schools vacated in protest (Tawfeeq, Wald, and Sterling 2008). Then in October 2008, thousands of Iraqis took to the streets of Sadr city and in the south-eastern province of Missan in support of Al-Sadr's concerns about the Status of Forces Agreement (SOFA), which had been negotiated by the US and Iraqi governments in 2008 and which would see the final withdrawal of all US forces by 31 December 2011. When the Iraqi Government ignored their protests and signed the deal, Al-Sadr's followers re-appeared in the streets and one of his senior supporters read a message from the cleric stating that,

> This crowd shows that the opposition to the agreement is not insignificant and parliament will be making a big mistake if it chooses to ignore it … The government must know it is the people who help it in the good and the bad times. If it throws the occupier out, we will stand by it (cited in Chulov 2008).

More recently, in early 2011, Al-Sadr spoke at a number of politico-religious rallies co-ordinated by his followers and attended by thousands of Iraqis (*Al-Jazeera* 2011a, Shadid 2011). In a style that has become the hallmark of Al-Sadr's campaign, he called on the crowd to resist US occupation 'through armed, cultural and all kinds of resistance', chanting slogans such as 'no, no to occupiers' (Al-Sadr cited in *Al-Jazeera* 2011b). At the same time, however, he also called for peace and unity between Iraqis and, referring to the brutal civil war of earlier years, pleaded with his followers: 'Whatever happened between brothers happened, but that page must be forgotten and turned forever' (Al-Sadr cited in Muir 2011).

The key reason the Shia Arab protests have been so effective is that they make up the majority of Iraq's population whereas the Sunni Arabs (around 20 per cent), the Kurds (around 20 per cent) and the Iraqi Christians (around 3 per cent) simply cannot command such impressively large demonstrations. Nonetheless, these smaller minorities have also been able to utilize the power of the streets in order to air their concerns and advocate political change. The Sunni Arab minority conducted some of their earliest protests in the form of general strikes in resistance to US blockades of Sunni cities. In Ramadi the entire town shut down for two days as US troops launched a major offensive across the Sunni region. As Sheikh Majeed Al-Gaood described it, 'a call came from the mosques for a general strike in Ramadi and neighboring towns. Schools, markets and offices shut down in protest at the blockade' (Al-Gaood cited in Assaf 2005). The Sunni Arab protests were to gather increased momentum as the former ruling minority found itself increasingly ostracized by the Shia Arab and Kurdish dominated central government. In 2005, Sunni Arab demonstrations were held in the towns of Hit, Ramadi, Samarra and Mosul to protest the US and Iraqi Government plan for a nation-wide referendum in October 2005 that was designed to ratify the Iraqi constitution drawn up by the government. The Sunnis felt that they had had little say in the creation of the constitution and took to the streets *en masse* to air their concerns (Nasr 2005). In northern cities such as Kirkuk and Mosul the Sunni Arabs have frequently taken to the streets in protests against what they see as the Kurdish domination of Nineveh's regional administration (Nourredin 2005). In 2008 the Sunni Arab population of the Baghdad suburb of Adhamiyah protested against moves by the Kurds to incorporate the oil province of Kirkuk into the autonomous Kurdish region (*Agence France Presse* 2008).

At around the same time, the Kurds were also conducting their own protests regarding Kirkuk. Thousands gathered in cities such as Sulaymanyah, Arbil, Kirkuk and Dohuk after the Iraqi Parliament passed a law that would see a power-sharing arrangement devised for Kurdistan's multi-ethnic cities. In both Sulamanyah and Dohuk, the protestors submitted a warrant of protest to the UN Secretary General, the Iraqi President, the President of the Kurdistan Regional Government (KRG) and the Iraqi Parliament, asking the law to be revoked (*Voices of Iraq* 2008b, 2008c).The Kurds have also rallied against the inequities they see across their own region. During both March and August of 2006, and more recently in August of 2008, a series of largely peaceful demonstrations broke into angry protest against the KRG and its failure to provide basic public services to the region (Hama-Saeed 2007, Ridolfo 2006).

Caught in the political and sectarian cross-fire of post-Saddam Iraq, smaller ethno-religious minorities, such as the Turkomen, the Faili Kurds (Shiite Kurds) and the Christian minority of Iraq (made up mostly of Syriac-speaking Assyrians and Chaldeans) are often forgotten alongside the three larger ethno-sectarian groups. Unfortunately, these small Iraqi minorities have been the victims of much violence and harassment with many having left the country in fear of their lives. They have nonetheless been politically active with some minor successes such as their inclusion in various political coalitions, the creation of a small number of media outlets and a handful of political protests staged since 2003. In 2008, hundreds of Iraqi Christians demonstrated across key towns in northern Iraq including Qosh, Karabakh, Tell-esqope and Dohuk. The protesters chanted slogans and carried banners expressing their indignation at being denied the chance to elect their own representatives in the provinces in which they lived. They also called for autonomy in their ancestral homeland. The President of the Assyrian-Chaldean-Syriac Council, Jameel Zito, spoke to the crowds stating, 'Our rights to elect our own representation has been denied therefore we demand our right to self-government, because this is the only way to ensure our rights in our homeland' (Zito cited in Hakim 2008).

However, not all of the protests of post-Saddam Iraq have been conducted along ethno-religious lines. Iraq has also seen a variety of civil movements emerge that are not so much concerned with issues regarding ethno-religious rights, resistance to the occupation or a rejection of state policy, but rather the plight of normal Iraqi citizens – ordinary people who demand better working conditions, higher salaries, safer environs and better infrastructure. While many of these protests have occurred in very specific ethno-religious areas and are at times made up entirely of one particular ethno-religious group, the main impetus of these protests is the people's struggle for a more inclusive and equitable future. The Iraqi people have repeatedly protested against corruption and nepotism in their local and national governments and called for the resignation of several senior officials (*Al-Jazeera* 2008, *Voices of Iraq* 2008a).

Women's rights have also become a particular concern in post-Saddam Iraq with Iraqi women of all ethnicities and religious persuasions initiating their own powerful protest campaigns since the 2003 US invasion. Several women's rights and social justice activists have joined forces in a group known as 'Women's Will' that has organized a boycott of the US goods which have flooded the Iraqi market since the invasion. One of the leaders of the group is reported to have argued:

> We are now living under another dictatorship, you see what kind of democracy we have, seems more like bloodocracy. You see what kind of liberation they brought: unemployment, murder and destruction. We must resist this, it is the right of any occupied people to resist. Especially the women, we can use the simplest weapons of resistance, a financial boycott (cited in Carr 2005).

Similarly, June 2005 saw massive protests organized by various Islamic human rights and women's rights organizations in Mosul which pressed for the immediate release of all Iraqi women in US custody. So effective was this campaign that the US was forced to release 21 Iraqi women in Mosul who had been held as a bargaining chip against relatives suspected of resistance against US forces (Al-Din and El-Yassari 2005). Both during and after the 2010 elections, women's rights became a major issue when several women's groups highlighted the various challenges women face, especially in terms of safety, and their gross underrepresentation in Iraqi politics (*Aswat Al-Iraq* 2010b, 2010d, 2010g).

As well as protests against corruption, nepotism and women's rights, in recent years, Iraq has also seen a collection of powerful workers' movements emerge. Iraqi doctors, nurses, taxi drivers, university staff, police, customs officers and emergency service personnel have repeatedly used non-violent protests, strikes, sit-ins and walk-outs. They have done so in order to draw attention to important issues such as their poor working conditions, the interference they are subjected to from various forces, the pressures under which they work, unfair dismissals, ineffectual government regulation and the dangerous nature of their jobs (Al-Dulaimy and Allam 2005, Al-Khairalla 2005a, Assaf 2005, Hassan 2005).

Perhaps the best examples of civil protest in Iraq have been those coordinated by the nation's largest and most powerful independent union, the General Union of Oil Employees (later renamed the Iraqi Federation of Oil Unions [IFOU]). The union is led by President Hassan Jumaa Awwad Al-Asady and has over 26,000 members. The IFOU really began to flex its political muscles in May 2005 when it held a conference against the privatization of Iraq's oil industry. Aiming directly at certain

Iraqi politicians complicit in US plans to privatize Iraqi oil, the conference called upon 'members of Parliament … to take a firm stand against political currents and directives calling for the privatization of the public sector in Iraq' (cited in *Uruknet* 2005). In June 2005, some 15,000 workers conducted a peaceful 24 hour strike, cutting most oil exports from the south of Iraq. This particular strike was in support of demands made by Basra Governor Mohammad Al-Waili that a higher percentage of Basra's oil revenue be invested back into the region's deplorable infrastructure. At the time, Al-Waili was quoted as saying that, 'Faced with a pathetic and unjust situation, our moral responsibility leads us to demand in the name of our people a fair share of resources' (Al-Waili cited in *Global Resistance News* 2005). The IFOU also demanded the removal of 15 high ranking Baath loyalists in the Ministry of Oil as well as a salary increase for the workers (*BBC* 2005).

Two years later, in May 2007, the IFOU threatened to strike again, but this was delayed when a meeting with Iraqi Prime Minister Nouri Al-Maliki resulted in the formation of a committee tasked with working on finding solutions acceptable to both sides. When the government failed to deliver on any of its promises, however, the oil workers went on strike across southern Iraq, bringing an immediate halt to the free flow of oil products, kerosene and gas to much of the country. A few days later, the Iraqi government responded by issuing arrest warrants for leaders of IFOU including Awwad in an attempt to clamp down on industrial action. At the time, Sami Ramadani (who runs IFOU's support committee in the UK) pointed out that, issuing a warrant for the arrest of the oil workers leaders is an outrageous attack on trade union and democratic freedom. In the face of such intimidation the union held firm, taking the bold step of closing the main distribution pipelines, including supplies to Baghdad. After several days of meetings and much political deliberation, Awwad released a statement which claimed 'Finally the workers have won in demanding their legitimate rights … And after deliberations … the two sides agreed to halt the strike and to use dialogue in dealings to resolve the outstanding issues' (Awwad 2007).

Throughout 2010 and into 2011 all of these divergent aspects of Iraq's various protest movements have converged. Religious figures, political parties, women's groups and civil rights movements have banded together in a series of protests that have been a great demonstration of the Iraqi people's understanding of the mechanisms of democracy. In the middle of 2010, as the government deadlock continued and Iraqis sweltered in the heat of summer with only sporadic electricity to fuel their air conditioners and poor access to drinking water, frustrations literally reached boiling point. Several protests and sit-ins erupted across Iraq, the largest and longest of which were held at Nasiriyah and Basra. These protests prompted Nuri Al-Maliki to send a delegation to Basra in order to look into the problem, but he remained adamant that electricity officials should be the ones held accountable for the shortages, leading Iraq's electricity minister, Kareem Waheed, to offer his resignation (Alwan and Fadel 2010, Fadel 2010). Aside from electricity and water issues underpinning these protests was a broad sense of dissatisfaction with the ongoing political stalemate, now well into its third month. As Iraq's foreign minister, Hoshyar Zebari, put it 'People are tired of a lack of services, lack of action, and all this debate on television about government formation and positions. The public sense is one of anger and tiredness' (Zebari cited in *Al-Jazeera* 2010).

However, no one could have predicted the dramatic sequence of events that would sweep across the Middle East and North Africa in late 2010 and through 2011 as long lasting and deeply entrenched regimes fell in Tunisia, Egypt and Libya (Isakhan, et al. 2012). Civil movements gained credible if faltering momentum across the region and Iraqis were confronted with the failures of their own democracy to deliver on the many promises made to them since 2003. This led to weeks of scattered protests across Iraq. As with the other protests across the Middle East, organizers used Facebook and other social media and new technologies to promote the rallies, disseminate opinion and stimulate debate. What differentiated them from protests elsewhere was the fact that, while other Middle Eastern protestors focused on overthrowing governments, the protests in Iraq mostly addressed issues such as corruption, the country's chronic unemployment and shoddy public services like electricity, and included calls for the resignation of provincial governors (Sly 2011).

These events culminated in the 'Day of Rage' (25 February 2011) in which thousands of protestors took to the streets in at least 17 separate demonstrations across the country following Friday prayers (*Al-Jazeera* 2011c, 2011d). In smaller regions such as the southern province of Thi-Qar, 10,000 demonstrators gathered with one claiming that such protests 'proved that there is a new factor affecting the state's policy which is the citizen, who managed to demand his rights ... [constituting] a real challenge for democracy' (Al-Jaberi cited in *Aswat Al-Iraq* 2011). Similarly, across the north, tens of thousands of Kurds mimicked protestors in Cairo and elsewhere by setting up camp for days on end in central squares, including *Al-Saray* square in Sulaimaniya (Al-Khateeb 2011). Muhammed Tawfeek, a spokesman for *Gorran*, the Kurdish opposition party, claimed that 'People here are as frustrated as the rest of the Middle East ... It's all about democracy, separation of power and clean elections' (Tawfeek cited in Arango and Schmidt 2011). Meanwhile, in Baghdad's own *Tahrir* (liberation) square 5,000 protestors carrying Iraqi flags and various political banners gathered, chanting 'No to unemployment. No to the liar Maliki' (cited in *Al-Jazeera* 2011f). Reporting from Baghdad, Al-Jazeera's Jane Arraf gave the following description of events:

> The protests in Iraq are growing in size, partly because of the instability of the coalition government formed by Nouri Al-Maliki, the country's prime minister ... Iraqis are increasingly unwilling to accept the nature of the democracy that has emerged in years after Saddam's regime was overthrown ... This is a new democracy, it's an unusual democracy, and it's not exactly what people bargained for ... On top of that, people are looking around [at] protests in Egypt and Tunisia ... It has shown them, particularly these young people that if they come out and demand their rights, perhaps something will happen (Arraf cited in *Al-Jazeera* 2011e).

Unfortunately, key Iraqi political figures such as Maliki and Barzani reacted to these events in ways similar to dictators and autocrats across the region: they met Iraqi protests with a mixture of brutal suppression and modest political and economic concessions. For his part, Maliki offered concessions such as promising to cut his pay in half and to amend the Iraqi constitution so that no leader could serve more than two terms (Sly 2011). In terms of suppression, Maliki ordered the closure of the offices and newspapers of the Iraqi Nation Party and the Iraqi Communist Party, both of which had been critical in organizing the protests (Schmidt and Healy 2011). Maliki also ordered a brutal crackdown on the Iraqi protestors, journalists, and civil and political activists who have been involved in the events. The ISF and the protestors clashed frequently, leading to many arrests, beatings and deaths. In the Kurdish north, Barzani employed a similar strategy, sending in a thousand of his *Peshmerga* militia to quell demonstrations that demanded his departure (Al-Khateeb 2011, Al-Laithi 2011).

While such developments do not bode well for Iraqi democracy, the protests of the Re-Colonial period nonetheless indicate the continuing struggle of the Iraqi people towards democracy and also shed light on the complex nature of politics post-Saddam. Commenting on these events, one anonymous editorial printed in *Azzaman* at the time of the 'Day of Rage' protests captures this complexity:

> Iraqis are supposed to have been 'liberated' by their U.S. occupiers. They are supposed to be enjoying the fruits of their occupation by the world's most powerful nation. They are supposed to have democracy, unlike other Arab countries whose nations are rising against their dictators. The U.S., childishly, thought it could bring democracy to Iraq … It thought it could bring its own lackeys and install them as satraps to rule the country democratically. And today, the lackeys it brought with its invasion, who are ruling the country, including its semi-independent Kurdish north, find that their own people are rising against them the way the people of Libya and other Arab countries are revolting against their dictators … Iraqis, who think of themselves as the real revolutionaries of the Arab world, are embarrassed and ashamed. They wanted to have the change on their own, the way the Egyptians toppled Mubarak's presidency … How glad we the Iraqis would have been if we today, like other Arabs, rose against our dictator and had him toppled. We need to remove this stigma of shame by overthrowing the lackeys the U.S. brought with it and installed over us, whether in the Kurdish north or the Arab centre and south (*Azzaman* 2011).

Conclusion

A close inspection of the Re-Colonial period, therefore reveals an unrivalled upsurge in media freedoms that have played a central role in promoting a succession of Iraqi elections and referendums since 2005. Similarly, the many protest movements that have spread across Iraq in the Re-Colonial period have allowed ordinary people to express their concerns or air their grievances in a relatively peaceful and democratic way. These indigenous, localized and highly co-ordinated media and protest movements reveal the strength of the Iraqi people's will towards democracy and that, when given the opportunity to make this will a reality, they are more than capable of utilizing democratic mechanisms independent of foreign interference. They also indicate the degree to which democratic practices and culture are familiar to the people of Iraq. The Iraqi people implicitly understand that by critiquing their government in the press or by taking to the streets to protest key decisions, they are able to hold their democratically elected representatives to account. The fact that Iraqi citizens of all ethno-religious persuasions and professions have actively utilized the mechanisms of democratic deliberation to effectively voice their concerns and influence politics is at odds with the prevailing western view that the streets of Iraq are the locus solely of spontaneous acts of violence.

The Re-Colonial period also contradicts the view that the West has a unique proclivity for democracy and the Iraqi people have been able to successfully expose the fallacy of the US's self-appointed mission to bring democracy to the Middle East. The argument can be made that whatever its shortcomings, democracy exists in Iraq today because Iraqis demanded it, not because US idealists imposed it. Together, the actions of both the US and the Iraqi people during the recent past assert an alternative history of Iraq, an alternative history that is written each day by the many Iraqis who are deeply concerned with the future of their nation.

Conclusion

Men make their own history, but they do not make it just as they please; they do not make it under circumstances chosen by themselves, but under circumstances directly encountered, given and transmitted from the past. The tradition of all the dead generations weighs like a nightmare on the brain of the living. And just when they seem engaged in revolutionising themselves and things, in creating something that has never yet existed, precisely in such periods of revolutionary crisis they anxiously conjure up the spirits of the past to their service and borrow from them names, battle cries and costumes in order to present the new scene of world history in this time-honoured disguise and this borrowed language.

Marx 1963 [1869]: 15

Salvaging Democracy from Discourse

As the curtains part on the 2007 high-grossing action blockbuster *300*, the audience is immediately greeted with a sense of foreboding. The story's narrator, Dilios, recounts for us the intense military training that Spartan men had to endure from childhood in order to protect the people from their dark enemies, enemies who wish to destroy the city-state and remove its virtues from the annals of history. This destruction has never been more imminent, it seems, than with the recent encroachment of Persian forces into Greece and the beginning of the Greco-Persian Wars of 480–479 BCE. 'A beast approaches' says Dilios,

> patient and confident, savouring the meal to come. But this beast is made of men and horses, swords and spears. An army of slaves vast beyond imagining, ready to devour Greece, ready to snuff out the world's one hope for reason and justice. A beast approaches (Snyder, Johnstad, & Gordon 2007).

To combat this beast the Spartan king, Leonidas, assembles 300 of his finest warriors who are later joined by other soldiers from the various city-states of Greece. Together these men head towards Thermopylae where Leonidas believes the narrow gorge and steep sea cliffs will make the vast numbers of the Persian army count for nothing. It is here that the Greeks, and especially the 300 Spartans, confront the Persians, enduring wave after of wave of attack until their ultimate defeat which, in turn, inspires the armies of Greece to repel the Persians the following year.

At the time of its release *300* sparked a wave of controversy as a plethora of blogs, film reviews, news reports and short academic papers sought to point out the film's historical inaccuracies, one-dimensional characters and overly simplistic plot (Cartledge 2007, Lytle 2007, Vergano 2007). Inside Iran, the film was greeted with outrage and indignation with President Mahmoud Ahmadinejad accusing the film of being part of an elaborate US psychological warfare program against his country (Jaafar 2007, Moaveni 2007). Overall, however, much of the criticism of the film focused on the racialist and pejorative nature of the text which relied heavily on its negative and stereotypical portrayal of Iran/Persia and the broader Middle East (Farrokh 2007, Scott 2007, K. Smith 2007).

It would be easy to demonstrate how this film represents the epitome of what Edward Said was referring to in his work on *Orientalism*. Throughout the film, the Persians are constructed as the other of Greece. Their army is made up of ghouls, freaks, ogres, unworldly beasts and immortals, who are mostly dressed in black and repeatedly described in terms such as 'beasts from the blackness', 'hunters of men's souls' and 'motherless dogs' (Snyder, et al. 2007). The Spartans, on the other hand, are the model of Greco-Roman hyper-masculinity, dressed in red capes and leather briefs, they possess 'superior fighting skills' and 'march for honour's sake, for duty's sake, for glory's sake' (Snyder, et al. 2007). This is not at all inconsistent with the findings of a number of other studies which have sought to investigate the portrayal of Middle Eastern people in Hollywood blockbusters (M. Bernstein & Studlar 1997, Khatib 2006, Semmerling 2006). Perhaps foremost among these is Jack Shaheen's *Reel Bad Arabs: How Hollywood Vilifies a People* in which he analyses more than 900 Hollywood films from 1896 to 2001.[1] 'Seen through Hollywood's distorted lens', writes Shaheen in his Introduction, the people of the Middle East 'look different and threatening ... brutal, heartless, uncivilized religious fanatics and money-mad cultural "others" bent on terrorizing civilized Westerners' (Shaheen 2001: 2).

What is even more interesting here is that, within this Orientalist framework, *300* also makes clear the distinction between the discourses of Western democracy and Oriental despotism. Consider for example the actions of King Leonidas versus those of the Persian king, Xerxes. Leonidas is not only depicted as strong, virtuous and brave, he is also seen to have great respect for the rule of law, for individual freedoms and for the democratic mechanisms of ancient Sparta – virtues he is prepared to die for. Despite his recalcitrant and bellicose nature, Leonidas consults with the religious clergy of Sparta, the Ephors, and heeds the advice of the Oracle. Similarly, he respects the jurisdiction of the Spartan council and is careful not to offend them or to contravene Spartan law. Here, the power of King Leonidas is tempered by the machinations of the state and, despite his obvious desire to summon the entire Spartan army, he instead leads his personal bodyguard, a

---

1   It should be noted here that Shaheen's study focuses on the construction of Arab peoples in Hollywood films, while *300* is about Persians. Arabs and Persians are, of course, distinct ethnically, culturally and linguistically. However, the fact that there are remarkably similar portrayals of Arabs and Persians in Western motion pictures indicates the homogenising force of Orientalism where the complex differences of the Orient are reduced to negative portrayals and stereotypes (Said 1981: 80–3, Shaheen 2001: 29).

small battalion of 300 'free' men, to their certain death. Xerxes on the other hand wishes to control all that he sees, demanding absolute submission from his people and complete obedience to his every whim. He considers himself a 'god-king', indulges his every fantasy and is in command of a vast army of 'slaves'. There is no consultation with religious or political bodies, no legal system with which to contend and no personal freedom for his subjects. There is only the arbitrary despotism of his absolute power.

This juxtaposition of Leonidas and Xerxes, and of the civilizations and political systems they represent, is particularly evident when they meet at the end of the first day of fighting at Thermopylae. Here, Xerxes, sitting atop a massive and overly ornate throne carried by his dutiful slaves, demands Leonidas's submission and threatens him with complete annihilation. When this fails to intimidate Leonidas, the Persian king attempts a bribe, offering to make him 'warlord of all Greece' (Snyder, et al. 2007). Leonidas refuses to be seduced by this offer, however, and an enraged Xerxes promises to 'erase even the memory of Sparta from the histories … the world will never know you existed at all' (Snyder, et al. 2007). To this Leonidas retorts 'The world will know that free men stood against a tyrant. That few stood against many' (Snyder, et al. 2007).

This kind of juxtaposition continues throughout the film where the plot moves the viewer several times back and forth between the sophisticated politics of the Spartan court and that of the depraved and imperious Persian Empire. In the court of King Xerxes for example, musicians play exotic instruments as semi-naked and disfigured women writhe and dance and seduce. Ram-headed men look on as bejewelled freaks appear to smoke opium and engage in acts of moral decadence and sexual depravity. The camera pans through this seamy interior as it follows the deformed Spartan outcast, Ephialtes, and his betrayal of King Leonidas. His reward, according to Xerxes, will be 'Everything you could ever desire. Every happiness you can imagine. Every pleasure your fellow Greeks and your false gods have denied you, I will grant you … Embrace me as your king and as your god' (Snyder, et al. 2007).

The Persian court is then sharply contrasted against the image of the Spartan council, where wise bearded men in white robes are seen deliberating and debating over the key issues of the state. It is here that Leonidas' wife, Queen Gorgo, gives an impassioned and skilled oration, imploring the council to send the entire Spartan army to Thermopylae. 'Send the army for the preservation of liberty' argues the Queen, 'Send it for justice. Send it for law and order. Send it for reason. But most importantly, send our army for hope' (Snyder, et al. 2007). Sadly, Gorgo's address comes too late as the 300 Spartans are finally overcome by the might of the nefarious Persian hordes. Fortunately, before he dies, Leonidas sends Dilios back to Sparta and asks him to spread the story of the brave 300 and warn Greece about the likely Persian invasion. Dilios succeeds in his mission and, as the movie draws to a close, he is seen walking amongst the vast Greek army, rallying them to battle with the words from free Greek to free Greek, the word was spread that bold Leonidas and his 300, so far from home, lay down their lives, not just for Sparta, but for all Greece and the promise this country holds. Now, here on this rugged patch of earth called Plataea, Xerxes hordes face obliteration! Just there, the barbarians huddle, sheer terror gripping tight their hearts with icy fingers ... This day we rescue a world from mysticism and tyranny, and usher in a future brighter than anything we can imagine. Give thanks, men, to Leonidas and the brave 300! To victory! (Snyder, et al. 2007).

The story of the 300 Spartans and their final stand against all odds at Thermopylae has been a consistent motif in popular Western culture. The 2007 film was based on the earlier graphic novel of the same name by Frank Miller (Miller 1998), itself inspired by the 1962 film *The 300 Spartans* (St.George, Callegari, DelGrosso, d'Eramo, & Liberatore 1962). More broadly, the story of the 300 Spartans has been recounted by novelists, film-makers and artists, from Jacques-Louis David's 1814 *Portrait of Leonidas* (David 1814) to Steven Pressfield's novel *Gates of Fire* (Pressfield 1998). In turn, each of these texts has taken their inspiration from what is arguably the best account of the Greco-Persian Wars: Herodotus' *Histories* (Herodotus 1996 [460 BCE]).

What is particularly problematic about this is not only that Herodotus, as demonstrated in Chapter 1, used typically Orientalist language to explain away the non-Western world, but he was also among the first to argue that the West was inherently democratic while the East was prone to despotism and tyranny. As demonstrated, the distinction between Western democracy and Oriental despotism has a long history that can be traced right through the canon of Western scholarship. This reveals the Eurocentric nature of the historical narrative that accompanies and underscores democracy itself. It is widely seen as a form of government forged and designed by the great nations of the rational and free West, a form of government whose actions, practices and movements have an exclusively Occidental heritage. This has left us with a false dualism between the virtues of the West and the backward, savage, cruel and inherently despotic people of the Orient.

Given that this false dualism can be traced throughout history from Herodotus to Hollywood, it is not surprising that the idea has been frequently invoked in academic, bureaucratic and popular media discourses on Iraq. By moving beyond the simplistic textbook analysis of Iraq's political history as one of despotism and violence and uncovering instead a more nuanced and complex picture, it is possible to find an alternative vision of Iraq that emphasizes those instances of egalitarianism, collective governance and democratic reform. The foremost contribution of this study has been to problematize the dialectic between Western democracy and Oriental despotism via an analysis of five key phases of Iraq's political history.

The first phase included the participatory institutions, practices and discourses of ancient Mesopotamia. Chapter 2 revealed that from among the early myths and epics recounted by the Sumerians to the grand empires of the Babylonians and Assyrians, can be found very sophisticated and inclusive forms of governance.

Along similar lines, Chapter 3 demonstrated that the democratic ethos was at work from the very earliest days of Islam up until the fall of the Ottoman Empire at the beginning of the twentieth century. Far from Oriental despotism, ancient and Islamic Iraq reveal a complex political landscape where, at particular times and locations, the broader polity was encouraged to participate in the machinations of the state. This is particularly significant because this is the first known study to examine the origins of ancient or Islamic democracy and discuss them in relation to contemporary political events such as the democratisation of Iraq. It is also the first to argue that such democracies raise pertinent questions about the history of Western democracy and point to important flaws in the notion that the Orient has always been prone to despotism.

This book then examined the public sphere during three phases of Iraq's more recent history. Chapter 4 looked at the Colonial period of Iraq (1921–58), which began with the arrival of the British at the close of the First World War and ended with the Revolution of 1958. In Chapter 5 the Post-Colonial era of Iraq's history (1958–2003) was examined by focusing on the series of autocratic regimes which governed Iraq from 1958 until the US invasion of 2003. Finally, Chapter 6 focuses on Re-Colonial Iraq (2003–11), the period of US occupation and forced democratisation amid horrific violence. What these three chapters have in common is that, despite Western interference, oppressive tyrants and seemingly inhospitable conditions, Iraq is home to a lively, if sometimes clandestine or partisan, public sphere. This inverts the traditional dualism between the discourses of democracy: it highlights the contradictory nature of the West which advocates democratic practices while interfering in Iraqi politics; it demonstrates that even domestic attempts to manipulate the discourses of democracy met with a virulent culture of resistance; and it highlights that, through it all, the myriad Iraqi people's movements, political parties and newspapers criticised their elites and overlords and agitated for a more democratic order.

The point here is not whether or not Iraq will become a democracy or how such a goal might be achieved, but that Iraq has a complex history of participatory politics and a rich civic culture that is rarely acknowledged. Iraq may never become a truly robust democracy. The increasingly authoritarian tendencies emerging among elements of Iraq's political elite, especially in the wake of the extended political stalemate of 2010, has left an Iraqi populace that is increasingly disillusioned about the efficacy of democracy and its ability to meet their many urgent needs. Recent escalations in violence following the withdrawal of all US troops at the end of 2011 mean that the future of Iraq's security and stability remain uncertain at best. Given these circumstances, it is possible that whatever exists of Iraq's complex public sphere today may erode within a year or two and any dream of a democratic and egalitarian Iraq may become a nightmare. While these possibilities must be understood and dealt with realistically, the alternative must also be acknowledged. As this study has shown, there is nothing in Iraqi history, culture or society that is absolutely antithetical to democratic forms of governance and no implicit reason why Iraq should become a failed state under the auspices of a despotic government. Contrary to the pervading assumptions about Iraq's political history, a more thorough analysis of the nation's past has revealed a sophisticated and diverse political landscape that has long fought against tyranny and oppression, that has asserted alternative visions of a more inclusive political order and is demonstrative of the Iraqi people's will toward democracy.

In a sense then, while this study does not contain any step-by-step guide to building democracy in Iraq, it does suggest that further analyses of Iraq's political history, such as that conducted here, may go some way towards bolstering and legitimating democratic movements within Iraq today. If Iraq is ever to emerge successfully from foreign occupation to form a robust and egalitarian democracy then an open and frank assessment of the nation's past will be necessary. However, as demonstrated, most Iraqis have learned about the past through a Baathist lens: a tyrannical kaleidoscope of state propaganda, a history re-written to both justify oppression and coerce people into patriotism. This was underpinned by a very complex cultural-discursive campaign in which the history of Iraq was commandeered by the state and embedded with Baathist ideology.

Nonetheless, many Iraqis have maintained an intimate and acute relationship with their own political history. No matter what their religious or political persuasion, or their ethnic or cultural identity, for most Iraqis the past is not a distant or irrelevant discourse, it is a tangible force that informs the present. They feel a deep sense of pride in the achievements of ancient Mesopotamia and regularly acknowledge Iraq as the birthplace of human civilization and of the written word. Likewise, not only are most Iraqis deeply religious, the religion of Islam and the legacy of Islamic Baghdad continues to inform everything from the poetry recited in cafes to the affairs of the state. Certain events of the Colonial period, such as the Great Iraqi Revolution and the Wathba, are also enshrined in popular memory and remain symbols of defiance and solidarity in the face of foreign interference. More problematic are the painful memories of the Post-Colonial period, which brought suppression and violence, but also planted the seeds of opposition and made Iraqis cynically aware of the manipulation of discourse for political purposes. Finally, all Iraqis have witnessed first-hand both the tragedies and the advances of Re-Colonial Iraq. In terms of their experiences with democracy: they have felt the excitement of voting in free and fair elections for the first time; read long editorials or watched extended TV programs about key policies and parties; and they have taken to the streets alongside their fellow Iraqis to hold the government to account or to advocate change. What is evident here is that Iraq is a complex ideological landscape in which political history plays a central role in the day-to-day lives of ordinary citizens.

The task here is to make sure that this political history is not commandeered by those who would mimic the Baath and others by turning it into a tool of oppression and coercion. Instead, the former occupying forces, the Iraqi government and the nation's intellectuals, writers, journalists and teachers – both at home and in Diaspora – have a responsibility to make sure that the 'historical memories' of democratic Iraq are discussed and debated in the contemporary public sphere.

Such an open and critical engagement with Iraq's democratic history will not only create avenues of intercommunity dialogue and help placate ethno-religious violence and sectarianism, it may also facilitate the establishment of an inclusive political order – giving the Iraqi people a sense of 'ownership' over democracy rather than viewing it as a foreign and largely Western imposition irrelevant to their own cultural heritage.

This has been one of the central arguments of a number of recent studies on Iraq's political history which have asserted that the nation's democratic past could become a powerful political and discursive tool, used to engender wider support and participation in contemporary political developments (Al-Musawi 2006, Bashkin 2009, Davis 2005b, Dawisha 2005a, 2009). Amongst these, Eric Davis has been the most adamant arguing that while 'historical memory will not provide a panacea for Iraq's political problems' the nation's democratic past 'can help to inspire Iraqis to regain a sense of civic pride and trust in their ability to forge ahead with democratisation' and to 'deprive those who seek to return Iraq to an authoritarian past' (Davis 2005a: 244).

If such a project is to be successful in Iraq and further abroad, however, we must move beyond the age-old and deep-seated framework provided for us by the false dichotomy between Western democracy and Oriental despotism. To some extent this means re-examining and re-writing the history of democracy itself. It means expanding the Eurocentric narrative that underpins democracy to one that is more inclusive of those democratic practices, movements and histories that fall outside this limited rubric. This does not mean that important moments such as the rise of the *polis* in ancient Athens or the French Revolution should be discarded, nor should the iconic works of writers such as Aristotle, Montesquieu or Weber, but rather that they should be incorporated into a much broader narrative. In the case of Iraq, this broader narrative would necessarily include pre-Athenian democratic developments such as those of ancient Mesopotamia, it would also incorporate Islamic elements as well as the various political movements that have played such an important role in Iraq throughout the Colonial, Post-Colonial and Re-Colonial periods.

To paraphrase Marx, overcoming the ideologies inherited from the past is no easy feat. As has been demonstrated, the discourses of democracy studied here are so deeply enmeshed into the Western scholarly and literary canon that they surface in everything from major works on history, philosophy and politics through to recent art, literature and major motion pictures, achieving a weight and a common sense value via repetition. Democracy, however, is worth salvaging from the series of overlapping and interconnected discourses which have constructed it. It contains, as Derrida has pointed out, an 'emancipatory promise' towards which society must strive (Derrida 2006 [1993]: 74). Hidden beneath the layers of Eurocentric history and racialist ideology, 'rule by the people' carries with it a quintessentially human notion that is at once both pragmatic and utopian, something that must be fought for and defended daily and is also always yet 'to come' (Derrida 2005 [2003]: 78–94, 2006 [1993]: 108, 212). Thus, any advancement in Iraq's long and multifarious move towards collective governance is not only a step in the direction of a more egalitarian and inclusive Iraq, but another affront to the discourses of democracy that have for so long clouded our ability to see beyond their simple dualism to the broader story of humankind's collective struggle towards democracy.

References

Abbas, S. (2007, 20 August). The government is feeble and so is the opposition. *Azzaman*.

Abdalla, M. (2007). Ibn Khaldun on the fate of Islamic science after the 11th century. *Islam & Science*, 5(1), 61–70.

Abdel-Malek, A. (1963). Orientalism in crisis. *Diogenes*, 44, 103–40.

Abdul-Jabar, F. (ed.). (2002). *Ayatollahs, Sufis and Ideologues: State, Religion and Social Movements in Iraq*. London: Saqi.

Abdulsalam, F. (2006a, 7 September). Iraq's last 'SOS'. *Azzaman*.

Abdulsalam, F. (2006b, 7 December). U.S. concept of victory in Iraq is laughable. *Azzaman*.

Abdulsalam, F. (2007a, 14 January). Coddling the militias. *Azzaman*.

Abdulsalam, F. (2007b, 2 January). A country where violations are legal! *Azzaman*.

Abdulsalam, F. (2007c, 18 August). The losses and benefits of a U.S. withdrawal. *Azzaman*.

Abdulsalam, F. (2007d, 3 July). Our abnormal government! *Azzaman*.

Abdulsalam, F. (2007e, 9 April). U.S. army and Iraqi people can never reconcile. *Azzaman*.

Abdulsalam, F. (2007f, 3 February). U.S. troop 'surge' to protect government and not Iraqi people. *Azzaman*.

Abdulsalam, F. (2009, 28 October). Iraqi leaders lack vision. *Azzaman*.

Aburish, S. K. (2000). *Saddam Hussein: The Politics of Revenge*. London: Bloomsbury.

Aeschylus. (1961 [472 BCE]). The Persians (P. Vellacott, trans.) *Prometheus Bound, The Suppliants, Seven Against Thebes and The Persians* (pp. 122–52). Harmondsworth: Penguin.

Agence France Presse. (2008, 4 August). Hundreds protest in Baghdad over Kirkuk's status.

Al-Aasam, A. A.-M. (2004, 29 February). Commentary. *Azzaman*.

Al-Adala. (2005, 17 February). Organization of the Islamic Conference calls on Iraqis to form a representative government.

Al-Ansari, A. (2005, 17 October). We cannot wait for others to make our future. *Al-Adala*.

Al-Atiyyah, G. (2002a, 29 January). Fear of 'alternative' to Saddam need not inhibit Washington. *The Daily Star*.

Al-Atiyyah, G. (2002b, 15 January). Iraq must clear the Turkish hurdle in the way of democratic change. *The Daily Star*.

Al-Atiyyah, G. (2002c, 26 February). What would Baghdad be like without Saddam? *The Daily Star*.

Al-Baldawi, A. T. (2005, 28 February). The government must tackle corruption. *Azzaman*.

Al-Basair. (2005, 23 January). Iraqi people are divided into two major groups on elections.

Al-Bayan. (2005a, 17 February). Attempts to form new government begin.

Al-Bayan. (2005b, 27 January). The countdown has begun for a great, historic day.

Al-Bayan. (2005c, 3 February). A historic day.

Al-Bayan. (2005d, 8 February). With their voting papers, our people have placed their full trust in the members of the new parliament.

Al-Baynah. (2005, 7 February). Our fellows are welcome to join us in rebuilding Iraq.

Al-Din, O. S. and El-Yassari, K. Y. (2005, 19 June). Criminal Violation of Law of Land Warfare Confirmed Again: U.S. Officers Forced to Release Women Hostages. *Islam Online*.

Al-Dulaimy, M., and Allam, H. (2005, 30 May). Welcome to liberated Iraq: Students non-violently protesting U.S. occupation raids on their campus get a quick response: More raids. *Global Resistance News*.

Al-Dulaymi, K. L. (2005, 23 January). The upcoming elections: 'a poisonous honey'. *Al-Basa'ir*.

Al-Farabi, A. N. (1962 [935]-a). The attainment of happiness (M. Mahdi, trans.) *Philosophy of Plato and Aristotle*. Glencoe: Free Press.

Al-Farabi, A. N. (1962 [935]-b). *Philosophy of Plato and Aristotle* (M. Mahdi, trans.). Glencoe: Free Press.

Al-Farabi, A. N. (1996 [948]). *La Citta Virtuosa* (M. Campanini, trans.). Milan: Rizzoli.

Al-Farabi, A. N. (2001 [930–45]). *The Political Writings, 'Selected Aphorisms' and Other Texts* (C. Butterworth, trans.). Ithaca: Cornell University Press.

Al-Furat. (1920a). 7 August.

Al-Furat. (1920b). 14 August.

Al-Furat. (1920c). 15 September.

Al-Hakim, M. B. (2001). Statement by Ayatollah Mohammed Baqir Al-Hakim. In J. Ehrenberg, J. P. McSherry, J. R. Sanchez and C. M. Sayej (eds), *The Iraq Papers* (pp. 318–19). Oxford: Oxford University Press.

Al-Hilfi, Q. (2010, 8 March). Voters bid Farewell from their martyrs and insisted on the ballot: the terrorists were slapped by their own crime. *Al-Sabah*.

Al-Iraq. (1979). 30 October.

Al-Iraq. (1989a). 1 March.

Al-Iraq. (1989b). 4 February.

Al-Iraq. (1989c). 4 March.

Al-Iraq. (2003a). 20 March.

Al-Iraq. (2003b). 21 March.

Al-Iraq. (2003c). 28 January.

Al-Jazeera. (2008, 9 March). Mass protest over Basra insecurity.

Al-Jazeera. (2010, 21 June). Iraq power outages provoke protests.

Al-Jazeera. (2011a, 5 January). Al-Sadr back in Iraq stronghold.

Al-Jazeera. (2011b, 8 January). Al-Sadr calls on Iraqis 'to resist'.

Al-Jazeera. (2011c, 26 February). Deadly protests rock Iraq.

Al-Jazeera. (2011d, 18 February). Fresh protests hit Iraqi cities.

Al-Jazeera. (2011e, 4 March). Protestors converge on Iraq capital.

Al-Jazeera. (2011f, 25 February). Tensions flare in Iraq rallies.

Al-Jumhuriyya. (1968). 22 September.

Al-Jumhuriyya. (1980). 1 January.

Al-Juwari, A.-a.-B. (2005, 18 January). Elections are the Beginning of The New Way. *Al-Adala*.

Al-Khafaji, A. (2006, 17 July). U.S. Iraq rhetoric is shallow, naive and childish. *Azzaman*.

Al-Khairalla, M. (2005a, 19 July). Baghdad hospital doctors on strike against soldiers. *Reuters*.

Al-Khairalla, M. (2005b, 9 April). Iraqis protest on anniversary of Saddam's Fall. *Common Dreams*.

Al-Khalil, S. (1991). *The Monument: Art, Vulgarity and Responsibility in Iraq*. Berkeley: University of California Press.

Al-Khateeb, B. (2011, 11 March). Iraqi Kurdish protestors to press demands for freedom and transparency. *Azzaman*.

Al-Laithi, N. (2011, 2 March). Tensions rise in Iraq's Kirkuk as Kurdish leader sends in militias. *Azzaman*.

Al-Lami, S. (2009, 28 October). Elections could save Iraq. *Al-Mashriq*.

Al-Mada. (2005a, 8 February). Election results spur intensive contacts between political forces.

Al-Mada. (2005b, 17 February). Electoral commission denies defining seats, percentages for political entities.

Al-Marashi, I. (2007). The dynamics of Iraq's media: Ethno-sectarian violence, political Islam, public advocacy, and globalisation. *Cardozo Arts and Entertainment Law Journal*, 25(95), 96–140.

Al-Mashriq. (2005, 13 February). Corruption and government's poor performance.

Al-Muqdadi, K. (2005, 5 January). Neither the current nor the elected government will be able to control the situation. *Azzaman*.

Al-Musawi, M. J. (1991). The socio-political context of the Iraqi short story, 1908–68. In E. Davis and N. Gavrielides (eds), *Statecraft in the Middle East: Oil, Historical Memory, and Popular Culture* (pp. 202–7). Miami: Florida International University Press.

Al-Musawi, M. J. (2006). *Reading Iraq: Culture and Power in Conflict*. London: I. B. Tauris.

Al-Mutamar. (2005a, 3 February). New dawn for democracy and a ray of hope for new Iraq.

Al-Mutamar. (2005b, 17 February). Zebari: No pre-fixed coalitions to form government.

Al-Pachachi, A. (2005, 5 January). Why the upcoming elections should be postponed. *Al-Mutamar*.

Al-Qadisiyya. (1989). 18 March.

Al-Qadisiyya. (1992). 21 January.

Al-Qassab, N. (2005, 27 January). Iraq's Unity and the Elections. *Al-Mutamar*.

Al-Rahim, A. H. (2005). The Sistani Factor. *Journal of Democracy*, 16(3), 50–53.

Al-Rashid, A. R. (2010, 5 April). Intimidating the Iraqis. *PUK Media*.

Al-Raziqi, H. M. (2005, 12 January). Holding election on time is a natural right of the Iraqi people. *Al-Bayan*.

Al-Rikabi, S. H. (2010, 12 November). Iraqi parliament gives birth to government. *Al-Akhbaar*.

Al-Rubaie, M., Allawi, A. and Al-Hakim, S. (2002). Declaration of the Shia of Iraq. In J. Ehrenberg, J. P. McSherry, J. R. Sanchez and C. M. Sayej (eds), *The Iraq Papers* (pp. 313–15). Oxford: Oxford University Press.

Al-Sanduq, L. (2005, 3 February). The citizens are no longer deprived of a role in making the decisions. *Azzaman*.

Al-Shaboot, M. (2007, 6 September). Maliki's government is in denial. *Azzaman*.

Al-Shahid. (2005, 17 October). The Iraqi government is now required to take action and implement the constitution.

Al-Shammari, S. (2005, 18 January). Iraqi elections a positive step of democracy. *Al-Mutamar*.

Al-Shaykh, B. (2004, 3 April). A limitless inferno. *Al-Dustour*.

Al-Shaykh, B. (2005a, 5 January). Advocates of fake agendas had better steer away from Iraq. *Al-Dustour*.

Al-Shaykh, B. (2005b, 12 January). Iraqis are now closer to finding a way out of the ordeal. *Al-Dustour*.

Al-Shaykh, B. (2005c, 5 January). Iraqis will no longer accept someone dictating to them what to do. *Al-Dustour*.

Al-Shaykh, B. (2005d, 6 February). Let's purge government departments of corrupt practices inherited from the past. *Al-Dustour*.

Al-Shaykh, B. (2005e, 17 January). Only with love will Iraqis live. *Al-Dustour*.

Al-Shaykh, B. (2005f, 15 January). Some political entities take advantage of religious symbols. *Al-Dustour*.

Al-Shaykh, B. (2005g, 4 January). Wisdom and its opposite. *Al-Dustour*.

Al-Shimmari, S. (2005, 12 January). Holding election on time scheduled; a victory over the forces of sabotage. *Al-Mutamar*.

Al-Sukuti, A. (2009, 28 October). Iraq's neighbours are to blame. *Al-Mada*.

Al-Taakhi. (1972). 21 November.

Al-Thawra. (1969). 29 January.

Al-Thawra. (1977). 15 June. Democracy: A source of strength for the individual and society.

Al-Thawra. (1989). 16 February.

Al-Thawra. (2002). 18 October.

Al-Thawra. (2003). 21 March.

Al-Tikriti, H. F. (2005, 28 February). The burdens of the upcoming government. *Al-Bayan*.

Al-Ubaydi, S. d. (2005, 5 January). The government has failed to address the collective Iraqi psyche positively. *Azzaman*.

Al-Uloom, M. B. (2002, 14 December). Iraq After Saddam. *Dar Al-Hayat*.

Al-Zahir, R. (2005, 28 February). Distinguishing between a national accord and reconciliation. *Tariq Al-Shab*.

Alatas, S. H. (1977). *The Myth of the Lazy Native*. London: Frank Cass.

Aldred, C. (1998). *The Egyptians* (3rd ed.). London: Thames and Hudson.

Ali, T. (2003). *Bush in Babylon: The Re-colonisation of Iraq*. London: Verso.

Allo, I. (2007, 6 March). The benefits of U.S.-style democracy. *Azzaman*.

Almond, G. A. and Verba, S. (1989 [1963]). *The Civic Culture: Political Attitudes and Democracy in Five Nations*. Newbury Park: Sage.

Alon, I. (1991). *Socrates in Mediaeval Arabic Literature* (3rd ed.). Leiden: Brill.

Alwan, A. and Fadel, L. (2010, 20 June). Protest in Basra over sporadic electricity, lack of potable water leaves 1 dead. *Washington Post*.

Amin, A. (2010, 5 August). Excessive or rightful demands. *PUK Media*.

Anderson, L. and Stansfield, G. (2004). *The Future of Iraq: Dictatorship, Democracy, or Division?* New York: Palgrave Macmillan.

The Anglo-French Declaration. (1918, 8 November). *Proclamation No. 32*.

Annual Report and Press Freedom Index. (2009). *Reporters Without Borders*.

Annual Report and Press Freedom Index. (2010). *Reporters Without Borders*.

Arango, T. and Schmidt, M. S. (2011, 18 May). Anger lingers in Iraqi Kurdistan after a crackdown. *The New York Times*.

Aristotle. (1943 [350 BCE]). *Politics* (B. Jowett, trans.). New York: The Modern Library.

Aristotle. (1984 [332 BCE]). *The Athenian Constitution* (P. J. Rhodes, trans.). Harmondswoth: Penguin.

Arjomand, S. A. (2004). Coffeehouses, guilds and Oriental despotism: Government and civil society in late 17th to early 18th century Istanbul and Isfahan, and as seen from Paris and London. *European Journal of Sociology*, 45(1), 23–42.

Armstrong, K. (2000). *Islam: A Short History*. London: Phoenix.

Arnold, T. W. (1961 [1913]). *The Preaching of Islam: A History of the Propagation of the Muslim Faith*. Lahore: Ashraf.

Asad, M. (1980 [1961]). *The Principles of State and Government in Islam*. Gibraltar: Dar Al-Andalus.

Asad, T. (1973a). Two European images of non-European rule. *Economy and Society*, 2(3), 268–89.

Asad, T. (ed.). (1973b). *Anthropology and the Colonial Encounter*. London: Ithaca.

Assaf, S. (2005, 21 May). General strike against occupation in Iraqi city of Ramadi. *Socialist Worker Online*.

Aswat Al-Iraq. (2008a, 21 December). 800,000 to cast their votes in Anbar.

Aswat Al-Iraq. (2008b, 5 November). Women satisfied with Kurdish Parliament's amendments to personal law.

Aswat Al-Iraq. (2009a, 26 January). Cultured citizens say elections will not make big change.

Aswat Al-Iraq. (2009b, 18 January). Elections offer opportunity for change – Basra intellectuals.

Aswat Al-Iraq. (2009c, 12 November). Iraqis show varied reactions to new election law.

Aswat Al-Iraq. (2009d, 22 January). Vote buying indicates political bankruptcy – observers.

Aswat Al-Iraq. (2009e, 12 January). We will never boycott elections again – Mosul citizens

Aswat Al-Iraq. (2009f, 25 July). Yazidis unsatisfied with their regional representation.

Aswat Al-Iraq. (2010a, 1 July). Al-Maliki to form new government under conditions – analysts.

Aswat Al-Iraq. (2010b, 9 December). 'Anti-woman violence gives us sleepless nights', Kurdistan Minister says.

Aswat Al-Iraq. (2010c, 25 February). Deaf-mute people pin hope on coming elections.

Aswat Al-Iraq. (2010d, 9 February). Iraqi women pessimistic regarding elections.

Aswat Al-Iraq. (2010e, 7 January). Kirkuk council members welcome high number of election participants.

Aswat Al-Iraq. (2010f, 8 March). Parties, organizations in Thi-Qar hail elections' success.

Aswat Al-Iraq. (2010g, 26 December). Woman activist calls for unification of efforts to avoid 'woman's marginalization in Iraq'

Aswat Al-Iraq. (2011, 3 March). Calls in Thi-Qar for Friday protests.

Australian. (2006, 23 January). Another positive step.

Avineri, S. (ed.). (1968). *Karl Marx on Colonialism and Modernization: His Dispatches and Other Writings on China, India, Mexico, the Middle East and North Africa*. New York: Double Day.

Awwad, H. J. a. (2007, 11 June). Iraqi oil workers claim tactical victory as negotiations resume and Ministry of Oil rebuked. *Naftana*.

Ayalon, A. (1995). *The Press in the Arab Middle East: A History*. New York: Oxford University Press.

Azzaman. (2005, 17 February). Unofficial list of Assembly members.

Azzaman. (2011, 25 February). Iraqis revolt against their 'liberation' by the U.S.

Babil. (2002). 18 October.

Baghdad. (2005, 3 February). Iraq is first winner in the elections.

Bailkey, N. (1967). Early Mesopotamian constitutional development. *The American Historical Review*, 72(4), 1211–36.

Balfour-Paul, H. G. (1982). Iraq: The fertile crescent dimension. In T. Niblock (ed.), *Iraq: The Contemporary State* (pp. 7–26). London: Croom Helm.

Baram, A. (1981). The June 1980 elections to the National Assembly in Iraq: An experiment in controlled democracy. *Orient*, 22, 391–412.

Baram, A. (1983). Mesopotamian identity in Ba'thi Iraq. *Middle Eastern Studies*, 19, 426–55.

Baram, A. (1989). The ruling political elite in Bathi Iraq, 1968–1986: The changing features of a collective profile. *International Journal of Middle East Studies*, 21(4), 447–93.

Baram, A. (1991). *Culture, History and Ideology in the Formation of Ba'thist Iraq, 1968–1989*. London: Macmillan.

Baram, A. (1994). A case of imported identity: The modernizing secular ruling elites of Iraq and the concept of Mesopotamian-inspired territorial nationalism, 1922–92. *Poetics Today*, 15(2), 279–319.

Baram, A. (1998). *Building Toward Crisis: Saddam Husayn's Strategy for Survival*. Washington: The Washington Institute for Near East Policy.

Bashkin, O. (2009). *The Other Iraq: Pluralism and Culture in Hashemite Iraq*. Stanford: Stanford University Press.

Bashkin, O. (2010). Iraqi democracy and the democratic vision of 'Abd Al-Fattah Ibrahim. In A. Baram, A. Rohde and Z. Ronen (eds), *Iraq Between Occupations: Perspectives from 1920 to the Present* (pp. 103–114). New York: Palgrave Macmillan.

Batatu, H. (1982 [1978]). *The Old Social Classes and the Revolutionary Movements of Iraq: A Study of Iraq's Old Landed and Commercial Classes and of its Communists, Ba'thists and Free Officers*. Princeton: Princeton University Press.

BBC. (2005, 17 July). Basra oil workers out on strike.

Beckett, K. S. (2003). *Anglo-Saxon Perceptions of the Islamic World*. Cambridge: Cambridge University Press.

Beckman, G. (1982). The Hittite assembly. *Journal of the American Oriental Society*, 102(2), 435–42.

Bede. (2008 [700]). *On Genesis* (C. B. Kendall, trans.). Liverpool: Liverpool University Press.

Bengio, O. (1992). *Baghdad Between Shi'a and Kurds* (Policy Focus No. 18). Washington: Washington Institute for Near East Policy.

Bengio, O. (1998). *Saddam's Word: Political Discourse in Iraq*. New York: Oxford University Press.

Bengio, O. (2003). Pitfalls of instant democracy. In M. Eisenstadt and E. Mathewson (eds), *U.S. Policy in Post-Saddam Iraq: Lessons from the British Experience*. Washington: Washington Institute for Near East Policy.

Bengio, O. (2004). In the eyes of the beholder: Israel, Jews and Zionism in the Iraqi media. In T. Parfitt and Y. Egorova (eds), *Jews, Muslims and Mass Media: Mediating the 'Other'* (pp. 109–119). London: Routledge Curzon.

Benjamin, W. (2003 [1940]). On the concept of history (E. Jephcott, trans.). In H. Eiland and M. W. Jennings (eds), *Walter Benjamin: Selected Writings 1938–1940* (vol. 4, pp. 389–400). London: Balknap.

Bennison, A. K. (2009). *The Great Caliphs: The Golden Age of the Abbasid Empire*. New Haven: Yale University Press.

Benomar, J. (2004). Constitution-making after conflict: Lessons for Iraq. *Journal of Democracy*, 15(2), 81–95.

Bermant, C. and Weitzman, M. (1979). *Ebla*. London: Weidenfeld and Nicolson.

Bernal, M. (1991 [1987]). *Black Athena: The Afroasiatic Roots of Classical Civilisation, Volume I: The Fabrication of Ancient Greece 1785–1985*. London: Vintage.

Bernal, M. (2001). *Black Athena Writes Back*. Durham: Duke University Press.

Bernhardsson, M. T. (2005). *Reclaiming a Plundered Past: Archaeology and Nation Building in Modern Iraq*. Austin: University of Texas Press.

Bernstein, J. (2008). *The Mesopotamia Mess: The British Invasion of Iraq in 1914*. Redondo Beach: InterLingua.

Bernstein, M. and Studlar, G. (eds). (1997). *Visions of the East: Orientalism in Film*. New Brunswick: Rutgers University Press.

Bhabha, H. K. (1990). The Third Space: Interview with Homi Bhabha. In J. Rutherford (ed.), *Identity, Community, Culture, Difference* (pp. 207–21). London: Lawrence and Wishart.

Bhabha, H. K. (1994). *The Location of Culture*. London: Routledge.

Bhabha, H. K. (ed.). (1995 [1990]). *Nation and Narration*. London: Routledge.

Black, A. (2001). *The History of Islamic Political Thought: From the Prophet to the Present*. New York: Routledge.

Bohnstedt, J. W. (1968). The infidel scourge of God: The Turkish menace as seen by German pamphleteers of the Reformation Era. *Transactions of the American Philosophical Society*, 58(9), 1–58.

Bonneterre, D. (1995). The structure of violence in the kingdom of the Mari. *The Bulletin of the Canadian Society for Mesopotamian Studies*, 30, 11–22.

Booth, W. (2003, May 14). In Najaf, new mayor is outsider viewed with suspicion. *Washington Post*.

Booth, W. and Chandrasekaran, R. (2003, 28 June). Occupation forces halt elections throughout Iraq. *Washington Post*.

Brévart, F. B. (1988). The German volkskalender of the fifteenth century. *Speculum*, 63(2), 312–42.

Brown, J. (2006). Orientalism revisited: The British media and the Iraq War. In A. G. Nikolaev and E. A. Hakanen (eds), *Leading to the 2003 Iraq War: The Global Media Debate* (pp. 97–111). New York: Palgrave Macmillan.

Bryce, J. (1921). *Modern Democracies* (vol. I). London: Macmillan.

Bulliet, R. W. (1978). Local politics in Eastern Iran under the Ghaznavids and Seljuks. *Iranian Studies*, 11(1), 35–56.

Burke, E. (1988). Islam and social movements: Methodological reflections. In E. Burke and I. M. Lapidus (eds), *Islam, Politics and Social Movements* (pp. 17–36). Berkeley: University of California Press.

Burns, J. F. (2002, 23 October). In opening the gates of its gulag, Iraq unleashes pain and protest. *New York Times*.

Bush, G. W. (2003a, 17 March). Address to the Nation. *The White House*.

Bush, G. W. (2003b, 19 March). Address to the Nation: Operation Iraqi Freedom. *The White House*.

Bush, G. W. (2003c, 6 November). Remarks by the President at the 20th Anniversary of the National Endowment for Democracy. *The White House*.

Bush, G. W. (2003d, 29 January). State of the Union Address. *Congress of the United States of America*.

Byman, D. L. (2003a). Building the new Iraq: The role of intervening forces. *Survival*, 45(2), 57–71.

Byman, D. L. (2003b). Constructing a democratic Iraq: Challenges and opportunities. *International Security*, 28(1), 47–78.

Byock, J. (2002). The Icelandic Althing: Dawn of parliamentary democracy. In J. M. Fladmark (ed.), *Heritage and Identity: Shaping the Nations of the North* (pp. 1–17). Shaftesbury: Donhead.

Campanini, M. (2008 [2004]). *An Introduction to Islamic Philosophy* (C. Higgitt, trans.). Edinburgh: Edinburgh University Press.

Carl, T. (2005, 10 April). Iraqi protesters call for U.S. pullout. *Associated Press*.

Carr, J. (2005, 3 June). Don't pay money for the enemy's weapons: Iraqi activists plan to boycott US goods. *Electronic Iraq*.

Cartledge, P. (2007, 2 April). Another view. *The Guardian*.

Catherwood, C. (2004). *Winston's Folly: Imperialism and the Creation of Modern Iraq*. London: Constable & Robinson.

Cawkwell, G. (1986 [1972]). Introduction *The Persian Expedition*. Middlesex: Penguin.

Chardin, J. (1720 [1686]). *Sir John Chardin's Travels in Persia*. London: J. Smith.

Choudhury, G. W. (1990). *Islam and the Contemporary World*. London: Indus Thames.

Chulov, M. (2008, 22 November). Shias stage protests against Iraq-US pact. *The Guardian*.

Cicero, M. T. (1998 [54 BCE]). *The Republic and The Laws* (N. Rudd, trans.). Oxford: Oxford University Press.

Clemons, S. (2005, 20 December). The jury still out on Iraqi democracy. *The Australian*, 12.

Cochrane, P. (2006). The 'Lebanonization' of the Iraqi media: An overview of Iraq's television landscape. *Transnational Broadcasting Studies*, 16.

Cockburn, P. (2008). *Muqtada Al-Sadr and the Battle for the Future of Iraq*. New York: Scribner.

Cogan, M. (2003). Achaemenid inscriptions: Cyrus cylinder. In W. W. Hallo and K. L. Younger (eds), *The Context of Scripture: Monumental Inscriptions from the Biblical World* (vol. 2). Leiden: Brill.

The Constitution of Iraq. (2010 [2005]). In J. Ehrenberg, J. P. McSherry, J. R. Sanchez and C. M. Sayej (eds), *The Iraq Papers* (pp. 306–12). Oxford: Oxford University Press.

Cordesman, A. H. and Hashim, A. S. (1997). *Iraq: Sanctions and Beyond*. Colorado: Westview.

Crone, P. (1980). *Slaves on Horses: The Evolution of the Islamic Polity*. Cambridge: Cambridge University Press.

Curtis, M. (2004). *Unpeople: Britain's Secret Human Rights Abuses*. London: Vintage.

Dahl, R. A. (1971). *Polyarchy: Participation and Opposition*. New Haven: Yale University Press.

Dahl, R. A. (1998). *On Democracy*. New Haven: Yale University Press.

Dahl, R. A. (2005 [1961]). *Who Governs?: Democracy and Power in an American City* (2nd ed.). New Haven: Yale University Press.

Dandamayev, M. (1995). Babylonian popular assemblies in the first millennium B.C. *The Bulletin of the Canadian Society for Mesopotamian Studies*, 30, 23–29.

Daniel, N. A. (1979). The impact of Islam on the laity in Europe from Charlemagne to Charles the Bold. In A. T. Welch and P. Cachia (eds), *Islam: Past Influence and Present Challenge* (pp. 105–25). Edinburgh: Edinburgh University Press.

Daragahi, B. (2003). Rebuilding Iraq's media. *Columbia Journalism Review*, 42(2), 45–50.

David, J.-L. (Artist). (1814). *Leonidas at Thermopylae* [Oil on Canvas].

Davis, E. (1992). State-building in Iraq during the Iran–Iraq War and the Gulf Crisis. In M. I. Midlarsky (ed.), *The Internationalization of Communal Strife* (pp. 69–92). London: Routledge.

Davis, E. (2005a). History matters: Past as prologue in building democracy in Iraq. *Orbis*, 49, 229–244.

Davis, E. (2005b). *Memories of State: Politics, History, and Collective Identity in Modern Iraq*. Berkeley: University of California Press.

Davis, E. (2005c). The new Iraq: The uses of historical memory. *Journal of Democracy*, 16(3), 54–68.

Davis, E. and Gavrielides, N. (1991). Statecraft, historical memory, and popular culture in Iraq and Kuwait. In E. Davis and N. Gavrielides (eds), *Statecraft in the Middle East: Oil, Historical Memory, and Popular Culture* (pp. 116–48). Miami: Florida International University Press.

Dawisha, A. (2005a). Democratic attitudes and practices in Iraq, 1921–1958. *The Middle East Journal*, 59(1), 11–30.

Dawisha, A. (2005b). The new Iraq: Democratic institutions and performance. *Journal of Democracy*, 16(3), 35–49.

Dawisha, A. (2009). *Iraq: A Political History from Independence to Occupation*. Princeton: Princeton University Press.

Dawisha, A. and Diamond, L. J. (2006). Electoral systems today: Iraq's year of voting dangerously. *Journal of Democracy*, 17(2), 89–103.

de Tocqueville, A. (1864 [1835]). *Democracy in America* (H. Reeve, trans. 4th ed. vol. 1). Cambridge: Sever and Francis.

de Tocqueville, A. (2001 [1833–47]). *Writings on Empire and Slavery* (J. Pitts, trans.). Baltimore: The Johns Hopkins University Press.

de Tocqueville, A. (2001 [1841]). Essays on Algeria (J. Pitts, trans.) *Writings on Empire and Slavery* (pp. 59–116). Baltimore: The Johns Hopkins University Press.

de Tracy, D. (1811). *A Commentary and Review of Montesquieu's Spirit of Laws* (T. Jefferson, trans.). Philadelphia: William Duane.

Democracy's Century: A Survey of Global Political Change in the 20th Century. (1999). New York: Freedom House.

Derrida, J. (1973 [1967]). *Speech and Phenomena* (D. Allison, trans.). Evanston: Northwestern University Press.

Derrida, J. (1976 [1967]). *Of Grammatology* (G. C. Spivak, trans.). Baltimore: Johns Hopkins University Press.

Derrida, J. (2003 [1967]). *Writing and Difference* (A. Bass, trans.). London: Routledge.

Derrida, J. (2005 [2003]). *Rogues: Two Essays on Reason* (P. A. Brault and M. B. Naas, trans.). Stanford: Stanford University Press.

Derrida, J. (2006 [1993]). *Spectres of Marx: The State of the Debt, the Work of Mourning, and the New International* (P. Kamuf, trans.). New York: Routledge.

Diamond, L. J. and Plattner, M. (eds). (1996 [1990–1995]). *The Global Resurgence of Democracy* (2nd ed.). Baltimore: Johns Hopkins University Press.

Dodge, T. (2005 [2003]). *Inventing Iraq: The Failure of Nation-Building and a History Denied*. New York: Columbia University Press

Downs, A. (1957). *An Economic Theory of Democracy*. New York: Harper and Row.

Dryzek, J. S. (2000). *Deliberative Democracy and Beyond: Liberals, Critics, Contestations*. Oxford: Oxford University Press.

Dunn, J. (ed.). (1992). *Democracy: The Unfinished Journey, 508 BC to AD 1993*. Oxford: Oxford University Press.

Duss, M. and Juul, P. (2009). *The Fractured Shia of Iraq: Understanding the Tensions within Iraq's Majority*. Washington: Centre for American Progress.

Easton, S. C. (1970). *The Heritage of the Ancient World* (2nd ed.). Sydney: Holt, Rinehart & Winston.

Edwards, M. U. (2003). Luther's polemical controversies. In D. K. McKim (ed.), *The Cambridge Companion to Martin Luther* (pp. 192–206). Cambridge: Cambridge University Press.

Ehrenberg, J., McSherry, J. P., Sanchez, J. R. and Sayej, C. M. (eds). (2010). *The Iraq Papers*. Oxford: Oxford University Press.

Esposito, J. L. and Voll, J. O. (1996). *Islam and Democracy*. New York: Oxford University Press.

Etherington, M. (2005). *Revolt on the Tigris: The Al-Sadr Uprising and the Governing of Iraq*. London: C. Hurst & Co.

Euripedes. (1973 [400 BCE]). The Bacchae (P. Vellacott, trans.) *The Bacchae and Other Plays*. London: Penguin.

Evans, G. (1958a). Ancient Mesopotamian assemblies. *Journal of the American Oriental Society*, 78(1), 1–11.

Evans, G. (1958b). Ancient Mesopotamian assemblies – an addendum. *Journal of the American Oriental Society*, 78(2), 114–15.

Fadel, L. (2010, 23 June). Lack of electricity and water puts Iraqis on edge during heat of summer. *Washington Post*.

Fairclough, N. (1995). *Media Discourse*. London: Edward Arnold.

Fakhry, M. (2004 [1970]). *A History of Islamic Philosophy* (3rd ed.). New York: Columbia University Press.

Fanon, F. (2005 [1963]). *The Wretched of the Earth*. New York: Grove Press.

Farrokh, K. (2007). *300: Separating Fact from Fiction*. Oxford: Osprey.

Feldman, N. (2003). *After Jihad: America and the Struggle for Islamic Democracy*. New York: Farrar, Straus and Giroux.

Feldman, N. (2005). The democratic fatwa: Democracy in the realm of constitutional politics. *Oklahoma Law Review*, 58(1), 1–9.

Fernea, R. A. and Louis, W. R. (eds). (1991). *The Iraqi Revolution of 1958: The Old Social Classes Revisited*. London: I. B. Tauris.

Finley, M. I. (1973). *Democracy Ancient and Modern*. New Brunswick: Rutgers University Press.

Finn, E. (2004, 4 February). Grand Ayatollah Sayyid Ali Husaini Sistani: Why we'd better listen to Iraq's influential cleric. *Slate*.

Fleming, D. E. (2004). *Democracy's Ancient Ancestors: Mari and Early Collective Governance*. Cambridge: Cambridge University Press.

Fontana, B. (1992). Democracy and the French Revolution. In J. Dunn (ed.), *Democracy: The Unfinished Journey 508 BC to AD 1993* (pp. 107–24). Oxford: Oxford University Press.

Forsdyke, S. (2001). Athenian democratic ideology and Herodotus' histories. *American Journal of Philology*, 122(3), 329–58.

Foucault, M. (1961). *Madness and Civilisation: A History of Insanity in the Age of Reason*. London: Tavistock.

Foucault, M. (1970). *The Order of Things*. London: Tavistock.

Foucault, M. (1981). *The History of Sexuality I: An Introduction*. Harmondsworth: Penguin.

Foucault, M. (1990 [1976]). *The History of Sexuality I: An Introduction*. New York: Vintage.

Foucault, M. (1991 [1979]). *Discipline and Punish: The Birth of the Prison*. New York: Vintage.

Foucault, M. (2005 [1969]). *The Archaeology of Knowledge*. London: Routledge.

Frankfort, H. (1968). *The Birth of Civilization in the Near East*. London: Ernest Benn.

Frankfort, H. (1978 [1948]). *Kingship and the Gods: A Study of Ancient Near Eastern Religion as the Integration of Society and Nature*. Chicago: The University of Chicago Press.

Frankfort, H. and Frankfort, H. A. (1977). Myth and reality. In H. Frankfort, H. A. Frankfort, J. A. Wilson, T. Jacobsen and W. A. Irwin (eds), *The Intellectual*

Adventure of Ancient Man: Essays on Speculative Thought in the Ancient Near East (pp. 3–27). Chicago: The University of Chicago Press.

Fukuyama, F. (1989). The end of history? *The National Interest*, 16, 1–18.

Gandolfo, K. L. (2011). Birthing democracy: The role of women in the democratic discourse of the Middle East. In B. Isakhan and S. Stockwell (eds), *The Secret History of Democracy*(pp. 177–90). London: Palgrave Macmillan.

Gardiner, A. (2004). *The Egyptians: An Introduction* (9th ed.). London: Folio.

Gerber, H. (2002). The public sphere and civil society in the Ottoman Empire. In M. Hoexter, S. N. Eisenstadt and N. Levtzion (eds), *The Public Sphere in Muslim Societies* (pp. 65–82). Albany: State University of New York Press.

Gettleman, J. (2004, 29 March). G.I.'s padlock Baghdad paper accused of lies. *The New York Times*.

Gibb, H. A. R. and Bowen, H. (1950). *Islamic Society and the West: Islamic Society in the Eighteenth Century* (vol. 1). Oxford: Oxford University Press.

Gibson, M. and Biggs, R. (eds). (1987). *The Organisation of Power: Aspects of Bureaucracy in the Ancient Near East* (2nd ed.). Chicago: The Oriental Institute of the University of Chicago.

Glantz, A. (2005). IRAQ: Some Saddam men make it to the election list. *Inter Press Service*.

Global Resistance News. (2005, 17 July). Iraqi oil exports suspended for few hours by strike.

Goedicke, H. (1975). *The Report of Wenamun*. Baltimore: Johns Hopkins University Press.

Goode, S. (1975). *The Prophet and the Revolutionary: Arab Socialism in the Modern Middle East*. New York: Franklin Watts.

Goody, J. (2006). *The Theft of History*. Cambridge: Cambridge University Press.

Gopal, P. and Lazarus, N. (2006). Editorial. *New Formations*, 59, 7–9.

Gore, R. (2004, October). Who were the Phoenicians?: New clues from ancient bones and modern blood. *National Geographic*, 206, 26–49.

Gramsci, A. (1971 [1929–1935]). *Selections from the Prison Notebooks* (Q. Hoare and G. N. Smith, trans.). New York: International.

Gramsci, A. (1978 [1921–1926]). *Selections from Political Writings, 1921–1926* (Q. Hoare, trans.). London: Lawrence and Wishart.

Gran, P. (1996). *Beyond Eurocentrism: A New View of Modern World History*. Syracuse: Syracuse University Press.

Gregory, D. (2004). *The Colonial Present: Afghanistan, Palestine, Iraq*. Oxford: Blackwell.

Grossrichard, A. (1998 [1979]). *The Sultan's Court: European Fantasies of the East* (L. Heron, trans.). London: Verso.

Grunebaum, G. E. v. (1946). *Medieval Islam: A Study in Cultural Orientation*. Chicago: University of Chicago Press.

Gurney, O. R. (2004 [1952]). *The Hittites* (9th ed.). London: Folio.

Habermas, J. (1987 [1981]). *The Theory of Communicative Action* (T. McCarthy, trans.). Boston: Beacon.

Habermas, J. (1989 [1962]). *The Structural Transformation of the Public Sphere* (T. Burger and F. Lawrence, trans.). Cambridge: MIT Press.

Habermas, J. (1996 [1989]). The transformation of the public sphere's political function. In W. Outhwaite (ed.), *The Habermas Reader* (pp. 28–31). Cambridge: Polity.

Habermas, J. (1996 [1992]). *Between Facts and Norms: Contributions to a Discourse Theory of Law and Democracy* (W. Rehg, trans.). Cambridge: Polity.

Haj, S. (1997). *The Making of Iraq, 1900–1963: Capital, Power, and Ideology.* New York: State University of New York Press.

Hakim, R. (2008, 3 October). The largest Assyrian-Chaldean demonstration in northern Iraq. *Ankawa.*

Hall, J. A. (1985). *Powers and Liberties: The Causes and Consequences of the Rise of the West.* Harmondsworth: Penguin.

Hama-Saeed, M. (2007, 26 March). Media in Iraq at Risk. *Assyrian International News Agency.*

Hartog, F. (1988 [1980]). *The Mirror of Herodotus: The Representation of the Other in the Writing of History* (J. Lloyd, trans.). Berkeley: University of California Press.

Hassan, A. (2005, 12 July). The real terrorists in this country are the police. *Reuters.*

Hassouna, H. A. (2001). Arab Democracy: The Hope. *World Policy Journal*, 18(3), 49–52.

Hatim, L. (1992). Yes for a national comprehensive and transitional government. *Al-Thaqafa Al-Jadida*, 39(5).

Hawlati. (2005a, 2 February). 65% of Kirkukis Voted for Fraternity List.

Hawlati. (2005b, 2 February). KDP Wins 21 Seats in Erbil, PUK 17 and Yakgirtu 3.

Haykal, M. H. (1976). *The Life of Muhammad* (I. Al-Faruqi, trans. 8th ed.). New York: North American Trust Publication.

Hechter, M. and Kabiri, N. (2004). *Attaining Social Order in Iraq.* Paper presented at the Order, Conflict and Violence Conference, Yale University, USA.

Hegel, G. W. F. (1952 [1837]). The philosophy of history. In M. J. Adler (ed.), *Great Books of the Western World: Hegel* (vol. 46, pp. 153–369). Chicago: Encyclopaedia Britannica.

Held, D. (2006 [1987]). *Models of Democracy* (3rd ed.). Stanford: Stanford University Press.

Hendawi, H. (2003, 20 May). Shiites mount anti-U.S. protests. *The Russia Journal*, p. 5.

Herodotus. (1996 [460 BCE]). *Histories* (G. Rawlinson, trans.). London: Wordsworth Classics.

Hil, R. and Wilson, P. (2007). *Dead Bodies Don't Count: Civilian Casualties and the Forgotten Costs of the Iraq Conflict.* Burleigh: Zeus.

Hitti, P. K. (1968). *The Arabs: A Short History.* London: Macmillan.

Hittinger, J. (2003). *Liberty, Wisdom and Grace: Thomism and Modern Democratic Theory.* Lanham: Lexington.

Hobson, J. M. (2004). *The Eastern Origins of Western Civilisation*. Cambridge: Cambridge University Press.

Homer. (1950 [700 BCE]). *The Iliad* (E. V. Rieu, trans.). London: Penguin.

Hooglund, E. (1990). Government and politics. In H. C. Metz (ed.), *Iraq: A Country Study* (pp. 177–211). Washington: United States Government.

Horkheimer, M. (2007 [1937]). Traditional and critical theory. In C. Calhoun, J. Gerteis, J. Moody, S. Pfaff and I. Virk (eds), *Classical Sociological Theory* (pp. 347–61). Oxford: Blackwell.

Hourani, A. (2005 [1991]). *A History of the Arab Peoples*. London: Faber and Faber.

Houtsma, M. T., Wensinck, A. J., Gibb, H. A. R. and Heffening, W. (1993). *The First Encyclopaedia of Islam 1913–1936* (vol. VI). New York: E. J. Brill.

Humadi, A. S. (2005, 4 January). Upcoming elections will transfer Iraq from dictatorship to ballot era. *Al-Bayan*.

Huntington, S. P. (1968). *Political Order in Changing Societies*. New Haven: Yale University Press.

Huntington, S. P. (1984). Will more countries become democratic? *Political Science Quarterly*, 99(2), 193–218.

Huntington, S. P. (1987). The goals of development. In M. Weiner and S. P. Huntington (eds), *Understanding Political Development* (pp. 3–32). New York: Harper Collins.

Huntington, S. P. (1991). *The Third Wave: Democratization in the Late Twentieth Century*. Norman: University of Oklahoma Press.

Huntington, S. P. (1998 [1996]). *The Clash of Civilizations and the Remaking of World Order*. London: Touchstone.

Hurrat, K. S. and Leidig, L. I. (1994). Iraq. In Y. R. Kamalipour and H. Mowlana (eds), *Mass Media in the Middle East: A Comprehensive Handbook* (pp. 96–108). Westport: Greenwood.

Husry, K. S. (1974a). The Assyrian Affair of 1933 (I). *International Journal of Middle East Studies*, 5(2), 161–76.

Husry, K. S. (1974b). The Assyrian Affair of 1933 (II). *International Journal of Middle East Studies*, 5(3), 344–60.

Ibrahim, A. (1992). On the draft of the internal by-laws and the political programme and other thoughts. *Al-Thaqafa Al-Jadida*, 39(4).

Ibrahim, Y. M. (1995, 15 October). Iraqis go to polls: Guess who will win. *New York Times*.

Iraq Daily. (2002). 18 October.

Iraq TV. (2003a). 19 March.

Iraq TV. (2003b). 20 March.

Iraq TV. (2003c). 21 March.

Ireland, P. W. (1970 [1937]). *Iraq: A Study in Political Development*. New York: Russell & Russell.

Isakhan, B. (2006). Read all about it: The free press, the public sphere and democracy in Iraq. *Bulletin of the Royal Institute for Inter-Faith Studies*, 8(1&2), 119–53.

Isakhan, B. (2007a). Engaging 'Primitive Democracy': Mideast roots of collective governance. *Middle East Policy*, 14(3), 97–117.

Isakhan, B. (2007b). Media discourse and Iraq's democratisation: Reporting the 2005 Constitution in the Australian and Middle Eastern print media. *Australian Journalism Review*, 29(1), 97–114.

Isakhan, B. (2008a). 'Oriental despotism' and the democratisation of Iraq in *The Australian. Transformations*, 16.

Isakhan, B. (2008b). The post-Saddam Iraqi media: Reporting the democratic developments of 2005. *Global Media Journal*, 7(13).

Isakhan, B. (2009a). *Discourses of Democracy: 'Oriental Despotism' and the Democratisation of Iraq*. Unpublished PhD, Griffith University, Australia.

Isakhan, B. (2009b). Manufacturing consent in Iraq: Interference in the post-Saddam media sector. *International Journal of Contemporary Iraqi Studies*, 3(1), 7–26.

Isakhan, B. (2010a). Military orientalism and the occupation of Iraq. *International Journal of Contemporary Iraqi Studies*, 4(1and2), 211–15.

Isakhan, B. (2010b). Orientalism and the Australian news media: Origins and questions. In H. Rane, J. Ewart and M. Abdalla (eds), *Islam and the Australian News Media* (pp. 3–25). Melbourne: Melbourne University Press.

Isakhan, B. (2011a). The streets of Iraq: Protests and democracy after Saddam. In B. Isakhan and S. Stockwell (eds), *The Secret History of Democracy* (pp. 191–203). London: Palgrave Macmillan.

Isakhan, B. (2011b). Targeting the symbolic dimension of Baathist Iraq: Cultural destruction, historical memory and national identity. *Middle East Journal of Culture and Communication*, 4(2), 257–81.

Isakhan, B. (2011c). What is so 'primitive' about 'primitive democracy'? Comparing the Ancient Middle East and Classical Athens. In B. Isakhan and S. Stockwell (eds), *The Secret History of Democracy* (pp. 19–34). London: Palgrave Macmillan.

Isakhan, B. (2012a). The Assyrians. In B. Isakhan and S. Stockwell (eds), *The Edinburgh Companion to the History of Democracy*. Edinburgh: Edinburgh University Press.

Isakhan, B. (2012b). The complex and contested history of democracy. In B. Isakhan and S. Stockwell (eds), *The Edinburgh Companion to the History of Democracy*. Edinburgh: Edinburgh University Press.

Isakhan, B. (2012c). Iraq. In B. Isakhan and S. Stockwell (eds), *The Edinburgh Companion to the History of Democracy*. Edinburgh: Edinburgh University Press.

Isakhan, B., Mansouri, F. and Akbarzadeh, S. (eds). (2012). *The Arab Revolutions in Context: Civil Society and Democracy in a Changing Middle East*. Melbourne: Melbourne University Press.

Isakhan, B. and Stockwell, S. (2011). Introduction: Democracy and history. In B. Isakhan and S. Stockwell (eds), *The Secret History of Democracy* (pp. 1–18). London: Palgrave Macmillan.

Ishaq, I. (2003 [725]). *The Life of Muhammad: Apostle of Allah.* London: The Folio Society.

Ismael, T. Y. (2008). *The Rise and Fall of the Communist Party of Iraq.* Cambridge: Cambridge University Press.

Istanbuli, Y. (2001). *Diplomacy and Diplomatic Practice in the Early Islamic Era.* Oxford: Oxford University Press.

Jaafar, A. (2007, 21 March). Iran president irked by '300'. *Variety.*

Jacobsen, T. (1970 [1943]). Primitive democracy in Ancient Mesopotamia. In W. L. Moran (ed.), *Toward the Image of Tammuz and Other Essays on Mesopotamian History and Culture* (pp. 157–170). Massachusetts: Harvard University Press.

Jacobsen, T. (1970 [1957]). Early political development in Mesopotamia. In W. L. Moran (ed.), *Toward the Image of Tammuz and Other Essays on Mesopotamian History and Culture* (pp. 132–56). Massachusetts: Harvard University Press.

Jacobsen, T. (1977 [1951]). The cosmos as a state. In H. Frankfort, H. A. Frankfort, J. A. Wilson, T. Jacobsen and W. A. Irwin (eds), *The Intellectual Adventure of Ancient Man: Essays on Speculative Thought in the Ancient Near East* (pp. 125–84). Chicago: The University of Chicago Press.

Jamail, D. (2004, 19 January). Shiites unity challenges U.S. plan in Iraq. *The New Standard.*

Jameelah, M. (1971). *Islam and Orientalism.* Lahore: M. Y. Khan.

Jamil, A.-a.-R. (2005, 17 January). The country is built by hands, not skulls. *Al-Dustour.*

Jasim, A. (2005, 9 April). Massive 'End the Occupation' protest in Baghdad dwarfs the 'Saddam Toppled' rally. *China Daily.*

Jervis, R. (2003). Understanding the Bush doctrine. *Political Science Quarterly*, 118(3), 365–388.

Jiwa, S. (1992). Fatimid-Buyid diplomacy during the reign of Al-Aziz Billah (365/975–386/996). *Journal of Islamic Studies*, 3(1), 57–71.

Joseph, J. (1975). The Assyrian Affair: A historical perspective. *International Journal of Middle East Studies*, 6(1), 115–17.

Kammunah, S. A. A.-A.-H. (2005, 6 January). We are approaching a great democratic process. *Al-Mutamar.*

Kamrava, M. (1998). *Democracy in the Balance: Culture and Society in the Middle East.* New York: Seven Bridges.

Katzman, K. (2000). *Iraq's Opposition Movements.* Washington: Congressional Research Services Report for Congress.

Kayali, H. (1995). Elections and the electoral process in the Ottoman Empire, 1876–1919. *International Journal of Middle East Studies*, 27(3), 265–86.

Kedourie, E. (1970). The kingdom of Iraq: A retrospect *The Chatham House Version and Other Middle Eastern Studies* (pp. 236–285). London: Weidenfeld and Nicolson.

Kedourie, E. (1994). *Democracy and Arab Political Culture* (2nd ed.). Washington: Washington Institute for Near East Policy.

Kee, M. S. (2007). The heavenly council and its type-scene. *Journal for the Study of the Old Testament*, 31(3), 259–73.

Keeble, R. (1997). *Secret State, Silent Press: New Militarism, the Gulf and the Modern Image of Warfare*. Bedfordshire: University of Luton Press.

Keeble, R. (1998). The myth of Saddam Hussein: New militarism and the propaganda function of the human interest story. In M. Kieran (ed.), *Media Ethics* (pp. 66–81). London: Routledge.

Kellner, D. (1995). Reading the Gulf War: Production / text / reception *Media Culture* (pp. 198–228). London: Routledge.

Kennedy, H. (1986). *The Prophet and Age of the Caliphates: The Islamic Near East from the Sixth to the Eleventh Century*. London: Longman.

Kennedy, H. (2005). *When Baghdad Ruled the Muslim World: The Rise and Fall of Islam's Greatest Dynasty*. Cambridge: Da Capo.

Kennedy, H. (2008). *The Great Arab Conquests: How the spread of Islam changed the world we live in*. London: Phoenix.

Kent, M. (1976). *Oil and Empire: British Policy and Mesopotamian Oil, 1900–1920*. London: Macmillan.

Khadduri, M. (1960 [1951]). *Independent Iraq, 1932–1958: A Study in Iraqi Politics*. London: Oxford University Press.

Khaldun, A. A.-R. I. (1967 [1377]). *The Muqaddimah: An Introduction to History* (F. Rosenthal, trans.). Princeton: Princeton University Press.

Khalidi, R. (1984). The 1912 election campaign in Syria. *International Journal of Middle East Studies*, 16, 461–74.

Khatab, S. and Bouma, G. D. (2007). *Democracy in Islam*. London: Routledge.

Khatib, L. (2006). *Filming the Modern Middle East: Politics in the Cinemas of Hollywood and the Arab World*. London: I. B. Tauris.

Khlayf, A. (2005, 17 October). Democracy and freedom have been created in Iraq. *Al-Adala*.

Khudayyir, W. (2005, 10 January). Postponing elections meant to achieve more important aim. *Al-Bayynah*.

Kilcullen, J. (1999). Ockham's political writings. In P. V. Spade (ed.), *The Cambridge Companion to Ockham*. Cambridge: Cambridge University Press.

Kinross, L. (2003 [1977]). *The Ottoman Empire*. London: Folio.

Kissinger, H. and Shultz, G. (2005, 28 January). Don't trust the exit plan. *The Australian*, 13.

Klausner, C. L. (1973). *The Seljuk Vezirate: A Study of Civil Administration, 1055–1194*. Cambridge: Harvard University Press.

Klein, J. (2005, 31 October). Look who's back! *Time*, 43, 25.

Klein, N. (2007). *The Shock Doctrine: The Rise of Disaster Capitalism*. New York: Allen Lane.

Krader, L. (1975). *The Asiatic Mode of Production: Sources, Development and Critique in the Writings of Karl Marx*. Assen: Van Gorcum.

Kraemer, J. L. (1992 [1986]). *Humanism in the Renaissance of Islam: The Cultural Revival During the Buyid Age* (2nd ed.). Leiden: Brill.

Kramer, S. N. (1963). Society: The Sumerian city *The Sumerians: Their History, Culture and Character* (pp. 73–111). Chicago: The University of Chicago Press.

Kurdistani Nuwe. (2005a, 25 January). KRG to close Kurdistan Intl. borders, restrict inter-city movements before, during elections.

Kurdistani Nuwe. (2005b, 2 February). Majority said voted for Kurdish sovereignty in election day survey.

Laclau, E. and Mouffe, C. (1985). *Hegemony and Socialist Strategy: Towards a Radical Democratic Politics*. London: Verso.

Lapidus, I. M. (1973). The Evolution of Muslim Urban Society The evolution of Muslim urban society. *Comparative Studies in Society and History*, 15, 21–50.

Lapidus, I. M. (1975). The separation of state and religion in the development of early islamic society. *International Journal of Middle East Studies*, 6(4), 363–85.

Larsen, M. T. (1976). *The Old Assyrian City-State and Its Colonies*. Copenhagen: Akademisk Forlag.

Lassner, J. (2000). *The Middle East Remembered: Forged Identities, Competing Narratives, Contested Spaces*. Ann Arbor: The University of Michigan Press.

Lazarus, N. (2006). Postcolonial studies after the invasion of Iraq. *New Formations*, 59, 10–22.

Leick, G. (2001). *Mesopotamia: The Invention of the City*. London: Penguin.

Levine, P. (2004). Journalism and democracy: Does it matter how well the press covers Iraq? *Civic Review*, 93(3), 16–24.

Lewis, B. (1961). *The Emergence of Modern Turkey*. London: Oxford University Press.

Lewis, B. (1964). *The Middle East and the West*. New York: Harper.

Lewis, B. (1990). The roots of Muslim rage: Why so many Muslims deeply resent the West, and why their bitterness will not easily be mollified. *The Atlantic*, 266(3), 47–60.

Lewis, B. (2002). What went wrong? *The Atlantic Monthly*, 289(1), 43–5.

Lijphart, A. (1977). *Democracy in Plural Societies: A Comparative Exploration*. New Haven: Yale University Press.

Lings, M. (1983). *Muhammad: His Life Based on the Earliest Sources*. Vermont: Inner Traditions International.

Lipset, S. M. (1971 [1959]). *Political Man: The Social Basis of Politics*. London: Heinemann.

Litvak, M. (1998). *Shi'i Scholars of Nineteenth-Century Iraq: The 'Ulama of Najaf and Karbala*. Cambridge: Cambridge University Press.

Lombard, M. (1975). *The Golden Age of Islam* (J. Spencer, trans.). Amsterdam: North Holland.

London Times. (1920, June 21). Letter to the Editor.

Longrigg, S. H. (2002 [1925]). *Four Centuries of Modern Iraq*. Reading: Garnet.

Lukitz, L. (1995). *Iraq: The Search for National Identity*. London: Frank Cass.

Luther, M. (1974 [1529]). On war against the Turk (C. M. Jacobs, trans.). In J. M. Porter (ed.), *Luther: Selected Political Writings* (pp. 121–31). Philadelphia: Fortress.

Lytle, E. (2007, 11 March). Sparta? No. This is madness. *The Star*.

Mackey, S. (2002). *The Reckoning: Iraq and the Legacy of Saddam Hussein*. New York: W. W. Norton.

Majd, M. G. (2006). *Iraq in World War I: From Ottoman Rule to British Conquest*. Lanham: University Press of America.

Makiya, K. (1993). *Cruelty and Silence: War, Tyranny, Uprising, and the Arab World*. (Pseudonym: Samir Al-Khalil). New York: W. W. Norton.

Makiya, K. (1998 [1989]). *Republic of Fear: The Politics of Modern Iraq*. (Pseudonym: Samir Al-Khalil). Berkeley: University of California Press.

Malmesbury, W. (1895 [1120]). *Chronicle of the King's of England: From the Earliest Period to the Reign of King Stephen* (J. A. Giles, trans.). London: George Bell & Sons.

Maraai, H. (2006a, 17 August). A barrel of democracy. *Azzaman*.

Maraai, H. (2006b, 20 September). Mortar attacks signal start of civil war. *Azzaman*.

Mardin, S. (1969). Power, civil society and culture in the Ottoman Empire. *Comparative Studies in Society and History*, 11(3), 258–81.

Margoliouth, D. S. (1919, 22 January). Meeting with Sir Percy Cox.

Markoe, G. E. (2005). *The Phoenicians*. London: Folio.

Marr, P. (2004 [1985]). *The Modern History of Iraq* (2nd ed.). Westview: Boulder.

Martin, M. and Snell, D. C. (2005). Democracy and freedom. In D. C. Snell (ed.), *A Companion to the Ancient Near East* (pp. 397–407). Malden: Blackwell.

Marx, K. (1963 [1869]). *The Eighteenth Brumaire of Louis Bonaparte*. New York: International.

Marx, K. (1973 [1853]). The British rule in India. *Karl Marx and Frederich Engels: Selected Works* (vol. 1, pp. 488–493). Moscow: Progress.

Marx, K. (1977 [1887]-a). *Capital: A Critique of Political Economy* (S. Moore and E. Aveling, trans. vol. 1). Moscow: Progress.

Marx, K. (1977 [1887]-b). *Capital: A Critique of Political Economy* (S. Moore and E. Aveling, trans. vol. 2). Moscow: Progress.

Marx, K. and Engels, F. (1974 [1846]). *The German Ideology* (2nd ed.). London: Lawrence & Wishart.

Matthiae, P. (1980). *Ebla: An Empire Rediscovered*. London: Hodder & Stoughton.

McDowell, D. (2000 [1996]). *A Modern History of the Kurds* (2nd ed.). London: I. B. Tauris.

McFadden, T. J. (1953). *Daily Journalism in the Arab States*. Columbus, Ohio.

Mez, A. (1937). *The Renaissance of Islam* (S. K. Bakhsh and D. S. Margoliouth, trans.). Patna: Jubilee

Mill, J. (1972 [1817]). *The History of British India*. London: Associated.

Mill, J. S. (1962 [1861]). *Considerations on Representative Government*. Indiana: Gateway Editions.

Miller, F. (1998). *300*. Milwaukie: Dark Horse Comics.

Misterek, M. (2005). Free speech, measured in Watts. *The News Tribune*.

Moaveni, A. (2007, 13 March). *300* sparks an outcry in Iran. *Time*.

Montesquieu, C. L. (1923 [1721]). *Persian Letters*. London: G. Routledge & Sons.

Montesquieu, C. L. (1949 [1748]). *The Spirit of the Laws* (T. Nugent, trans.). New York: Hafner.

Moran, W. L. (ed.). (1992). *The Amarna Letters*. Baltimore: Johns Hopkins University Press.

Muir, J. (2011, 8 January). Iraq Shia cleric Moqtada Sadr urges Iraqis to unite. *BBC*.

Mulhim, R. A. (2005, 7 February). A need for a comprehensive national dialogue. *Al-Mutamar*.

Nakash, Y. (2003 [1994]). *The Shi'is of Iraq*. Princeton: Princeton University Press.

Nasr, M. A. (2005, 13 October). Demonstrations sweep Iraqi towns. *Free Arab Voice*.

New York Times. (1995, 17 October). No Surprise in Iraqi Vote.

Nieuwenhuis, T. (1982). *Politics and Society in Early Modern Iraq: Mamluk Pashas, Tribal Shayks and Local Rule Between 1802 and 1831*. The Hague: Martinus Nijhoff.

Nourredin, N. (2005, 30 October). Sectarian protest rocks key north Iraq province. *Reuters*.

Oppenheim, A. L. (1964). *Ancient Mesopotamia: Portrait of a Dead Civilization*. Chicago: The University of Chicago Press.

Oppenheim, A. L. (1967). *Letters from Mesopotamia: Official, Business, and Private Letters on Clay Tablets from Two Millennia*. Chicago: The University of Chicago Press.

Oppenheim, A. L. (1969). Mesopotamia: Land of many cities. In I. M. Lapidus (ed.), *Middle Eastern Cities: A Symposium on Ancient Islamic and Contemporary Middle Eastern Urbanism*. Berkeley: The University of California Press.

Osman, H. (2002, 23 September). Iraqi Kurds fear loss of freedom. *BBC News*.

Ottaway, M. and Kaysi, D. (2010, 15 November). Can Iraq's political agreement be implemented? *Carnegie Endowment for International Peace*.

Otterman, M. and Hil, R. (2010). *Erasing Iraq: The Human Costs of Carnage*. London: Pluto.

Paine, T. (1856 [1791]). *The Rights of Man: Being an Answer to Mr. Burke's Attack on the French Revolution*. London: Holyoak and Co.

Parpola, S. (2000). The Mesopotamian soul of western culture. *Bulletin of the Canadian Society for Mesopotamian Studies*, 35, 29–34.

Pasha, S. H. (1993). Towards a cultural theory of political ideology and mass media in the Muslim world. *Media, Culture and Society*, 15, 61–79.

Pateman, C. (1999 [1970]). *Participation and Democratic Theory*. London: Cambridge University Press.

Paz, M. A. and Aviles, J. A. G. (2009). Demonizing the tyrant: Saddam Hussein's image in Spanish news programs during the Second Persian Gulf War. *International Journal of Contemporary Iraqi Studies*, 3(1), 53–74.

Peters, R. (2006, 2 November). Last gasp in Iraq. *USA Today*.

Philo, G. and McLaughlin, G. (1995). The British media and the Gulf War. In G. Philo (ed.), *Glasgow Media Group Reader* (vol. 2, pp. 146–56). Glasgow: Glasgow University Press.

Pipes, D. (1983). *In the Path of God: Islam and Political Power*. New York: Basic.

Plato. (1975 [360 BCE]). *The Laws* (T. J. Saunders, trans. 3rd ed.). London: Penguin.

Plato. (1975 [380 BCE]). *The Republic* (D. Lee, trans. 2nd ed.). London: Penguin.

Polybius. (1889 [150 BCE]). *The Histories of Polybius* (E. Shuckburgh, trans.). London: Macmillan.

Porter, P. (2009). *Military Orientalism: Eastern War Through Western Eyes*. London: C. Hurst & Co.

Poster, M. (1984). *Foucault, Marxism and History*. Cambridge: Polity.

Pressfield, S. (1998). *Gates of Fire: An Epic Novel of the Battle of Thermopylae*. New York: Doubleday.

Preston, Z. (2003). *The Crystallisation of the Iraqi State: Geopolitical Function and Form*. Bern: Peter Lang.

Program of the Arab Baath Socialist Party. (1965). Paper presented at the Eighth National Conference of the ABSP, Baghdad.

Propaganda and activities against participation in Iraq elections. (1922, 10 November). *Abstract of Police Intelligence*.

Qassim, M. (2010, 12 November). A surreal government. *Sot Al-Iraq*.

Quesnay, F. (1946 [1767]). Despotism in China (L. A. Maverick, trans.). In L. A. Maverick (ed.), *China a Model for Europe* (pp. 139–304). San Antonio: Paul Anderson.

Rahman, H. (1997). *The Making of the Gulf War: Origins of Kuwait's Long-Standing Territorial Dispute with Iraq*. Reading: Ithaca.

Rasul, S. (2005a, 28 February). Iraqi people are in bad need of services and power. *Al-Bayan*.

Rasul, S. (2005b, 4 January). Reasons behind the anti-Iraqis stance regarding the Arab media. *Al-Bayan*.

Reid, D. M. (1993). The postage stamp: A window on Saddam Hussein's Iraq. *The Middle East Journal*, 47(1), 77–89.

Rice, T. T. (1961). *The Seljuks in Asia Minor*. London: Thames and Hudson.

Richardson, J. E. (2004). *(Mis)Representing Islam: The Racism and Rhetoric of British Broadsheet Newspapers*. Amsterdam: John Benjamins.

Richardson, J. E. (2007). *Analysing Newspapers: An Approach from Critical Discourse Analysis*. Hampshire: Palgrave Macmillan.

Ridolfo, K. (2006, 25 August). Iraq: Security, political pressure affect media performance. *Radio Free Europe: Radio Liberty*.

Rodinson, M. (2002 [1980]). *Europe and the Mystique of Islam* (R. Veinus, trans.). London: I. B. Tauris.

Romano, A. (2005). Asian journalism: News, development and the tides of liberalisation and technology. In A. Romano and M. Bromley (eds), *Journalism and Democracy in Asia* (pp. 1–14). London: Routledge.

Rose, S. and Baravi, A. (1998). The meaning of Halabja: Chemical warfare in Kurdistan. *Race and Class*, 30(1), 74–7.

Roth, M. T. (1997 [1995]). *Law Collections from Mesopotamia and Asia Minor* (2nd ed.). Atalanta: Scholars.

Rugh, W. A. (1979). *The Arab Press: News Media and Political Process in the Arab World*. London: Syracuse University Press.

Rugh, W. A. (2004). *Arab Mass Media: Newspapers, Radio, and Television in Arab Politics*. Westport: Praeger.

Rushd, A. A.-W. M. I. (1974 [1165]). *Commentary on Plato's Republic* (R. Lerner, trans.). Ithaca: Cornell University Press.

Sachedina, A. (2001). *The Islamic Roots of Democratic Pluralism*. New York: Oxford University Press.

Sadiki, L. (2004). *The Search for Arab Democracy: Discourses and Counter-Discourses*. New York: Columbia University Press.

Sadowski, Y. (1993). The new Orientalism and the democracy debate. *Middle East Report*, 183, 14–21, 40.

Saggs, H. W. F. (2004). *The Babylonians: A Survey of the Ancient Civilizations of the Tigris-Euphrates Valley* (9th ed.). London: Folio.

Said, E. W. (1979). *The Question of Palestine*. New York: Vintage.

Said, E. W. (1981). *Covering Islam: How the Media and the Experts Determine how we see the Rest of the World*. New York: Pantheon.

Said, E. W. (1994 [1993]). *Culture and Imperialism*. London: Vintage.

Said, E. W. (2003 [1978]). *Orientalism*. London: Penguin.

Said, E. W. (2004). *Humanism and Democratic Criticism*. New York: Columbia University Press.

Said, E. W. (2004 [2002]). Israel, Iraq and the United States *From Oslo to Iraq and the Road Map* (pp. 213–27). New York: Pantheon.

Saliba, G. (2007). *Islamic Science and the Making of the European Renaissance*. Cambridge: MIT Press.

Salih, S. (1992). The new draft programme document between discourses and questions of the new reality. *Al-Thaqafa Al-Jadida*, 39(5).

Salucci, I. (2005). *A People's History of Iraq: The Iraqi Communist Party, Worker's Movements, and the Left 1924–2004*. Chicago: Haymarket.

Salvatore, A. (1996). Beyond Orientalism? Max Weber and the displacements of 'essentialism' in the study of Islam. *Arabica*, 43(3), 457–85.

Sami, Q. (2006, 6 November). President Bush wants nothing less than victory in Iraq; but over whom? *Azzaman*.

Saward, M. (2003). *Democracy*. Cambridge: Polity.

Sawer, M. (1977). *Marxism and the Question of the Asiatic Mode of Production*. The Hague: Martinus Nijhoff.

Schemeil, Y. (2000). Democracy before democracy? *International Political Science Review*, 21(2), 99–120.

Schmidt, M. S. and Healy, J. (2011, 4 March). Iraq shuts office of protest organizers. *New York Times*.

Schultz, J. P. (1981). *Judaism and the Gentile Faiths: Comparative Studies in Religion*. London: Associated University Press.

Schumpeter, J. (2011 [1947]). *Capitalism, Socialism, and Democracy* (2nd ed.). Mansfield: Martino.

Scott, A. O. (2007, 9 March). Battle of the manly men: Blood bath with a message. *The New York Times*.

Semmerling, T. J. (2006). *'Evil' Arabs in American Popular Film: Orientalist Fear*. Austin: University of Texas Press.

Shadid, A. (2011, 8 January). Iraqi cleric embraces state in comeback speech. *New York Times*.

Shaheen, J. G. (2001). *Reel Bad Arabs: How Hollywood Vilifies a People*. New York: Olive Branch.

Shaw, S. J. (1976). *History of the Ottoman Empire and Modern Turkey* (vol. 1). Cambridge: Cambridge University Press.

Shmuelevitz, A. (2004). Zionism, Jews and Muslims in the Ottoman Empire as reflected in the weekly Hamevasser. In T. Parfitt and Y. Egorova (eds), *Jews, Muslims and Mass Media: Mediating the 'Other'* (pp. 28–34). London: Routledge Curzon.

Silverfarb, D. (1986). *Britain's Informal Empire in the Middle East: A Case Study of Iraq, 1929–1941*. Oxford: Oxford University Press.

Silverfarb, D. (1994). *The Twilight of British Ascendancy in the Middle East: A Case Study of Iraq, 1941–1950*. Basingstoke: Macmillan.

Silvestro, F. (1965). *Voices from the Clay: The Development of Assyro-Babylonian Literature*. Norman: University of Oklahoma Press.

Simon, E. (1988). *The 'Türkenkalender' (1454) Attributed to Gutenberg and the Strasbourg Lunation Tracts*. Cambridge: Medieval Academy of America.

Sina, A. A. A.-H. (1973 [1012]). *The Metaphysics* (P. Morewedge, trans.). London: Routledge.

Skinner, Q. (1992). The Italian city-republics. In J. Dunn (ed.), *Democracy: The Unfinished Journey 508 BC to AD 1993* (pp. 57–69). Oxford: Oxford University Press.

Sluglett, P. (2007). *Britain in Iraq: Contriving King and Country*. London: I.B. Tauris.

Sly, L. (2011, 5 February). Iraq's Maliki says he won't seek 3rd term, in possible reverberations from Egypt. *The Washington Post*.

Smith, K. (2007, 9 March). Persian Shrug: Designer carnage kills and thrills in bloody '300'. *New York Post*.

Smith, R. O. (2007). Luther, the Turks, and Islam. *Currents in Theology and Mission*, 34(5), 351–64.

Snell, D. C. (2001). *Flight and Freedom in the Ancient Near East*. Leiden: Brill.

Snyder, Z., Johnstad, K. and Gordon, M. B. (Writer). (2007). 300 [Film]. USA: Warner Bros. Entertainment.

Soroush, A. (2000). *Reason, Freedom, and Democracy in Islam* (M. Sadri and A. Sadri, trans.). Oxford: Oxford University Press.

Spencer, R. (2006). Edward Said and the war in Iraq. *New Formations*, 59, 52–62.

Springborg, P. (1992). *Western Republicanism and the Oriental Prince*. Cambridge: Polity.

St. George, G., Callegari, G. P., DelGrosso, R., d'Eramo, G. and Liberatore, U. (Writer). (1962). The 300 Spartans [Film]. USA: Twentieth Century Fox.

Stansfield, G. (2003). *Iraqi Kurdistan: Political Development and Emergent Democracy*. London: Routledge Curzon.

Stansfield, G. (2007). *Iraq: People, History, Politics*. Cambridge: Polity.

Stark, F. (1951). *Beyond Euphrates: Autobiography 1928–1933*. London: John Murray.

Stewart, R. (2006). *Occupational Hazards: My Time Governing in Iraq*. London: Picador.

Stivers, W. (1982). *Supremacy and Oil: Iraq, Turkey, and the Anglo-American World Order, 1918–1930*. New York: Cornell University Press.

Stockwell, S. (2011a). Before Athens: Early popular government in Phoenicia and Greek city states. In B. Isakhan and S. Stockwell (eds), *The Secret History of Democracy* (pp. 35–48). London: Palgrave Macmillan.

Stockwell, S. (2011b). Democratic culture in the early Venetian Republic. In B. Isakhan and S. Stockwell (eds), *The Secret History of Democracy* (pp. 105–19). London: Palgrave Macmillan.Stockwell, S. (2012). Venice. In B. Isakhan and S. Stockwell (eds), *The Edinburgh Companion to the History of Democracy*. Edinburgh: Edinburgh University Press.

Storm, R. (2003). *Myths and Legends of the Ancient Near East*. London: Folio.

Tabor, K. (2002). The press in Iraq. *Frontline World*.

Talabani, Q. J. (2010a, 30 May). Iraq's year of transition. *PUK Media*.

Talabani, Q. J. (2010b, 15 March). The Iraqi elections. *PUK Media*.

Tawfeeq, M., Wald, J. and Sterling, J. (2008, 25 March). Peaceful Iraq protests spark clashes; 50 reported dead. *CNN*.

Thoman, R. E. (1972). Iraq under Ba'thist rule. *Current History*, 62(365), 31–7.

Tibawi, A. L. (1964). *English Speaking Orientalists: A Critique of Their Approach to Islam and Arab Nationalism*. London: Luzak.

Tomanic-Trivundza, I. (2004). Orientalism as news: Pictorial representations of the US attack on Iraq in Delo. *Journalism*, 5(4), 480–99.

Toth, J. (1992). Demonizing Saddam Hussein: Manipulating racism as a prelude to war. *New Political Science*, 11(1&2), 5–39.

Tripp, C. (2000). *A History of Iraq*. Cambridge: Cambridge University Press.

Tripp, C. (2007). ' In the name of the people': The 'People's Court' and the Iraqi revolution (1958–1960). In J. C. Strauss and D. B. C. O'Brien (eds), *Staging Politics: Power and Performance in Asia and Africa* (pp. 31–48). London: I. B. Tauris.

Tripp, C. (2007 [2000]). *A History of Iraq* (3rd ed.). Cambridge: Cambridge University Press.

Turner, B. S. (1974). *Weber and Islam: A Critical Study*. London: Routledge.

Turner, B. S. (1978). *Marx and the End of Orientalism*. London: Allen & Unwin.

Turner, B. S. (1994). *Orientalism, Postmodernism and Globalism*. London: Routledge.

Turner, B. S. (1996 [1981]). Weber's Orientalism *For Weber: Essays on the Sociology of Fate* (2nd ed., pp. 257–286). London: Sage.

Uruknet. (2005, 17 July). Iraqi oil workers hold 24-hour strike – oil exports shut down.

Usher, S. (2004). Radio station to help Iraqis decide. *BBC News*.

Usher, S. (2005a). Hard TV sell for Iraqi electorate. *BBC News*.

Usher, S. (2005b). Iraqi media urges high turnout. *BBC News*.

Vagelpohl, U. (2008). *Aristotle's Rhetoric in the East: The Syriac and Arabic Translation and Commentary Tradition*. Leiden: Brill.

Van den Boorn, G. P. F. (1988). *The Duties of the Vizir: Civil Administration in the Early New Kingdom*. London: Kegan Paul.

Vergano, D. (2007, 5 March). This is Sparta? The history behind the movie '300'. *USA Today*.

Voices of Iraq. (2008a, 24 August). Dozens rally demonstrations to protest corruption in Muthana.

Voices of Iraq. (2008b, 31 July). Duhuk demo ends by presenting warrant of protest against elections law.

Voices of Iraq. (2008c, 31 July). Protestors in Sulaimaniya present warrant of protest against election law.

Voltaire, F. M. A. (1963 [1756]). *Essay on the Customs and Spirit of the Nations and the Principal Facts of History from Charlemagne to Louis XIII*. Paris: Garnier.

Voltaire, F. M. A. (1994 [1779]). First conversation: On Hobbes, Grotius and Montesquieu (D. Williams, trans.). In D. Williams (ed.), *Voltaire: Political Writings* (pp. 87–100). Cambridge: Cambridge University Press.

Walker, J. (2005, 8 March). Behind the Cedars: Nonviolent protest in the Middle East. *Reason Online*.

Walzer, R. (2007). Platonism in Islamic Philosophy. In I. R. Netton (ed.), *Islamic Philosophy and Theology* (vol. I: Legacies, Translations and Prototypes, pp. 160–74). London: Routledge.

Warriner, D. (1962 [1957]). *Land Reform and Development in the Middle East: A Study of Egypt, Syria, and Iraq* (2nd ed.). Westport: Greenwood.

Watt, W. M. (1972). *The Influence of Islam on Medieval Europe*. Edinburgh: Edinburgh University Press.

Watt, W. M. (1987 [1962]). *Islamic Philosophy and Theology*. Edinburgh: Edinburgh University Press.

Weber, J. (2006). Strassburg, 1605: The origins of the newspaper in Europe. *German History*, 24(3), 387–412.

Weber, M. (1992 [1904–5]). *The Protestant Ethic and the Spirit of Capitalism* (T. Parsons, trans.). London: Routledge.

Wein, P. (2006). *Iraqi Arab Nationalism: Authoritarian, Totalitarian, and Pro-Fascist Inclinations, 1932–1941*. London: Routledge.

Wellhausen, J. (1975 [1901]). *The Religio-Political Factions in Early Islam* (R. C. Ostle and S. M. Walzer, trans.). Amsterdam: North Holland Publishing Company.

West, D. (2006, 12 June). Forget false democracy, stop real terrorism. *Jewish World Review*.

Wien, P. (2006). *Iraqi Arab Nationalism: Authoritarian, Totalitarian, and Pro-Fascist Inclinations, 1932–1941*. London: Routledge.

Wilson, A. (1919). Telegram to the British Foreign Office.

Wimmer, A. (2003). Democracy and ethno-religious conflict in Iraq. *Survival*, 45(4), 111–34.

Wittfogel, K. (1957). *Oriental Despotism: A Comparative Study of Total Power*. New Haven: Yale University Press.

Wolf, C. U. (1947). Traces of rimitive democracy in Ancient Israel. *Journal of Near Eastern Studies*, 6(2), 98–108.

Xebat. (2005a, 2 February). 425,000 Kirkukis Voted, Fraternity List on Top.

Xebat. (2005b, 25 January). Barzani Meets Separately with Turcomans, Christians and Ezidians.

Xenophon. (1986 [360 BCE]). *The Persian Expedition* (R. Warner, trans.). Middlesex: Penguin.

Yaphe, J. S. (2008). After the surge: Next steps in Iraq. *Strategic Forum*, 230, 1–6.

Yassin, J. (2002, 7 December). The predicament of Iraqi intellectuals. *Dar Al-Hayat*.

Young, R. J. C. (1995). Foucault on race and colonialism. *New Formations*, 25, 57–65.

Zaki, K. (2005, 28 February). Acts of corruption and embezzlement. *Al-Mutamar*.

Zaydan, I. (2005a, 6 January). It is not right to accuse all of the candidates of being Iranian agents. *Al-Dustour*.

Zaydan, I. (2005b, 6 January). A need for a remedy to heal our wounds. *Al-Dustour*.

Zengerle, J. (2002, 24 January). Can the Iraqi exiles remake Iraq? At home abroad. *The New Republic*.

Zubaida, S. (2002). The fragments imagine the nation: The case of Iraq. *International Journal of Middle East Studies*, 34(2), 205–15.

Index